PENGUIN BOOKS

UNREAL ELECTIONS

C.S. Krishna is a self-proclaimed legendary development consultant. He wants to make it big as a public policy guru but three years of writing satire for *The UnReal Times* under the pseudonym Unreal Mama has rendered him incapable of thinking seriously. He has an engineering degree from IIT Bombay, MS from Ohio State University and an MBA from IIM-Ahmedabad.

Karthik Laxman has a degree in software engineering from BITS-Pilani and an MBA from IIM-Ahmedabad. In his career he has taken more U-turns than Mulayam Singh Yadav and Arvind Kejriwal put together, transitioning from a programmer to management consultant to development specialist to entrepreneur to sundry other roles, before finding his calling as a house-husband. He also writes for and manages *The UnReal Times*.

UNREAL
ELECTIONS

C.S. KRISHNA &
KARTHIK LAXMAN

PENGUIN BOOKS

PENGUIN BOOKS

Published by the Penguin Group

Penguin Books India Pvt. Ltd, 7th Floor, Infinity Tower C, DLF Cyber City, Gurgaon 122 002, Haryana, India

Penguin Group (USA) Inc., 375 Hudson Street, New York, New York 10014, USA

Penguin Group (Canada), 90 Eglinton Avenue East, Suite 700, Toronto, Ontario, M4P 2Y3, Canada

Penguin Books Ltd, 80 Strand, London WC2R 0RL, England

Penguin Ireland, 25 St Stephen's Green, Dublin 2, Ireland (a division of Penguin Books Ltd)

Penguin Group (Australia), 707 Collins Street, Melbourne, Victoria 3008, Australia

Penguin Group (NZ), 67 Apollo Drive, Rosedale, Auckland 0632, New Zealand

Penguin Group (South Africa) (Pty) Ltd, Block D, Rosebank Office Park, 181 Jan Smuts Avenue, Parktown North, Johannesburg 2193, South Africa

Penguin Books Ltd, Registered Offices: 80 Strand, London WC2R 0RL, England

First published by Penguin Books India 2014

Copyright © C.S. Krishna and Karthik Laxman 2014

All rights reserved

10 9 8 7 6 5 4 3

This book is a work of fiction. None of the events described in it actually took place—they are entirely the product of the authors' imagination. The names, persons, people, and places portrayed in the book are either fictitious or have been used fictitiously; they are not accurate portrayals of real persons, organizations or places, and they should not be construed as being accurate at all.

ISBN 9780143423119

Typeset in Sabon by R. Ajith Kumar, New Delhi
Printed at Thomson Press India Ltd, New Delhi

This book is sold subject to the condition that it shall not, by way of trade or otherwise, be lent, resold, hired out, or otherwise circulated without the publisher's prior written consent in any form of binding or cover other than that in which it is published and without a similar condition including this condition being imposed on the subsequent purchaser and without limiting the rights under copyright reserved above, no part of this publication may be reproduced, stored in or introduced into a retrieval system, or transmitted in any form or by any means (electronic, mechanical, photocopying, recording or otherwise), without the prior written permission of both the copyright owner and the above-mentioned publisher of this book.

A PENGUIN RANDOM HOUSE COMPANY

To Dr Kamala Devi, my ever-loving grandmother

C.S. KRISHNA

To Mom, Dad, Priya and Anjali

KARTHIK LAXMAN

Contents

Prologue

THE ENTREPRENEUR SAT HUNCHED in the living room of his four-bedroom apartment, his forehead creased with worry. He'd just had his fifth fight that month with his wife. She had come home exhausted after a long day at work, and found him laughing with his associates in the hall. What followed was a vicious tongue-lashing delivered to him right in front of his shocked colleagues that ended with her storming off into their bedroom slamming the door behind her.

He couldn't blame her though. While he loitered in the streets and hung around with his friends plotting insane schemes, she handled the household expenses, paid the home-loan instalment and looked after the children.

Suddenly the sky was rocked by the sound of thunder.

1

Smelling rain in the air, he pulled the thin shawl tighter around him, and wondered what the future held in store. Behind him his co-founders squabbled, arguing with each other on what they should name their fledgling enterprise.

It was pouring now. The Delhi NCR (National Capital Region) seemed to have received more than its share of thunderstorms this year. He trudged out into the balcony, rested his forearms on the railing and leaned over, staring emptily into the distance, when suddenly the lights in the streets went out, plunging the neighbourhood into darkness. 'Typical Ghaziabad,' he sighed.

He didn't see the point of going back in and fetching a kerosene lamp. He continued gazing into the darkness which seemed to symbolize his current predicament.

A flash of lightning lit up the neighbourhood. In that millisecond, he saw something monstrous hanging like a bat right in front of him. He leapt back instinctively and crashed into the wall behind him. For a moment, he lay on the floor, legs sprawled, wondering what the hell he'd seen.

Lightning flashed again, for him to make out what he thought he had seen earlier. A grotesque-looking creature draped in a dark cape hung upside down from the railings of the floor above.

The creature then unfolded its arms to reveal a fluorescent V etched brightly across its chest. In the dim light of the fluorescent V, the creature extended something towards him.

'Take it,' the creature rasped.

He swallowed hard, and slowly inched forward with his arm stretched out.

'Wh . . . what is this?' he managed to stammer.

'A gift.'

He eyed it warily, and risked a glance at the thing he now held. It was a large folder. Thunder rent the skies once again.

'Who are you?' he asked, and glanced up. But the creature was gone.

Utterly bewildered by the turn of events, he stumbled back into the living room, sat himself at a small table in a corner, and set down the folder near a kerosene lamp.

Then Arvind Kejriwal opened the folder and began reading the first of several documents, his eyes growing wider by the minute.

MATCH PREVIEW

'It's an electrifying atmosphere out there, looks like we have a cracker of a match here, folks.'

—Ravi Shastri

ONE

The family

THE FARMER STEPPED INTO the dim room, heart in his mouth. The door shut behind him with a click. The blinds of the full-length window on the wall opposite him were drawn, throwing many patterned shadows all around. Near the window stood Ajay Maken, dressed in a dark suit, sipping his glass of red wine. Behind him, in a shadowy corner, Jairam Ramesh sat cross-legged.

In the centre of the room, at an oak desk, a man was reclining on a chair. He wore a black suit and a bow tie. A red rose adorned his jacket pocket. His facial features stayed hidden under a shadow, but the light bounced off his slicked-back oiled hair. A tiny kitten stretched on his lap, pawing at him as he stroked it absently.

The farmer shivered. Summoning every ounce of courage within him, he took a step forward, bowed low towards the man, took his hand and kissed it.

'Godfather,' the farmer whispered.

Rahul Gandhi looked up at the farmer. The corner of his mouth went up in a half smile. With an imperious wave of his hand that at once screamed power and compassion, he gestured at the farmer to take a seat opposite him.

Beyond the far corner of the room, behind two spyholes, Sonia Gandhi and Ahmed Patel shook each other's hands in excitement.

'Your dream is coming true, madam!' whispered Ahmed Patel. 'Marlon Brando isn't a patch on our Rahul baba!'

'Shh! Let's watch,' Sonia Gandhi whispered back, barely concealing her elation.

The farmer sat quietly for a moment and then began.

'I believe in Haryana,' he said. 'I raised my son in the Haryanvi fashion. I gave him freedom but taught him never to dishonour the family.

'He found a friend,' the farmer continued. 'Not of the same *gotra*. They went to the movies. They stayed out late. But I didn't protest. Two weeks ago, he told us he'll introduce his life partner to us. We were happy. We were relieved that we didn't have to go to Kerala to find a bride. We eagerly awaited the day my son would walk in with our daughter-in-law.

'On the auspicious day, my wife swept the courtyard and prepared a delicious dinner for the couple. I came home from the field and found them standing side by side, holding hands. They looked really happy. But I couldn't stop crying. Our daughter-in-law was a boy.'

The farmer choked with emotion. Rahul made the slightest of gestures with his index and middle fingers. A man promptly emerged from the shadows, handed a tissue to the farmer and returned to the shadows. The farmer wiped his tears, struggling to regain his composure.

'I went to the khap panchayat, like a good Haryanvi. The two boys were brought to trial. The tau reprimanded them, and ordered them to stop eating chow mein.' The farmer's face contorted with pain and anguish. 'Stop eating chow mein?! They eloped that very day! I stood outside my house like a fool while the entire village laughed at me!'

Rahul Gandhi did not betray any emotion. Subconsciously, he scratched under the kitten's ear, listening to the farmer with the unhurried air of a man who knew exactly what he had to do, and when he had to do it.

The farmer's face cleared. He straightened in his chair, and said in a firm tone, 'Then I told my wife, we must go to Rahul baba. He would know how to handle such delicate situations.'

Rahul Gandhi stiffened. The kitten leapt off his lap with a meow, and scampered into the darkness. The aura of nonchalant power abruptly left him. Instead, a vacant expression materialized on his face, and he looked at the farmer blankly.

'Uh, can you check with Mummy on this?'

Behind the spyhole, Sonia Gandhi and Ahmed Patel slapped their foreheads in unison, and stood looking at each other in frustration.

'What do we do now?' said Sonia.

Ahmed opened his mouth to reply, when his phone buzzed.

'Ahmed,' he barked into the phone. 'Yes . . . yes . . . yes . . . WHAT!?'

A moment later, Ahmed slipped the phone back into his kurta pocket and turned to his boss. 'Madam, we have a serious problem.'

* * *

Around the time the most powerful woman in the subcontinent was preparing her firstborn to take charge of the family's affairs, trouble was brewing in her backyard. Arvind Kejriwal had torn into her son-in-law, Robert Vadra, demanding a probe into his real estate dealings. The tide of bad press against him showed no signs of abating, with allegations of Vadra's extraordinary feats popping up—such as buying 3.5 acres of land in Manesar for Rs 7.5 crore and then flipping it to DLF 65 days later for Rs 58 crore after the Haryana government allowed it to be developed for residential purposes.

The Congress PR machinery faced an uphill task in dispelling the notion that the first *jamai* was anything but a *dalal* who essentially made his money by obtaining regulatory clearances. And as frenzied media coverage reached a crescendo, it became difficult to differentiate between serious reportage and satire, with reports like these going viral on social media sites. (see image on page 11)

When the furore showed no signs of dying down, the Congress president convened an urgent meeting at 10 Janpath constituting the entire top brass to discuss the day's key agenda, succinctly titled 'Saving Private Vadra'.

The UnReal Times
India's favourite satire, spoof, parody and humour portal

| HOME | NATIONAL ▾ | CRICKET | SHOWBIZ ▾ | WORLD NEWS ▾ | MISC. ▾ | IN PICS |

About Us   Write for Us   Contact Us   Login

Kejriwal widens attack, demands thorough probe into how Priyanka could fall for a chap like Vadra

October 9, 2012 | Filed under: Featured,General,Latest National | 2, Posted by: UnReal Mama

Like 1,706 people like this. Be the first of your friends.   Follow @TheUnRealTimes

Arvind Kejriwal widened his attack on India's first son-in-law, demanding a thorough probe into how an ordinary chap like Robert Vadra, with such a weak balance sheet of personal assets and low human capital, could make Priyanka fall for him.

"Vadra's sweet-heart deal with DLF raises many questions but what makes no sense whatsoever is how a petty brass trader from Moradabad, who looks more like Priyanka's chauffeur than her significant other, could *patao* a Nehru-Gandhi scion and marry into India's most powerful political family. We demand that Vadra come clean on this," thundered the feisty Magsaysay award winner, during a televised press conference.

Sonia was seated at the head of the long conference table, with Ahmed Patel standing behind her with a note and pen in hand. To her right were ministers from the Union Cabinet, spokespersons and various advisors. To her left, after a few vacant seats, were a battery of Italian to English to Hindi to English to Italian translators. On the floor, further to the left of the table, DLF Chairman K.P. Singh held down Robert Vadra's legs as he performed a series of sit-ups without a second's rest. When everyone else had assembled, Sonia Gandhi coughed politely, and the meeting began.

Ahmed pressed a button, and the 60-inch plasma TV installed on the wall opposite Sonia came to life. Arnab Goswami's booming voice filled the room.

'The Nation wants to know, Mr Jha!' Arnab said. 'Why did DLF give unsecured, interest-free loans amount to crores to Mr Robert Vadra's company, Skylight?'

'Two quick points, Arnab. First, they were business advances, a standard business practice, but second and more importantly, Mr Modi, whose hands are still fresh with the blood of the 2002 riot victims . . .'

'Don't change the topic, Mr Jha and don't BS me. Are we given to understand that Mr Vadra was, to put it bluntly, a middleman?'

'Allow me to explain, Arnab . . .'

'No, you first listen to my question, Mr Jha. A financier lends Rs 5 crore to Mr Vadra to buy land and then buys back the land at triple the value to net Mr Vadra a humongous return . . .'

It looked like a tiger making short work of a tethered goat. Sonia winced.

'*Dannazione*! That's enough,' she shouted. 'Turn the damn thing off.'

Ahmed yanked out the power plug, and the room suddenly became quiet.

'A maverick civil society activist digs up an old *Economic Times* report to make allegations against my son-in-law and that becomes the national narrative? Are we still in power or am I hallucinating?' Sonia exclaimed, banging her hand on the table.

Ahmed cleared his throat. 'Er . . . Madam, should we plant a "Sonia is very unhappy with Robert?" article to . . .'

Sonia cut him off with a stern glare.

'I meant, "Sonia is very unhappy with Robert being accused" article, madam,' Ahmed hastened to clarify. 'It's slightly inconsistent with our policy, but should help under the circumstances.'

Sonia gave her assent by waving her hand impatiently. 'We need a new approach, team. This is not going anywhere. How am I supposed to win the election for you chaps if my son-in-law is being called a "dalal"?' she said, turning to her Union Cabinet and posse of spokespersons. 'You guys are supposed to be the best in the business. Then why is there not a single positive story about Rob?'

'Madam, I just wrote a column explaining why Vadra is a very nice person,' answered Sanjay Jha, still appearing a little frazzled after the encounter with Arnab a few hours earlier at the Times Now studio. 'No media house is willing to publish it, so I have put it up on HamaraCongress.com. Perhaps if Tharoor sir can retweet it, it would be great,' he said, passing a document to the Congress president.

'Apropos of Mr Jha's entreaty, I have indeed perused the content of the said epistle penned by Mr Jha, madam,' Tharoor said, flicking his hair, 'and upon intense cogitation, thought it politic if you were to also scan the missive and satisfy yourself that it would indeed serve the overarching objective, namely of repairing the battered reputation of Mr Vadra, before I comply with Mr Jha's supplication of sharing his expostulations on the microblogging site that goes by the onomatopoeic name Twitter.'

The Congress president blinked. There was a moment's silence, during which the members looked at each other and then at Tharoor leaning back in his seat with a satisfied smile, and then again at Sonia.

'Uh, come again?' she said.

'I think Shashi wants you to approve it before he can

retweet it,' whispered Ahmed into the Congress president's ear.

'Ah, I see,' said Sonia. 'Pass it over, please.' Jha anxiously looked on like a student waiting for feedback from the school principal while Sonia donned her spectacles to go through the article.

Why Robert Vadra will make a better PM: A SWOT analysis by Sanjay Jha

Dimension	Robert vs NaMo	Verdict
Meritocratic Rise	Narendra Modi may have risen from a humble background to become the CM of Gujarat but then Robert Vadra was also a rank outsider when he overnight propelled himself into the Congress party's top echelons. Despite lack of pedigree and connections, he vaulted his way into Priyanka's heart.	Vadra's rise has been far more meritocratic and inspiring to the youth of the country.
Family Values	Robert Vadra is the quintessential family man. In an earlier interview, he'd said, 'I've lost 20 kg in five years. And in this much time, if I'd wanted to, I could have become a big celebrity. It's been a fight to stay normal.' He insisted towards the end of the interview, 'I gave up my life for Priyanka, fighting every day to not be a celebrity.'	Robert has always placed family over self even at the cost of personal ambition. Contrast this with Modi's greed for power at the expense of domestic bliss.

Contd . . .

. . . contd

Dimension	Robert vs NaMo	Verdict
Electability	Robert Vadra once said, 'I can win an election from anywhere,' a level of confidence which Narendra Modi lacks. Ultimately, whichever constituency Vadra chooses to represent, he will make a huge difference to it, unlike Modi. For instance, the first family's citadels, Raebareli and Amethi, enjoy 24-hour power supply while most parts of Uttar Pradesh face power cuts. However, Narendra Modi's constituency Maninagar does not enjoy such privilege. It has 24-hour power supply, but then so does the rest of Gujarat.	Robert is a pan-Indian name with appeal not restricted to a particular state.
Self-abnegation	Vadra once memorably said, '*Abhi Rahul ka time chal raha hai, phir Priyanka ka time aayega, phir parivar ke doosre sadasyon ka.*' Contrast this with Modi's impatience to land the top job.	This shows that Robert Vadra, in the best traditions of Indian self-renunciation, is patient and is willing to wait for his turn, unlike Modi.
Business Acumen	Modi earned his business chops as a tea vendor. Roadside tea retailing, colloquially called *cutting chai* in urban India, has sound economics. It requires	Those who still think that Modi is more business savvy need to have a counselling session

Contd . . .

. . . contd

Dimension	Robert vs NaMo	Verdict
	little capital, has low cost manufacturing, and tends to have a diversified customer base and good customer loyalty. All it requires is for the entrepreneur to wake up at dawn and put in hard labour until dusk. As against Modi, Robert Vadra has built a successful business empire spanning real estate, hotels and many other sectors through sheer grit and shrewd judgement. Moreover, competitors can assault tea vendors but Robert Vadra's business is virtually unassailable by competition. It is so creditworthy that it can get loans at zero per cent interest rates, and its value increases 600 times in three years. Vadra's achievement is more commendable since he is married into a family which has a history of destroying businesses rather than creating them.	with DLF Chairman K.P. Singh.
Social Media Influence	Modi boasts of a huge following on Facebook and Twitter, overlooking the fact that quality is more important than quantity. How many updates by Modi on Facebook and Twitter can you remember? As against	Vadra has a higher social media quotient than NaMo.

Contd. . .

. . . contd

Dimension	Robert vs NaMo	Verdict
	this Robert Vadra's update on Facebook: 'Mango people in banana republic.' It has entered the hall of fame alongside *'Tum mujhe khoon do, main tumhe azadi dunga'* and *'Meri Jhansi nahi doongi.'*	
Physical Fitness	Narendra Modi inherited his so-called 56-inch chest from his parents whereas Robert Vadra worked hard to develop a rippled, sculpted look. While Modi does Pranayama and Yoga, Vadra engages in secular muscle-building routines. Hence, unlike Modi, Vadra is more likely to feel for people with underdeveloped physiques. This is precisely why he used to run a fitness bulletin on his Facebook page.	Vadra is India's Rambo, not Modi.

'Hope you liked it, madam?' asked Jha, grinning sheepishly.

Sonia put the clipping down and peered over her spectacles to glower at Jha. 'You jackass, you call this analysis or is it insidious satire? Whose side are you on, anyway?' she hissed. 'Take him away before he wastes some more of my time. And let me have a relook at his contract too!'

'Er . . . sorry, madam. I should have been more effusive in my praise,' stuttered Jha, as he was unceremoniously picked up from his seat and ushered out. 'One more chance, madam. I'll compare him to a breath of fresh air . . . madam, pleaaaaaaaaaase,' were his last words before he was ejected from the premises.

'As I was saying,' Sonia continued, 'we need a new approach, team. Out-of-the-box thinking. Come on, people, throw me a bone here.'

'DLF could sponsor the India Against Corruption agitation,' ventured K.P. Singh, much to everyone's amazement. 'You see, IAC has done for us in a matter of days what IPL title sponsorship for five years couldn't achieve. Namely, brand recall across the length and breadth of the country. Now even housewives and kids know of terms like "business advances", "sweetheart deals" while the phrase "doing a DLF on me" has become a buzzword in the workplace. Imagine the brand placement possibilities. New exposés by Arvind Kejriwal can be called a "DLF Maximum". We can rope in other sponsors too for the Kejriwal-led IAC realty show. A scam of over Rs 1000 crore can be called a "Citi moment of Excess". In fact, it will be a virtuous cycle. We sponsor Kejriwal who in turn unravels more DLF maximums which drives brand visibility and brings in more business, enabling Arvind to spawn more DLF maximums.'

The DLF chairman's passionate espousal of his business plan was cut short by Rahul Gandhi's entrance, in tow with Digvijaya Singh. Hair dishevelled, a glazed look in his eyes and sporting a four-day stubble, the Nehru–Gandhi scion stumbled towards the vacant chair next to Sonia, and flopped into it.

'Rahul, you are late, again,' Sonia chided.

'Sorry, Mamma, I was doing some . . . er . . . deep meditation with Diggy uncle,' he said, kissing his mother on her forehead. 'Anyway, sorry for interrupting you, KP uncle. That was some cool jazz you were spewing, boss. Brand visibility, market share and all. Reminds me of my days as a management consultant with that strategy consulting firm . . . what's its name . . . Gecko . . . no . . . Lizard Group . . . no . . . ah yes, Monitor Group!'

At this, Jairam Ramesh suddenly threw up his hands and whooped, startling the others. 'Yes! Rahul baba has shown us the way,' he exclaimed. 'All we need to say is that DLF had hired Robertji as a management consultant and paid him the big bucks for his consulting services to the real estate conglomerate during the 2007–10 period.

'After all,' he continued, 'DLF sponsored a shitty tournament like IPL for five years, forking out humungous sums to BCCI in the name of creating enterprise value. So it would be totally in line with their way of doing business to hire the services of management consultants as well. And it makes business sense to hire Vadra rather than McKinsey or BCG, no? What say, Mr KP?'

K.P. Singh pondered over this for a moment. 'Hmm . . . yeah sure,' he said, warming up to the idea. 'We could justify extending unsecured, interest-free loans to Robert as consideration for his strategic inputs. Come to think of it, we have indeed shelled out big bucks to receive advice on stuff like "which markets to play in", "how to become No. 1", "defining No. 1", "the need to be No. 1", and other pressing business challenges, through 1000 finely crafted PowerPoint slides replete with spiffy graphics, cryptic business jargon, and bleeding obvious insights. By jingo, this could work, Jairam!'

There was a murmur of approval from all the Congress

spokespersons. 'It's easier to go with this line than attempting to rationalize Rob's dealings with DLF as standard practice in the real estate business, ma'am,' said Abhishek Manu Singhvi, sounding relieved.

Singhvi was only echoing a wide-felt sentiment of his tribe. Analysing the curious balance sheets and P&L statements of Vadra's company and giving it a positive spin was proving to be a task of Himalayan proportions. Even IIMA students had been stumped when asked to prepare a P&L of Vadra's company for the 2007–10 period during an exam to test their grasp of accounting and had *gherao*ed the office of the Dean of Academic Affairs two days earlier, forcing the intervention of the HRD ministry.

'Insofar as allegations of Shri Vadraji acquiring assets disproportionate to known sources of income are concerned,' averred Manish Tewari, 'claiming he was a management consultant, juxtaposed with DLF's propensity to sponsor orgies such as IPL, will satisfy the public after they step back and take a holistic view. Indeed, Shri Vadraji's only disproportionate assets over which there would continue to be question marks after that would be his pectoral muscles.'

There was a chorus of 'ayes' followed by desk-thumping. Although Sonia had not fully followed the line of argument, she could discern the contours of a consensus emerging, and one of the hallmarks of her leadership style was not to get in the way when there was broad-based agreement on an issue. 'I think we have consensus here,' Sonia said, a little unsure of herself. 'Well done, Jairam.'

'No, all credit to Rahul, madam,' Jairam was quick to point out. 'It was his idea, really.' Jairam was always conscientious about acknowledging Rahul for intellectual inputs. Many months later, he would not only credit the Nehru–Gandhi scion for formulating, scoping, advocating, canvassing support for and finally suggesting the title—the Right to Fair Compensation and Transparency in Land Acquisition, Rehabilitation and Resettlement—for the Land Acquisition bill, but also go ahead and credit Rahul Gandhi for the idea to credit him.

Everyone seemed satisfied except Robert Vadra. 'Calling me a management consultant just to make your jobs easier? How is being dubbed a management consultant any better than being called a land shark?' he remonstrated, but his protests were drowned by rapturous cries of *'Sonia Gandhi ki jai'* and *'Rahul lao, desh bachao'* as the assembled members celebrated yet another demonstration of mind-blowing leadership by their beloved leaders.

When the chants died down, Sonia looked around the room with a satisfied smile. Her smile slowly turned into a frown, as she noticed something amiss.

'Where is Dr Singh?' she said.

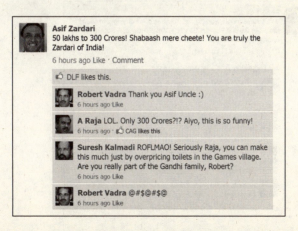

Asif Zardari
50 lakhs to 300 Crores! Shabaash mere cheete! You are truly the Zardari of India!
6 hours ago Like · Comment

👍 DLF likes this.

Robert Vadra Thank you Asif Uncle :)
6 hours ago Like

A Raja LOL. Only 300 Crores?!? Aiyo, this is so funny!
6 hours ago · 👍 CAG likes this

Suresh Kalmadi ROFLMAO! Seriously Raja, you can make this much just by overpricing toilets in the Games village. Are you really part of the Gandhi family, Robert?
6 hours ago Like

Robert Vadra @#$@#$@
6 hours ago Like

The Hindu
"Robert Vadra is a small farmer," says Bhoopinder Singh Hooda
6 hours ago · Like · Comment

  👍 DLF likes this.

  Ashok Khemka WTF?
  6 hours ago · 👍 Arvind Kejriwal and 1,394,304 others like this

  Robert Vadra :D Thinking of milking a cow. Pawar ji, can
  you help me?
  6 hours ago · Like

  Sharad Pawar Sure. Position yourself near the cow, and
  place a bucket between its legs, right under its udder
  6 hours ago · Like

  Robert Vadra Done. Then?
  6 hours ago · Like

  Sharad Pawar Now gently squeeze its teats one after the
  other.
  6 hours ago · Like

  Robert Vadra Yay! It's working. But Pawarji, the milk
  looks very watery and smells weird too. Also there's only
  one teat.
  6 hours ago · Like

  Sharad Pawar Huh? How's that possible? Can you send
  me a pic?
  6 hours ago · Like

  Robert Vadra Done. Check mail.
  6 hours ago · Like

  Sharad Pawar Uh, that's a bull.
  6 hours ago · Like

  Ashok Khemka ROFLMAO
  6 hours ago · 👍 Arvind Kejriwal and 2,545,434 others like this

Robert Vadra
Vadra surname not working out. Thinking of modifying it to sound
more like Gandhi. Perhaps Gandhi + Vadra = Gandra. Robert
Gandra! How does that sound?
6 hours ago · Like · Comment

  👍 Bhoopinder Singh Hooda, DLF like this.

  Priyanka Gandhi No Robert, people in the North will
  laugh at you
  6 hours ago · Like

  Robert Vadra Um, okay. How about Vadra + Gandhi =
  Vaandhi? Robert Vaandhi!
  6 hours ago · 👍 Subramanian Swamy likes this

  Priyanka Gandhi No Robert, Vaandhi means vomit in
  Tamil. People in the South will hold their noses near you
  6 hours ago · Like

  Robert Vadra Argh! This is so difficult. Wish it was as
  easy for me as it was Feroz ji
  6 hours ago · Like

TWO

The silent leader

NOVEMBER 2012

THE TOUR GUIDE IN London looked dismayed. Headed in his direction were a bunch of teenage girls and boys who, in all likelihood, were tourists from that infernal country. The girls wore tank tops and miniskirts, and giggled non-stop, while the boys wore shorts, vests and baseball hats turned sideways, and walked jauntily behind the girls flaunting their muscled arms, as if they owned the bloody place.

'Americans,' the tour guide muttered in disgust, and watched warily as two of them, the girls, made their way to him.

'Hi!' said the blonde, with a wide smile that revealed unnaturally white teeth and a blob of chewing gum stuck between them. 'We are from America. Do you mind showing us around?'

The tour guide swallowed his revulsion, and smiled politely. 'Of course! Welcome to Madame Tussauds!'

From his long experience as the museum's tour guide, he knew precisely what would tickle the American tourist's craving for a unique cultural experience. So he led them to the Hollywood section, and stood aside frowning, as the girls drove themselves silly photographing each other smooching Robert Pattinson, groping Brad Pitt's bum, hugging George Clooney and so on. When they were done, he took them to the music section, then to the sports section, and then after a moment's hesitation decided to risk taking them to his favourite section—world leaders. He figured he'd start with something his tourists would find familiar, so he led them to the replica of the most powerful office in the world.

'Welcome to the Oval Office,' he said, with an exaggerated sweep of his hand.

'Wow,' drawled the blonde, looking around the room with big eyes. 'Which country is this in?'

The tour guide's jaw dropped open. He blinked in disbelief. 'The United States of America,' he said, gritting his teeth.

The blonde looked at him vacuously for a second before breaking into a happy grin. 'That's ossum!'

Shaking his head, the guide herded the group into the room, towards the large desk near the tall French windows.

'This is the Resolute desk,' he said, gesturing at the mammoth wooden furniture, and slipped into his well-rehearsed monologue. 'It is called so because it was built with wood from the Arctic Rescue Ship called the *HMS Resolute*. In the first half of the nineteenth century, the ship got trapped in the Arctic ice and had to be abandoned. Later in 1856, an American whaler rescued the ship and returned it to Queen Victoria. The ship's timbers were then used to make the desk which the queen gifted to America in 1880,' he concluded, and turned to his group with a confident smile, only to discover that the girls weren't paying attention to him. Instead, they were bunched around the wax figure standing behind the desk.

'I love Obama!'

'He is so hot!'

'Like, so hot!'

The guide sighed, and walked over to them. 'As you no doubt have guessed, this is President Obama.'

After the girls were done oohing and aahing over Obama, they turned their eyes towards the other occupant of the room.

'Who is that guy?' asked the redhead, pointing at the wax model of a diminutive elderly man with a blue turban, standing across the desk facing the American president.

The tour guide frowned for a fleeting moment. 'Uh, that, ladies, is Dr Manmohan Singh,' he said. 'Dr Manmohan Singh is the prime minister of India, the world's largest democracy, and has been portrayed here in conversation with Barack Obama, the leader of the world's most powerful democracy,' he added with a flourish.

'While on paper Dr Singh is the most powerful man in India, he is widely considered to be a puppet controlled by his party's president Sonia Gandhi, an Italian-born woman who was married to former Indian Prime Minister Rajiv Gandhi,' the tour guide added, immensely pleased with himself for staying well versed with the nuances of politics in the subcontinent.

'This one isn't as good as the others,' said the redhead, walking around the replica of the Indian PM. 'Like, it clearly looks like a wax model,' she added and poked a finger into the wax model's side. 'Feels real though.'

The blonde, meanwhile, stood chewing her gum in front of the wax model, peering into its still eyes. The redhead circled around the figurine and joined her friend at the front. The blonde blew out a gum bubble that grew to the size of a golf ball and then went splat on her face. At which, the wax model blinked.

Startled out of their wits, the two girls shrieked and fled the room.

The tour guide gawked at the door in dumbfounded amazement for a few moments and then slowly turned around to find the erstwhile wax model gazing at him with a placid expression. He swallowed hard and looked away. In his mind, he cursed the front desk for not posting information about the visit of a state guest. After a minute, when he realized that Dr Singh stood unmoved from his spot, he mustered the courage to meet the Indian premier's gaze.

'Prime minister, I am so sorry for whatever I said about you. I did not mean any of it!' he despaired.

Dr Manmohan Singh stared at the guide for a long time. Then he mumbled, '*Theek hai*,' and turned on his heel to make his way out of the museum towards a waiting car that would take him to the airport and from thereon back to India, where he would answer his party president's urgent summons.

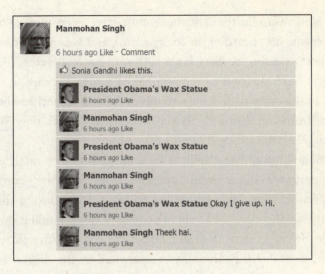

Manmohan Singh

6 hours ago Like · Comment

👍 Sonia Gandhi likes this.

President Obama's Wax Statue
6 hours ago Like

Manmohan Singh
6 hours ago Like

President Obama's Wax Statue
6 hours ago Like

Manmohan Singh
6 hours ago Like

President Obama's Wax Statue Okay I give up. Hi.
6 hours ago Like

Manmohan Singh Theek hai.
6 hours ago Like

* * *

If the Vadra exposés had lowered morale in the Congress camp, Kejriwal's follow-up sting operation on the Union Law Minister Salman Khurshid battered it. As it became increasingly clear that Salman Khurshid's Zakir Hussain Memorial Trust may or may not have embezzled funds amounting to no more than Rs 70 lakh meant for handicapped people, a pall of gloom hung over the corridors of 24 Akbar Road, the Congress headquarters.

'Of all the awesome things he could have done as the Union law minister with the power and financial outlays at his disposal, he has to get entangled in a petty scam like this that does not even breach the one crore mark. *Thoo*!' exclaimed a Congress Working Committee member from Kerala.

'Lot of soul-searching needs to be done,' averred his colleague. 'From the heady days of the multi-lakh crore 2G scam to this, the decline has been precipitous.'

Sonia Gandhi thought there must have been a mistake when she first heard of the 'baby scam', as it was referred to in party circles. 'Seventy lakhs? Ahmed, are you sure? You might have miscounted the number of zeroes. Perhaps, it is a 70-lakh crore scam,' she remarked. Ahmed rechecked and confirmed the figure. 'Only six zeroes, ma'am. It's only 70 lakh, I'm afraid.' Sonia almost fainted.

Salman would have to fight these allegations by himself as the party was quick to distance itself from the 'baby scam'. No leader was willing to come to his aid in refuting the charges. 'Shri Khurshid's entanglement in this scam, if it can even be called that, does not reflect the ethos of the party. The leadership is profoundly embarrassed by the cheapness of the allegations and the ridiculous proportions of the figures associated with it,' a senior leader opined.

There was even speculation that Khurshid might be asked to put in his papers.

It was in these circumstances that the Congress high command decided that nothing less than a complete overhaul of the government would do to redeem the party's image in the eyes of the public.

So for the second time that month, the party top brass met in 10 Janpath's conference room.

* * *

The room bore a markedly different look that day. The long conference table had disappeared and, instead, a circular table stood in the centre, with several chairs set around it, directed outwards. Each chair had a piece of paper stuck to its head.

Finance Minister, Home Minister, Law Minister, read some of the tags. A massive throne-like chair was set several feet away from this arrangement.

The door opened and in strode Sonia Gandhi, Rahul Gandhi, Dr Manmohan Singh and the entourage of UPA Cabinet ministers. Sonia walked straight to the throne-like chair and made herself comfortable, while the rest stood a few feet away with folded hands.

Sonia Gandhi swept the room with her gaze, and clapped twice. 'All right, it's time for the Cabinet reshuffle. Take your seats, gentlemen!'

The ministers whooped with joy and scrambled towards their respective seats. Dr Singh, meanwhile, padded towards Sonia Gandhi and murmured a greeting.

'Oh no, Dr Singh,' said Sonia, and gently pushed the prime minister towards the table. 'How can we play without you? Please join them.'

Sonia Gandhi gestured to Rahul, who clapped excitedly and ran towards the DVD player in the corner of the room.

'Ready?' cried Rahul, standing over the player. 'Go!' he barked, and pressed down the 'play' button.

Britney Spears's 'Oops! I did it again' filled the room. The ministers leapt from their respective seats and began jogging one after the other in a clockwise direction. As the beats gathered momentum, the ministers ran faster and faster, making Rahul more and more excited, until he finally plunged down the 'stop' button.

* * *

Meanwhile, political circles were abuzz as to which politician would be outed next. Kejriwal had hinted that it would be someone big from Maharashtra. And that could only mean the big daddy of them all—Sharad Pawar.

There was a glow on the face of the Maratha strongman, a spring in his step in the lead-up to the day of Kejriwal's press conference. To have the honour of being dishonoured by the anti-corruption crusader now carried a certain cachet, akin to a Bollywood diva being invited to endorse Lux, in a nod to her stardom. For a politician to be 'exposed' by Kejriwal was the equivalent of a model shooting into the big league by being exposed for the famed Kingfisher calendar by ace lensman Atul Kasbekar.

The Maratha strongman cancelled all engagements that fateful day to savour the moment in his penthouse in the company of his aides. He settled into his favourite seat, popcorn in hand, and switched on the widescreen plasma TV with all the excitement and eagerness of an avid Indian cricket fan waiting for the Indian run chase to begin in an ODI match. The news channels interrupted regular broadcast to bring the live footage from the Press Club of India, where Kejriwal's conference was about to begin.

'Today I am going to talk about a politician from Maharashtra. Someone who is a heavyweight in every sense of the term, a national leader,' Kejriwal began in an earnest tone. Pawar's chest swelled with pride, and he extended his hand to his aide to accept his congratulations in advance.

'*Jee haan, mein Gadkariji ki baat kar raha hoon,*' Kejriwal continued. '*Veh brashtachaar ke Maharathi hain.*'

Pawar felt his ego getting punctured like an over-inflated

tyre bursting. In a heartbeat, his smile turned into a scowl and he spat out the popcorn in his mouth.

'What the bloody hell is this? Are you sure this is live coverage?' he bellowed like a raging African bull elephant. A minion scrambled to change channels, but they all showed visuals of a rotund Gadkari, with Kejriwal's voice in the background chronicling his feats in the field of corruption. It was like a slap on the face of Sharad Pawar, much more painful than the one an irate Sikh had landed on his face a year ago. Even veteran, thick-skinned politicians felt viscerally the magnitude of the slight on one of their own.

The next day, a lesser-known activist, Y.P. Singh, tried to salvage the situation by doing a 'mercy exposé' on Sharadji at a hurriedly convened press conference, listing in awe the assets he had acquired during the course of his illustrious career, but it did little to pacify Pawar.

'I don't want to be exposed by some *do-takke-ka* activist. I want the best. I WANT KEJRIWAL!' he screamed, and threatened to retire from all walks of public life, triggering panic in the corridors of power. The stability of the government was at stake. Senior leaders rushed to the NCP supremo's residence to pacify and dissuade him from acting in haste, while Congress troubleshooters tried to work on Kejriwal, hoping to persuade him to do a Pawar exposé.

Kejriwal later issued a mea culpa, clarifying that his slight of the NCP supremo was unintentional. 'I meant no discourtesy to Shri Pawarji. I consider him to be as corrupt, if not more, as Vadraji, Khurshidji and other leaders. I just thought why not be considerate to the less corrupt and let them have their day in the sun. I promise I'll do an exclusive exposé on him soon. He deserves no less,' promised the feisty social-activist-turned-politician.

What was merely a pinprick to Sharad Pawar's ego turned out to be the kiss of political death for Nitin Gadkari, like the innocent extra getting killed in the crossfire between the cops and dacoits. Although Kejriwal's exposé was very mild—he had alluded to diversion—he had unwittingly opened the Pandora's box. The media took to investigating Gadkari's shady business dealings with the same gusto as a pack of hyenas biting into the juicy hinds of a corpulent water buffalo. The skeletons began to tumble out of Gadkari's closet: shell companies registered in slum colonies under the name of his driver, his accountant and employee's son listed as directors and so on. The deeper the reporters dug, the more bizarre the stories turned out to be. Even a fictitious report that Gadkari's pet Great Dane, Gundu, was registered as a director found traction with an incredulous public.

* * *

Later that evening in 10 Janpath, Sonia Gandhi sat watching the evening news, thoroughly enjoying BJP leaders stumbling over each other attempting to defend the allegations against their president Nitin Gadkari.

'These allegations are baseless, wrong and unfortunate!' huffed Nitin Gadkari at his press conference. 'I have been working in the area as a social entrepreneur for the benefit of farmers . . .'

Sonia threw her head back to laugh, and found Ahmed Patel standing quietly behind her couch.

'Oh, Ahmed, are you watching this?' said Sonia, guffawing. 'Every channel is going after him. This is priceless!'

'Ha ha ha, yes, madamji, it is,' Ahmed joined in politely, and the two laughed for a full minute, switching between the various channels telecasting Gadkari's press conference.

When his boss had finally calmed down, Ahmed bent towards her, and cleared his throat.

'Er . . . Soniaji, are you sure about today's changes in the Cabinet?' he asked in a low voice.

The Cabinet reshuffle had ended up cocking a snook at Kejriwal by 'rewarding' tainted leaders: Shashi Tharoor was re-inducted into the Cabinet as minister of state for HRD, Salman Khurshid was 'promoted' to Union foreign minister, the embarrassment he had caused to the party by getting entangled in a 70-lakh scam notwithstanding, and Manish Tewari was rewarded for putting in donkey's years defending the indefensible.

'Well, the idea was to send a strong signal to Kejriwal that the party is going to brazen it out and not get embarrassed by his provocations. It was a very pacifist, Gandhian-like response, akin to turning the other cheek and saying, "Come slap me again if you dare,"' explained Sonia Gandhi patiently.

Ahmed persisted. 'But, madam, won't this add to a growing sense of anti-incumbency that a political opponent might exploit to his or her advantage?'

Sonia Gandhi burst out laughing. 'And who's going to do that?' she pointed at the television. 'These jokers?'

* * *

Arvind Kejriwal
Just learnt that Bruce Wayne is Batman. Soon going to expose him to the entire world.

6 hours ago Like · Comment

👍 Joker, Harvey Dent like this.

 Morgan Freeman aka Fox Wait a minute. You are saying that my boss is a masked vigilante who beats up people with his bare hands, and your strategy is to blackmail him? *Smirk* Good luck

6 hours ago · 👍 Salman Khurshid likes this

 Arvind Kejriwal Ek Arvind ko maar doge, to 100 Arvind khade ho jayenge

6 hours ago Like

 Morgan Freeman aka Fox Er, let me check with Nolan on a comeback line

6 hours ago Like

THREE

The Gujarat lion

DECEMBER 2012

Dekho dekho kaun aaya, Gujarat ka sher aaya!

The sheets stirred.

Dekho dekho kaun aaya, Gujarat ka sher aaya!

The sheets parted. Narendra Modi stretched his arms wide in either direction and yawned.

Dekho dekho kaun aaya, Gujarat ka sher . . .

'*Jag gaya sher*,' said Modi, and silenced the customized SmartNaMo alarm clock with a quick tap on its head. It was three in the morning. Modi leapt out of his bed with the vitality of a teenager to begin yet another twenty-hour day.

In fifteen minutes, Modi had brushed his teeth with a neem stick from the forests of Vadodara, rinsed his face with a herbal soap made by the self-help groups of Kutch, gulped down a glass of milk from the dairies of Anand, and eased into the prayer pose of *suryanamaskar* in the space behind his house. He then began warming up with a series of basic yogic poses, his body gliding from one pose to another before slipping into the first of the difficult poses—the *shirshasana*, or the headstand. A few serene moments later, he fluidly moved into the *eka hasta vrksasana*, the one-handed tree pose, and calmly held his body's weight on his left hand for half a minute, before transitioning to the *taraksvasana*, or the handstand scorpion pose. Expertly balancing his body on both arms, he bent his legs backward all the way to the front of his face, like a scorpion coiling its tail.

After Modi had completed the ten toughest poses in yoga, he dropped down to the floor and began to do push-ups. Without breaking into a sweat or pausing for rest, he executed 300 push-ups with perfect form. When he was done, he bounced up, pulled a measuring tape and wrapped it around his chest.

'Fifty-five inches,' he muttered and frowned.

He dropped back to the floor, performed 100 more push-ups, and measured his chest again.

'Fifty-six inches,' he exclaimed. 'Yes!'

By 5 a.m., he had freshened up and moved to his study. With one hand holding I.E. Irodov's *Problems in General Physics* open midway, and the other scribbling away on a notepad of recycled paper, Modi solved five IIT problems in thirty minutes and pumped his fist in delight.

At 5.30 a.m., Modi opened his walk-in wardrobe, and stared at an assortment of kurtas with colours ranging from bright saffron to light pink. After scratching his beard for a moment, he picked a relatively new light-green kurta from a corner. He then proceeded to carefully iron out every crease from the garment, and stood back and nodded in satisfaction when he was done.

At 7 a.m., Narendra Modi sat in his apartment's living room, dressed and groomed for the day ahead, poring over the day's newspaper. A dozen other dailies were stacked next to him. Just as he was shaking his head ruefully at a headline, Amit Shah stumbled in, dazed and dishevelled, barely stifling a yawn.

'*Kya kya chaapte hain, yeh media waale,*' grumbled Modi. 'Look at these headlines: "Modi is India's answer to Hitler", "Modi is a dictator", "Modi is a . . . pariah",' Modi looked up at Shah. 'What's pariah?'

'Um, seems to stem from *pari*, Modibhai . . . uh, the Hindi word for fairy,' said Shah, scratching his bald head. 'Maybe pariah means a male fairy?' he asked eagerly.

Modi flicked his wrist, like Spiderman would, and a smartphone slid into his palm from under his sleeve. A few clicks on his phone later, 'According to Webster's, pariah means castaway, outsider, vagabond, derelict or persona non grata,' Modi folded his arms and set his mouth in a tight line. '*Dekh lunga saalon ko.*'

'*Chodiye na*, Modibhai,' said Shah, eager to cheer his boss up. 'Let's watch your favourite scene from your favourite movie.'

Shah slid a disc into the DVD player adjacent to the TV, and the screen came alive with a scene from the animated movie *The Lion King*, with the uplifting tune of Elton John's 'Circle of Life' filling the room. Modi's eyes lit up. He watched in rapt attention, as animals of various hues, shapes and sizes, travelled from far and wide towards the tall rock in the middle of the jungle, where the Lion King stood proudly, his regal mane fluttering in the breeze. The wise old monkey climbed onto the rock, greeted and hugged the Lion King, and together they walked to the queen to check on her little cub. The monkey smiled at the cub, dabbed paste on its forehead and lifted it.

'Now comes my favourite scene,' said Modi, reaching for Shah's hands, his eyes welling up with emotion.

And then the monkey hobbled to the very edge of the rock and held little Simba aloft. Down below, the zebras and the elephants and the giraffes and animals of every species went crazy, cheering and hooting and trumpeting their delight. Back in the living room, Modi and Amit Shah hugged each other and jumped excitedly.

When the two had calmed down, Modi wiped his eyes and handed his phone to Amit Shah.

'Call the Lion King . . . I mean, Advaniji,' said Modi. 'It's time for Simba to stake his claim.'

'Right away, Modibhai,' said Shah, dialling the BJP patriarch's landline number.

'Hello, is Advaniji home? Modiji wants to talk to him,' he said to the butler who answered the phone.

'Just a moment, he's in his study,' Advani's butler chirped. A few seconds later, Shah heard a loud slap. The butler returned to the call.

'He isn't at home,' he said, his voice a lot less chirpy this time.

'But . . .' started Shah, before the call disconnected with

the loud crack of the receiver being slammed down.

Modi ground his teeth. 'Never mind,' he said. 'Call Sushmaji.'

'She isn't picking, Modibhai,' said Shah, seconds later.

'Jaitleyji?'

'Busy . . .'

'Gadkariji?'

'Voicemail . . .'

'Prakash Javadekar?'

'He isn't picking . . .'

'Venkaiyah Naidu?'

'Not picking . . .'

'That *chaprasi* at the BJP office?'

'Not picking . . .'

'Maa Jagdamba!' screamed Modi. 'Why the hell is no one picking my call? It's like I am some . . . some . . .'

'Pariah, saheb?' supplied Amit Shah helpfully.

Modi threw him a murderous look, prompting Shah to take an involuntary step backwards.

Modi began pacing the room. '*Aise nahi chalega,*' he muttered, his brows furrowed. He stopped, set his jaw, picked up his briefcase and turned towards the door. 'Let's get to work,' he said, his eyes blazing with resolve. 'Assembly elections are upon us.'

* * *

The next day, Modi embarked on the Sadbhavna mission—a series of one-day fasts in various districts, interspersed with photo ops with people from various communities, castes and

religions—all aimed to tell the world, 'It's all cool here, yo!'
Funded by the state government, the Sadbhavna mission was
a roaring success, save for a brief flutter in between when
a Muslim cleric offered Modi a skullcap in full view of the
cameras. For the briefest of seconds, Modi stared at the
cleric as if it weren't a skullcap but a time bomb the cleric
was suggesting Modi wear as his headgear. The very next
moment, the seasoned political instinct in him took over, and
he smiled broadly. He politely refused the skullcap, accepted
a shawl instead, and hugged the cleric with great affection.

But the damage was already done. By the time the cleric
had left the stage, an NDTV scribe had already completed
his next 'Blow to Modi' story headlined 'Modi refuses cleric's
skullcap; offends minorities yet again' and sent it to her editor
for review. Secular leaders across the country whooped and
high-fived each other. Bihar CM Nitish Kumar fainted in
ecstasy. He would later recover to conceptualize and pioneer
the topi–tilak theory of secularism.

Nevertheless, the Modi juggernaut in Gujarat hurtled
ahead. Modi's next step was the Vivekananda Yuva Vikas
Yatra, a month-long tour around Gujarat, highlighting his
government's successes, and connecting with his electorate.
Wherever he went, vast crowds thronged to hear him speak,
and laugh at his jokes on Dr Manmohan Singh and Rahul
Gandhi. Ever the forward thinker, Modi measured the volume
of laughter with a sound meter, and assigned colour-coded
ratings to each of the jokes on his list, categorizing them into
three categories: LOL, ROFL and ROFLMAO, and at the
end of each day, filed away the gags marked ROFLMAO in
a folder labelled 2014.

Meanwhile, the Gujarat Congress decided that it was time to counter Modi with its own high-pitch campaign.

* * *

'Narendra Modi has been lying to the voters!' declared Gujarat Congress chief Arjun Modhwadia. 'His so-called development is a myth. The reality is that farmers are committing suicide, there's no drinking water, there's no electricity, there's no safety for women and children. The people of Gujarat are fed up with the Narendra Modi government and will give a befitting reply to Modi by electing the Congress . . . Congress to pow . . . BWAHAHAHAHAHA!'

Modhwadia's colleague Shaktisinh Gohil groaned. 'Not again, Arjunbhai! This is the fifth time you have lost it! We barely have an hour before the press conference. How will you be ready in time?'

'Can't do it . . . can't do it, yaar,' sputtered Modhwadia, his huge frame rocking with mirth. 'The very idea of the Congress coming back to power in Gujarat sends me over the edge. BWAHAHAHA!'

Gohil stared at his colleague in dismay, and was about to make an incisive remark when Modhwadia's phone rang aloud.

'Soniaji's call!' he exclaimed. The two leaders leapt off their seats, stood at attention and saluted smartly. Modhwadia then gingerly tapped a key on his mobile phone and put it to his ear.

'Soniaji!' he said, stooping almost all the way down to the ground. 'My day is made! I can't tell you how privileged I am that you've deemed it worth your while to call . . .'

'Save it,' Sonia barked. 'How is our campaign coming along?'

'Er . . . fantastic, madam. With Rahul baba and your blessings . . .'

'Whatever,' she interrupted. 'I noticed that Modi has been trumpeting his Gujarat model to all and sundry. People seem to be buying into it too. Why aren't we showcasing our alternative Gujarat model?'

'Our Gujarat model? Um . . . we don't have . . .'

'Then come up with one!'

'But, Soniaji . . .'

'No buts. I want to see the Congress's Gujarat model first thing tomorrow morning. Understood?'

'Er . . . yes, madam, but . . .' said Modhwadia, but Sonia had already hung up.

Modhwadia looked at his colleague desperately. 'Yaar, how do we come up with our own Gujarat model at such short notice?'

Shaktisinh Gohil put an arm around his distressed friend, and said, 'Leave that to me.'

* * *

The next day, a series of advertisements featuring Tulika Patel, a small-time Gujarati model and TV actress, hit national television. '*Disha badlo, dasha badlo,*' urged the petite Tulika, with a conviction greater than all of Gujarat's Congress leaders put together, highlighting the failures of the Modi government, and arguing that the Congress could do a far better job at governance. So ubiquitous was Tulika on TV, and so central she seemed to the Congress's election campaign that veteran Congress leaders soon began to wonder if she was the Congress's CM candidate for Gujarat.

Then Rahul Gandhi landed in Gujarat, giving a gentle fillip to the Congress's campaign and a massive boost to Modi's. The moment it was confirmed that Rahul would address a number of rallies, Modi set fire to all the documents that had his upcoming speeches which Amit Shah had painstakingly prepared over the past three weeks.

'What are you doing, Modibhai?' panicked Amit Shah.

'Rahul baba is here,' replied Modi.

'Oh,' said Shah, and after a moment's thought, added, 'Let me go open that bottle of champagne.'

* * *

Rahul kicked off his tour of Gujarat with rallies in all the Congress strongholds. Suffice to say, his calendar wasn't a particularly hectic one. His rallies were high-decibel events, with no one quite sure of what to expect. Rahul's most notable performance came in Sabarkantha district, where he wowed the masses as well as the intelligentsia with his groundbreaking theory on potatonomics.

'*Ek kilo aloo kitne ka bikta hai?*' he hollered at a rally, and cold-called a random chap from one of the front rows.

The poor chap who had been desperately waiting for the speech to get over so that he could collect the promised lunch packet and get back to his village to tend to his field blinked and said the first thing that came to his mind. '*Tees rupaye,*' he mumbled.

'Yes, *teen rupaye*!' exclaimed Rahul, and turned back to the audience at large to take his argument forward. 'A packet of potato chips costs 10 rupees. Whose loss is it? Farmers'!'

'But I said tees rupaye . . . thirty!' blurted the man, and was immediately slapped by a Youth Congress worker.

'If Rahulji says a kilo of potatoes costs 3 rupees, then it costs 3 rupees. Get it?' He wagged his finger menacingly.

'But . . .' he began in protest, and was promptly lifted off his feet by two burly men and dumped outside the rally grounds, wherefrom he made his way back to his village on an empty stomach.

Rahul then visited various colleges in Gujarat to interact with the youth to share his vision for their future. In one such visit, while Rahul was waxing eloquent on the importance of Internet at the school level, a student got up and asked, 'Mr Gandhi, how would you generate awareness on Internet among primary school students in government schools when they can't even read or write properly?'

Rahul gawked at the student for a moment. He had no frigging idea. Then he hit upon a way out, and smiled. 'Let me put that question to you. How would you do it?'

The student stared back undaunted. 'Please answer my question first, sir.'

'Try, try, how would you do it?' persisted Rahul.

'I'd thought about it, but since I didn't know I thought I'd ask you.'

'Just give it a shot. Try!'

Back and forth they went on, amidst growing boos, until Rahul's bodyguards realized that something was amiss, shoved the student aside and promptly whisked Rahul off the premises.

Sonia Gandhi
Modi raaj ma tamne kachbo nathi madyu.. Modi sarkar ne ukhadi feko!
6 hours ago Like · Comment

👍 Manmohan Singh and 25 others like this.

Arjun Modhwadia WELL SAID, SONIA JI! WELL SAID!
6 hours ago Like

Sushil Shinde Fantastic Gujarati, madam!
6 hours ago Like

Manish Tewari Mindblowingly holistic!
6 hours ago Like

Speechwriter Er, madam. The line's fine, except for one word. It's "kashu nathi madyu" which means "people got nothing" and not "kachbo nathi madyu" which means "people aren't getting tortoises under Modi rule"
6 hours ago · 👍 Narendra Modi and 6 Crore Gujaratis like this

Sonia Gandhi I see. Ahmed!
6 hours ago Like

Ahmed Patel Speechwriter, you're fired.
6 hours ago Like

Speechwriter NOOOOOOO!
6 hours ago Like

When the campaign was done and dusted, votes cast, counted, and the final tally made available, it was the Congress that erupted in jubilation and took to the streets celebrating the improvement in their tally by two seats from fifty-nine in 2007 to sixty-one in 2012. The ecstatic Congress workers gathered outside 10 Janpath to fete their great youth icon, but Rahul had already left for Spain. So the workers satisfied the uncontrollable urge to demonstrate their loyalty by feeding a massive three-tier butterscotch cake to Rahul's life-size poster.

Modi, meanwhile, returned to his Gandhinagar office, leaned back in his enormous chair, swung his legs over the desk, and flicked a *dhokla* into the air. The dhokla carved an elegant arc above him and landed perfectly into his open mouth.

The phone rang.

'*Kem cho*, Modibhai!' greeted a cheerful voice.

Even as he chomped on his dhokla, Modi's hirsute face broke into a broad smile.

'Long time no see, Bhagwatji!'

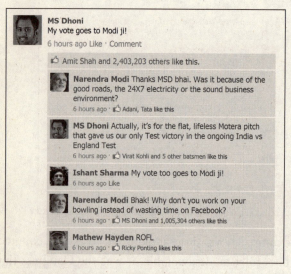

MS Dhoni
My vote goes to Modi ji!
6 hours ago Like · Comment

👍 Amit Shah and 2,403,203 others like this.

Narendra Modi Thanks MSD bhai. Was it because of the good roads, the 24X7 electricity or the sound business environment?
6 hours ago · 👍 Adani, Tata like this

MS Dhoni Actually, it's for the flat, lifeless Motera pitch that gave us our only Test victory in the ongoing India vs England Test
6 hours ago · 👍 Virat Kohli and 5 other batsmen like this

Ishant Sharma My vote too goes to Modi ji!
6 hours ago Like

Narendra Modi Bhak! Why don't you work on your bowling instead of wasting time on Facebook?
6 hours ago · 👍 MS Dhoni and 1,005,304 others like this

Mathew Hayden ROFL
6 hours ago · 👍 Ricky Ponting likes this

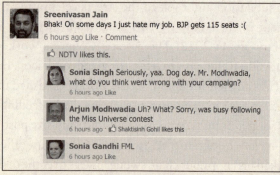

Sreenivasan Jain
Bhak! On some days I just hate my job. BJP gets 115 seats :(
6 hours ago Like · Comment

👍 NDTV likes this.

Sonia Singh Seriously, yaa. Dog day. Mr. Modhwadia, what do you think went wrong with your campaign?
6 hours ago Like

Arjun Modhwadia Uh? What? Sorry, was busy following the Miss Universe contest
6 hours ago · 👍 Shaktisinh Gohil likes this

Sonia Gandhi FML
6 hours ago Like

FOUR

The crown prince rises

FROM THE BALCONY, SONIA Gandhi watched her ecstatic party members dance around Rahul's portrait, celebrating the Congress's performance in Gujarat with gusto. From time to time they broke into chants of 'Rahul Gandhi *ki jai*', 'Sonia Gandhi *ki jai*' and, occasionally, 'Manmohan Singh *hai hai*'.

'Idiots,' muttered Sonia Gandhi.

As always, Ahmed silently crept up to her side, instinctively expecting a command from his supreme leader.

'We need to fast-track our plans of elevating Rahul. Enough games. Time to bite the bullet,' said Sonia. 'Arrange for a party conclave.'

Ahmed nodded. 'I hear Jaipur is great this time of the year,' he said.

* * *

The Birla auditorium in Jaipur, the venue for the Congress Chintan Shivir, was buzzing with activity. The top leaders of the party, including Sonia Gandhi, were seated on the stage, a giant poster of a dimpled, clean-shaven Rahul Gandhi adorning the backdrop. Nubile female members of the Youth Congress kept scurrying about in stage management activities, their lissom sari-clad figures providing much-needed eye candy to the bored delegates.

These conclaves, held every five years or so, are usually staid affairs. Meant to brainstorm solutions for pressing challenges confronting the nation and the party, they invariably degenerate into an abject display of fealty to the Nehru–Gandhis, ending in boisterous reaffirmations of faith in the leadership of Smt. Sonia Gandhi.

However, the three-day-long Jaipur Chintan Shivir in January 2013 promised to be a little different. Jaipur, with its romantic history, grand palaces and hoary forts, provided the perfect vista for one of the seminal succession events in India's history: Rahul Gandhi being formally recognized as number two in India's grand old party.

There had been some hiccups in the months leading up to Rahul's coronation, however. Rahul, in his Gautama Siddhartha act, had said he was neither interested in becoming PM nor even getting married. The Nehru–Gandhi scion had said: 'If I get married and have children, then I will become a status quoist and will be concerned about bequeathing my position to my children.'

The casual statement of renunciation of temporal vices led to a flurry of activity: Robert Vadra's DLF penthouse in Gurgaon became the political nerve centre for some time with many

Congress leaders making a beeline there to pay their respects to his son Rehaan. In parallel, jockeying also commenced for who would become Rahul's Manmohan. Some preferred to market their candidature through subtle imagery: A.K. Antony's starched white shirts now appeared a shade lighter, as though to highlight his squeaky clean image. Chidambaram, for his part, jettisoned quotes from the Thirukkural altogether for prophetic verses from the Bible about leading his flock to the Promised Land, Moses like. Some others preferred to be more blunt in signalling their eagerness. Mani Shankar Aiyar, never one for half measures, spammed Sonia's inbox with messages such as 'Madam, I see glimpses of Rajivji in him', while Diggy reminded Rahul of his 'guru dakshina'.

Fortunately, Rahul later retracted his statement and clarified that he was willing to take over the party, ostensibly out of a sense of noblesse oblige. And when he was spotted in one of Delhi's posh eateries in the company of a pretty lady, visits to Robert's residence also dwindled, paving the way for the Jaipur Chintan Shivir.

The 350 delegates settled into their seats on the first day of the shivir. Their moment of unbridled joy—Rahul's coronation—would have to wait for the following day, for day one was devoted to discussions on more mundane topics such as emerging socio-economic challenges, empowerment of women, bridging the gap between Bharat and India, and strengthening the Congress organizationally.

As A.K. Antony expatiated from the podium on the need to foster inclusive growth, a few frontbenchers began to nod off while a few others fidgeted in their seats. Even Sonia seemed bored, stifling a yawn.

'And may I now request Shri Digvijaya Singhji to share his considered views on social inclusion of marginalized communities,' the pretty Youth Congress general secretary announced. There were groans from the backbenches.

As Digvijaya rambled on, creases of worry and anxiety began to form on Sonia's face, but it had nothing to do with the torture of sitting through a Digvijaya Singh speech.

'Has Rahul finalized his speech?' she whispered to Ahmed Patel.

'He's not willing to take inputs from Jairam Ramesh or Shashi Tharoor, madam,' replied Ahmed. 'Insists he will write his own speech. He's watching some Hollywood superhero flicks to gain inspiration.'

'This is getting very tense for me. What if he chooses to speak extempore?' Sonia sighed.

'Don't worry, madam. Everything will be all right,' Ahmed tried to reassure, but Sonia's anxiety only deepened.

It was now the turn of Dr Veerappa Moily to take his turn at the podium to share his thoughts as the head of the subcommittee for organizational affairs on 'streamlining internal processes'.

'In our party, there are plenty of rules and guidelines to regulate party discipline, communication with the press, party hierarchies and what not,' he began in a low bass after the customary expression of gratitude to Sonia Gandhi and Rahul Gandhi. His audience by now was fast asleep.

After adjusting his oval-rimmed spectacles and taking a deep breath, Moily continued: 'But I ask you this today, friends. Are there guidelines on how to deal with the Nehru–Gandhis? Has anyone codified "best practices" in interacting with our beloved Soniaji? Do we have reference points for expressing admiration for Rahulji without going over the top and yet doing justice to his immense capabilities?'

His words sparked a frisson, jolting the assemblage out of its stupor.

'Look, we are not saying don't praise Rahulji or Soniaji for their abilities, looks or whatever it is that you think is great about them. No, no and no, for that would be bad politics. All I am saying is do it artfully and in the right amount. Sycophancy can be a double-edged sword that can cut both ways: do it right and you can rise to your full potential; do it wrong and you can kiss your career in the Congress goodbye. Like everything else in life, it is about striving for the golden mean. Today I intend to expound on how party members can achieve that balance.'

The assemblage erupted in hearty cheers, exhorting the petroleum and natural gas minister to press ahead.

'Here is rule one from "Moily's rules for climbing to the top of the greasy Congress pole of power",' he thundered, raising his pitch a few notes.

'Rule One: Express admiration, gratitude or fealty implicitly in concise language; allude to inherent merit, not inheritance; avoid hyperbole. For instance, take Union Rural Development Minister Jairam Ramesh's statement to the press on 8 September 2011 in the aftermath of the introduction of the Land Acquisition Bill.'

A statement flashed on screen behind him.

Without Rahul Gandhi's intervention and involvement in every step [the Land Acquisition Bill] would not have been prepared and introduced in fifty-five days.

'What class, what punch,' Moily raved, looking at the slide. 'In very few words, it showcases Rahul's policy smarts, influence, and effort in shaping a landmark bill.

'Now let me show you another, a statement made by Mani Shankar Aiyar after the 2009 General Elections:

> *Fortunately or unfortunately, the only thing written in Rahul's destiny is that he's bound to become prime minister, whether that's in 2012—as I hope—or 2014—as many expect—or 2019, if we don't do well in the next elections. That we'll have Rahul as PM is beyond question.*

'Well, what do you think of this one?'

'Spot on, sir,' a delegate answered. 'Just what the doctor ordered,' was another attendee's response. There was a murmur of approval.

Moily facepalmed himself.

'No, you bozos, this is total crap,' Moily screamed in frustration. 'It smacks of sarcasm and is satiric and insulting. It implies that Rahul will become PM because he is a Gandhi. In sum, it does more harm than good. Any wonder then that though both Jairam and Mani are Tam Brahms, the former handles the powerful rural development portfolio while the latter has been relegated to the backbenches of the Rajya Sabha.'

A murmur went through the crowd. Several attendees nodded thoughtfully.

'Now, moving on to rule number two: Metaphors are an important tool in a politician's rhetoric, but are better avoided when referring to the Nehru–Gandhis. They sow seeds of confusion, and provide fodder for the commentariat to indulge in scurrilous speculation. Take Salmanji's contention that Rahul should go beyond cameos. Rahul was flummoxed by this googly from the Union corporate minister so much so that he was summoned to 10 Janpath to clarify what he meant. Was Mr Khurshid implying that Rahul's interventions were mere item numbers, irrelevant to the overall narrative? If so, it was uncalled for. Any questions before I proceed?'

A member from the backbenches stood up. 'Sir, can you shed some light on how to celebrate Rahul baba's birthday without going over the top?'

'Excellent question,' said Moily. 'What do you think about congregating outside 10 Janpath on Rahul Jayanthi to get a darshan of our beloved leader?'

'Great idea,' many roared, followed by desk thumping.

'Lousy idea, you bozos,' Moily snapped. 'Rahul never celebrates his birthday in India and you are only wasting your time by insisting on catching a glimpse of his dimples on that day. The correct practice is to organize cake-cutting ceremonies in front of Rahul posters in your home states. The Congress Publicity and Propaganda wing maintains a huge stock of Rahul posters showcasing the Nehru–Gandhi scion in various attires and get-ups—Rahul sporting a tilak, Rahul donning a skullcap, a clean-shaven Rahul waving to the crows, a surly-looking stubbled Rahul channelling his inner Che Guevara, Rahul in a turban. So borrow them and feed them on the joyous occasion of his birthday. And in the highest traditions of simplicity and austerity, feed his posters with dal-chawal, not expensive cream cakes or ladoos. Recommended slogans for the happy occasion are "*Rahul lao, desh bachao*", "43 is the new 23", "I see Rajivji in him", the last one being my favourite.'

There was a round of applause before a delegate from Tamil Nadu raised his hand and posed a question: 'Sir, what if we run out of Rahul baba's posters?'

'Then make do with Rahul Bose's posters,' Moily answered, a little annoyed.

The Tamil Nadu Youth Congress in its exuberance to celebrate Rahul Jayanthi had mistakenly printed lakhs of Rahul Bose posters a few years back and they were lying unused.

'Now if these above rules seem too nuanced to be internalized, never mind,' continued Moily, 'but if one rule of being a good courtier must be internalized, it is this: Give a simple, direct answer to a simple, direct question from 10 Janpath, especially if it concerns succession at the top.

'I refer to it as the "playing with a straight bat and not fishing outside the off stump" rule. This rule can never be overemphasized. Occasionally, the Gandhis, in the context of succession, will bowl a teasing line in the corridor of uncertainty to test the batsman's temperament and technique. The time-tested response is to see it through to the wicketkeeper. One veteran Congress politician, now occupying the highest office of the land, learnt this rule the hard way. In response to a direct question, "Who will be the next PM?" posed immediately after Indira Gandhi's tragic assassination, this gentlemen is believed to have answered: "the seniormost leader". It was a blunder that saw the veteran sent back to the pavilion and out of the game for the next five years.

'Never ever make such a mistake. For instance, if someone asks, "Will Rahul be the Congress PM candidate in 2014?" the safe answer would be: "We all want him to be the prime minister. It's up to him and the family to decide though." With that, I conclude my speech.'

Moily's speech was met with thunderous applause, with chants of 'Moilyji ki jai' emanating from the back rows before being drowned out by more vociferous slogans of 'Soniaji ki jai' and 'Rahulji ki jai'. As Moily got off the stage, senior leaders, Cabinet ministers and office-bearers rushed to congratulate him for one of the all-time great speeches rendered in a Congress conclave. Later in the day, Ahmed Patel patted the minister and conveyed the high command's heartfelt appreciation for adumbrating on an issue close to their heart.

* * *

That night, Sonia kept tossing and turning. In a few hours, Rahul would have to give his acceptance speech, but the boy was nowhere ready. Like any other mother, Sonia wanted the best for her son. To see him go in the family way, and take over the reins of the party, albeit as number two, would be the fulfilment of her ardent desire. The fate of an entire party rested on what he would say and, more importantly, what he would not say. What if Rahul misspoke?

At 11 p.m., she decided to check on Rahul, lodged in the adjacent room in the posh five-star hotel. She knocked on his door and walked right into what seemed like a war scene.

Books and stationery were strewn all over. Broken china lay scattered on the floor. The window was shattered. Rahul was jumping around the room in a green outfit and what seemed like a massive pair of green styrofoam hands, in tandem with the Incredible Hulk on the widescreen plasma TV in the room.

'HULK SMASH!' he squealed, and flung a coffee mug across the room.

Sonia withdrew hastily, deciding to give him a little more time. At 1 a.m., Sonia tried her luck again. This time, she nudged open the door just enough to peep in cautiously. If anything, the room looked worse. Paint was peeling off in thin lines at various spots on the wall, as if an animal had slashed at it with its claws. On the TV, Wolverine of *X-men* was making short work of Magneto's sidekicks.

Rahul turned around with a start, and hid his hands behind him. 'Don't worry, Mummy. I should be done in a few hours. Just need that final dash of inspiration to write my speech,' he said with a guilty look on his face. Reassured, Sonia retreated to her room.

At 4 a.m., Sonia awoke with a start. There was no point trying to sleep any more. Wearily, she made her way to Rahul's room once again.

The door was ajar, and the lights were switched on. As Sonia tiptoed in, the visage of Batman interrogating The Joker came into view on the TV. Rahul was sprawled on the sofa with a glazed look, a half-eaten pizza by his side. Sprawled all over the floor were crumpled sheets.

'Rahul,' Sonia said in a stern maternal tone. 'What is the status? Please don't tell me you still haven't finalized your speech, let alone rehearsed it.'

'Oh, Mummy, this feels like one of those stupid high school assignments,' he whined. 'Just not getting the kick. I finished watching the entire *X-men* series and now have started on Nolan's trilogy, but just not getting the flow for my lines.'

'Oh dear,' Sonia gasped. 'Forget trying to write your own lines. Let me go and wake up Mani. He used to be your dad's favourite speech-writer. Nothing will please him more than the honour of writing your acceptance speech for becoming number two.'

'No!' shrieked Rahul, like a toddler whose lollipop was being snatched away from him. 'It is my speech and I will write it myself. No short cuts. I find his to be very long-winded, anyway.'

'Holy ravioli!' Sonia cried, 'this is turning out to be scarier than I thought.' She sank into a chair and began to sob uncontrollably.

Suddenly, the power went off, engulfing the room in darkness. 'Bloody Gehlot,' Sonia cursed. 'As though I didn't have enough to worry about, the power keeps going off. It is a poison!'

When the lights came back again, Rahul's countenance had changed, the vacuous lassitude replaced by a thoughtful calm.

* * *

The next day, Digvijaya rose to propose Rahul Gandhi as the vice president of the party, a statement that cut through the thick pall of listlessness hanging over the auditorium as attendees, who had been trying hard not to nod off, suddenly perked up. In what may or may not have been spontaneous, Sonia thumped her desk and wiped a tear from her eyes.

Rahul gingerly approached the podium, rolled up his sleeves, and delivered the line of the century.

'Last night, at four, my mother came to me and cried. Why did she cry? Because she understands that power is poison . . .'

The speech would go down in the annals of Congress history as one of the all-time great speeches, a perfect blend of corniness and maudlin sentimentality, up there with Nehru's 'tryst with destiny', Indira's *garibi hatao* and Rajiv's *nani yaad dila denge*.

As soon as Rahul finished his speech, the floodgates opened and a torrent of effusive praise gushed forth from the reservoir of pent-up emotions. 'The Obama moment of Indian politics,' raved Mani Shankar; 'One of the greatest speeches of contemporary Indian political history,' proclaimed Dr Tharoor; '*Rajivji . . . Rajivji ki yaad dila di*,' was the more earthy verdict of Haryana CM Bhupinder Singh Hooda.

The rain dance was well and truly under way. An ambience of revelry and giddy headedness engulfed the auditorium, and soon spread to the multitude of Congress workers assembled outside.

'And now Rahulji's aide Kanishka Singh will make an important declaration,' the pretty Youth Congress general secretary announced.

'Rahul has promised to usher in a new approach,' Kanishka began. The delegates cheered heartily.

'All of you have sung his praises, proclaimed your steadfast devotion and loyalty to his leadership. But the time has come to test it. You will all be administered an exam and your responses evaluated to rank you and objectively determine the pecking order,' he said.

'Bring it on,' a delegate shouted. 'I am ready to shoot for Rahul. What is a measly sycophancy exam compared to that?' bellowed another delegate from the middle section of the auditorium.

'But wait, there is a catch,' Kanishka said. 'What use is lavish praise if it is not heartfelt? What is the degree of truth in what they say? So we will also administer a polygraph test to record physiological responses such as blood pressure, pulse rate, perspiration and skin conductivity. This will help us score the responses for sincerity as well. For too long, we have ignored this dimension, but not any more. The new 360-degree exam will evaluate the delegates for not just their sycophancy, but also the sincerity behind the sycophancy to determine the new pecking order. Are you ready, fellow Congressmen?'

The words had punctured the bubble of euphoria. Jubilation gave way to panic. Faces turned pallid, the sparkle in the eyes gave way to fear—the look before being led to the guillotine. A wave of silence descended on the hitherto cacophonous auditorium.

A phalanx of Rahul's team, freshly minted MBAs attired in crisp business casuals, fanned out with question papers and an array of instruments to administer the polygraph test:

a) Did you think Rahul's acceptance speech was the Obama moment of Indian politics?

b) Did you feel that the ghost of Jawaharlal Nehru was speaking through Rahul baba?

c) Did you feel that his elevation to the post of vice president was the greatest day of your life?

d) Did you think, 'yawn . . . Same set of recycled clichés?' when he said the party has to change?

e) Did you feel like cringing when Rahul said that his mother told him 'power is poison'?

f) Did the thought 'when the f*** will we get rid of this family and institute internal democracy' ever cross your mind as Rahul concluded his nomination speech?

The procedure was a brainchild of Rahul Gandhi himself, a throwback to his brief stint as a management consultant. In addition to learning how to craft PPT slides that packed a lot of information but communicated very little, Rahul had imbibed faith in a data-driven, measurement-based approach to management and leadership in the first and only real job he would ever hold. The Rahul era was under way. An unwieldy, gargantuan century-old political party would be managed like a corporation with Rahul's laptop-wielding, MBA-degree-holding whiz-kids calling the shots.

As the exam got under way, many began to perspire profusely, grappling with the prospect of, for the first time in their lives, having to strike a balance between professing loyalty and admiration for the Nehru–Gandhi scion on the one hand and doing so truthfully, on the other.

One particular Congress leader aced the polygraph test as he proceeded to record his true feelings. Needless to say, he promptly tendered his resignation as soon as he completed the exam.

Many others failed to clear the cut-offs in sycophancy, with the polygraph spiking as they wrote paeans in praise of Rahul. However, there were winners as well such as Dr Shashi Tharoor, who dug deep within his reservoir of vocabulary, to formulate responses, such as:

Apropos of the Nehru–Gandhi scion's congenital traits, taken in conjunction with his innate capabilities undoubtedly moulded by the genetic traits of his forefathers and propinquity for wielding power which, if one thinks about it holistically and perspicaciously, is synonymous with toxicity, then one concludes that he is but a worthy heir to the throne after carefully defenestrating arguments of an ad hominem nature.

It ensured that he comfortably cleared the cut-offs in sincerity while gathering the benefit of doubt for sycophancy.

However, one man topped both the sycophancy and veracity charts to emerge at the top of the pecking order, at least in Rahul Gandhi's mind: Mani Shankar Aiyar. The former Union panchayati raj minister had long ago internalized his admiration and devotion to the Nehru–Gandhi family, especially Rajiv Gandhi, so much so that he genuinely believed in it. 'I just thought of the sweet, smiling face of Rajiv Gandhi and the words of praise flowed smoothly and truthfully from my pen,' he recalled, grinning from ear to ear like a Cheshire cat.

Meanwhile, outside the auditorium, away from all the

tension and the anxiety, the Congress workers danced with gusto, while journalists reported back to their respective TV houses.

'With Rahul's elevation, the Congress has paved the way for his projection as its prime ministerial candidate in 2014, and effectively thrown down the gauntlet at the BJP,' said NDTV's Sreenivasan Jain, shouting to make himself heard over the cacophony behind him.

'This comes as a major blow to Modi who is still only one among the many potential PM candidates for the BJP. Will BJP elevate Gujarat strongman Narendra Modi in response? Will 2014 be a Rahul versus Modi fight? With cameraman Ramesh, this is Sreenivasan Jain reporting from Jaipur. Back to you, Barkha,' Jain concluded, and took off dancing towards the Congress workers.

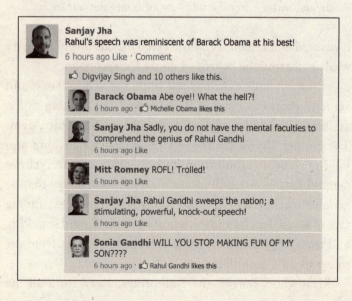

Sanjay Jha
Rahul's speech was reminiscent of Barack Obama at his best!
6 hours ago Like · Comment

👍 Digvijay Singh and 10 others like this.

Barack Obama Abe oye!! What the hell?!
6 hours ago · 👍 Michelle Obama likes this

Sanjay Jha Sadly, you do not have the mental faculties to comprehend the genius of Rahul Gandhi
6 hours ago Like

Mitt Romney ROFL! Trolled!
6 hours ago Like

Sanjay Jha Rahul Gandhi sweeps the nation; a stimulating, powerful, knock-out speech!
6 hours ago Like

Sonia Gandhi WILL YOU STOP MAKING FUN OF MY SON????
6 hours ago · 👍 Rahul Gandhi likes this

FIVE

The visionary socialist

'TIME IS RIPE TO launch a massive movement against rising prices, unemployment and corruption,' Prakash Karat declaimed.

'Mmm . . .' said Karunanidhi, sounding as excited as a person getting up on a Monday morning.

'We will fight them in the beaches, in the cities, in the villages. We will fight them tooth and nail, and not let the neo-liberal communal forces prevail,' Karat raved, channelling his inner Churchill.

Karunanidhi grunted, his face as dull as yesterday's coffee.

'The need of the hour, Karuna sir, is,' Karat continued, 'for the Third Front forces to coalesce to offer the masses a non-Congress, non-BJP government. One out of five children dying of starvation is from India. It is because of the neo-liberal policies of the UPA regime. Meanwhile, the rise of Modi threatens the social fabric of our society.'

It was hard to tell what impact Karat's passionate pitch was having on the DMK supremo.

'Karuna sir, we hope you will make yourself available for the conclave of the Third Front leaders. To have you on board will be a great boost to our efforts to forge a non-Congress, non-BJP secular alternative,' said Karat.

No response.

'Sir, hello? Are you with me?'

Karunanidhi may well have dozed off but there was no way of looking through his dark, forbidding goggles to discern if his eyes were shut. Karunanidhi's aide gestured that it was time for Karat to take leave. Karat picked up his tumbler, slurped the residual layer of filter coffee, and got ready to depart.

'Oh, before I leave, here is a bouquet of flowers for,' Karat paused, took a deep breath, and uttered the words slowly, 'Kani . . . mozhi.'

The word had an electrifying effect, jolting the DMK supremo out his reverie.

'Ca . . . can you repeat that again, *paa*?' the Kalaignar said, removing his goggles.

'Sure, please give my regards to . . .' Again the pause for dramatic effect. The conscious effort to get it right, and then the word: 'Kani-mozhi', just the way it ought to be pronounced with a twisting of the tongue to get the 'zh' right.

Karunanidhi lunged forward and planted a kiss on an unsuspecting Karat's face. 'Brilliant! At last someone has managed to not mangle my daughter's name. This is too much, *paa*,' he cried, tears rolling down his eyes.

At the height of the 2G scandal, it was not CAG's damning report, the CBI raids and interrogation, the arrest of Raja, the ignominy of Kani being taken to Tihar jail that had rankled. It had been the manner in which his beloved daughter's name had been abused by leaders, news anchors and media pundits. If the English anchors were bad enough by referring to her as 'Kanimozee', the Hindi ones were worse, calling her 'Kanimochee'.

'No big deal, sir,' Karat lied, wiping his face.

It was a big deal. It had taken him three months of practice to get the pronunciation right. And in the process, he had won the DMK supremo's undying loyalty.

In a burst of spontaneity, the DMK supremo composed a limerick in praise of the CPI(M) general secretary:

> *More loving than the cow to her calf can be,*
> *More bountiful than the waters of the Cauvery,*
> *Sweeter than the halwa of Tirunelveli,*
> *That is what you are for correctly pronouncing Kanimozhi,*
> *For some you may be Prakash Karat,*
> *But for me you are gold of 24 carat.*

Karat bowed graciously as he prepared to depart. 'I can see why the people of Tamil Nadu have honoured you with the epithet Kalaignar,' he said. 'I take it you will be allying with the non-BJP, non-Congress parties to . . .' 'To keep the communal forces at bay,' Karunanidhi completed the sentence, his voice animated, a smile on his face. 'Yes, of course, *paa*. We must keep the communal fascist forces at bay.' It was like music to Karat's ears.

After he was led out and the door had shut, Karat shouted, 'Yessss!' and pumped his fists in the air. The first of the many pieces of the jigsaw puzzle had fallen into place.

The quest for the formation of a non-Congress, non-BJP Third Front government is to the Left in India what the pursuit of a grand unified theory is to physicists, what the search for the Holy Grail had been to the Knights Templar of the medieval era. But for Karat, it was something more than chasing a pipe dream. He had made it his life mission.

Before passing on the baton of leading the CPI(M), his predecessor Comrade Harkishan Singh Surjeet had said to him, 'Comrade, in my lifetime I had fervently hoped for two things: one, the Indian cricket team discovers a genuine, tearaway fast bowler. Two, regional parties coalesce to form a stable Third Front government that lasts a full term. Alas, both wishes have remained unfulfilled. I hope in your term at least one of them gets realized.' 'I swear on the holy *Das Kapital*, comrade,' Prakash had cried then. 'I shall rededicate the rest of my life to the pursuit of one and only one goal: bringing all the regional parties together on the basis of a common minimum programme.' 'Well, all the best, son. Don't get too hung up on it,' a feeble Surjeet had responded.

Every year, Karat organized the Third Front conclave, a summit of regional, secular parties to explore the formation of the Third Front. The leaders would come, hold hands, make airy declarations and then go their separate ways: some to the BJP camp, most into the open arms of the Congress.

The biggest obstacle to the formation of a durable non-

BJP, non-Congress alliance was that these parties were pitted against each other rather than the two national parties in their home states: DMK vs AIADMK in Tamil Nadu, TMC vs the Left in West Bengal, BSP vs SP in UP.

How could he inspire the other leaders to sink their petty rivalries in pursuit of the larger objective if the Left in its own backyard was locked in a struggle against the TMC and not the Congress? If only he could get Mamata to attend his summit, stand on the dais and hold hands with him. The same Mamata whose skull the CPI(M) cadre had cracked.

And then the contours of a bold, even reckless, plan began to take shape in the left side of his brain . . .

OPENING OVERS

'The odd ball is keeping low. They are doing it in singles.
If India wants to win here, they'll need to play well.'

—Ravi Shastri

SIX

Her Majesty's agent

APRIL 2013

'WHAT INCOMPREHENSIBLE GIBBERISH IS this, my friend?' Law Minister Ashwani Kumar bellowed, waving a file in the face of CBI Director Ranjit Sinha seated opposite him in the minister's office in Shastri Bhavan. It was the CBI's draft status report on alleged irregularities in the allocation of coal blocks by the PMO.

'Er . . . we have tried to be as objectionable as possible, sir, considering it is a court-monitored probe,' replied Sinha, fidgeting uncomfortably in his chair.

'"Objective", not "objectionable",' Ashwani corrected him. 'And I'm referring to the report's purple prose and atrocious grammar, not its veracity. Malapropisms in lieu of elegant metaphors, idiocy in place of idiom, split infinitives where one would expect hair-splitting, nonsense when one is looking for nuance. You have murdered the language, many, many times over.'

And then the punch below the belt: '*UPSC mein kaunsa rank aaya?*'

'452, sir. I did very well in GK but scored poorly in the essay round.'

'No wonder. Looks like I'll have to rewrite the whole thing just to make it comprehensible,' muttered Ashwani, shaking his head in dismay.

It was the oldest trick in the book: the pucca brown sahib, Macaulay's legatee, pulling his weight and rank over the native subaltern by mocking his command over the Anglo-Saxon tongue.

The CBI director felt like hitting back with a volley of abuse in chaste Bhojpuri, but held himself in check and stared back poker faced. Sinha looked haggard and worn out, with dark circles under his puffy, sleep-deprived eyes. His work–life balance had gone out of whack ever since he had taken over as the CBI director six months back, his elevation coinciding with the exit of Mamata Banerjee from the UPA. This had meant that the UPA's survival depended on Mulayam's and Mayawati's support, which in turn meant more work for the CBI.

On his first day in office, he had been handed a file with the rubric 'Assets highly disproportionate to known sources of income' and under it in smaller-sized font, 'the murky shenanigans of Messrs Mulayam and Smt. Mayawati'.

The CBI director and his team had been unstinting in their efforts, sacrificing many a weekend to unravel the byzantine cross-holdings of Mulayam Singh Yadav's extended kin, putting in twenty hours a day to meticulously compile sundry transactions, all the while being driven hard by their political bosses to pile up the evidence. And then suddenly, a few days before the vote in Parliament, Sinha was told to drop the case and go back to the bench.

'But, sir, we have put in over 20,342 man-hours and are close to framing charges. You want us to close the case?' Sinha had remonstrated with his boss.

'All I am saying is press the pause button. Chill out for some time,' Home Minister Shinde chuckled in response.

The cycle of hot–cold would repeat over and over again. Just as Sinha was about to take off for vacation, he would be instructed to 'reactivate the M&M files'. Of late, Sinha had begun to complain of insomnia and BP triggered by the highly fluctuating nature of his workload. His friend in I-banking told him that even he did not have to put up with this much work-related uncertainty: 'Dealing with a highly random variable like Mulayam must be more stressful than grappling with the vagaries of the stock market, boss.'

And now to be upbraided for his English was the last straw. It was one thing to mess with a civil servant's work–life balance, quite another to be uncivil to him and hurt his ego.

'You may go now,' Ashwani said, dismissing him superciliously with a wave of the hand. 'Looks like I'll have to spend more time than I budgeted for . . . how should I put it . . . proofreading the report. And do me a favour, will you? Get yourself a copy of the Wren & Martin guide to grammar. Never too late to learn, you know.'

* * *

That night Sinha had trouble sleeping as he tossed and turned, the law minister's put-down still rankling him. Why did the law minister have to be so bloody snobbish? Couldn't he have been more down to earth, and said, '*Yaar, Ranjit, report ko thoda tweak kar de, yaar.* You know what I mean,' and perhaps winked. Ranjit would have understood and taken care of it. He was no novice in these matters, and understood the nuances of statecraft. But no, that Ashwani had to go and deride the report's English in that annoying accent of his.

Ranjit cursed softly. If only the UPSC had been exclusively in Hindi and there had been no bloody English essay, he would have cracked the IAS for sure. He did all the grunt work that kept this government afloat, and in return got mocked. Being the CBI director had to be the crappiest job in the world.

Sinha's reverie was interrupted by the sound of a faint knock against the windowpane of his first-floor bedroom. He was about to dismiss it as a monkey when the knocks grew louder followed by a high-pitched shriek, similar to the ululation of an owl. Sinha jumped out of bed to take a closer look.

The silhouette of a monstrous black creature clinging to the window railings came into view. A bright V shone on the top half of its body, and a black cape fluttered behind it.

Sinha was about to reach for the phone when the apparition said in what was a man's baritone, 'There is no need to call the cops, my friend. By the time they get here, I will have disappeared. I have come to help you in cleaning up the system.' The man-creature seemed to have a voice modulator that amplified his voice, even his inhalations and exhalations distinctly audible.

'Who . . . what are you?' Sinha stammered.

'I am who I am but the question is who are you? A CBI director or a football to be kicked around in a political minefield?'

Sinha gasped. The words had struck a chord, resonating with his ongoing conflict. 'What do you want?' he asked.

'The question is, what do you want?' the man-creature replied. 'To be the hero this nation needs or continue to be abused by your masters until retirement. If your choice is the former, then we can work together. If not, we can end this conversation and you will never see me again.'

Sinha nodded, gesturing the creature to go on.

The man-creature pulled out a stack of files tucked behind his neck, and pushed it through the railings. 'What you have here is a treasure trove of evidence to nail high-ranking ministers and bureaucrats. Call recordings, money trails, the works. If I were you, I would first start with the Cash for Railway Post scam involving the railway minister's nephew. The bugger has been taking cash to dole out jobs in the railway board.'

Sinha browsed through the files and looked up slack-jawed at the weird upside-down man.

'Wow. Batman's hood and cape, Phantom's eye band, Darth Vader's voice. *Aap to Krrish ke bhi baap nikle.*'

The vigilante bristled at the facetious observation. 'I am not a third-rate Bollywood superhero. I am V-man,' he squeaked. The voice modulator seemed to have stopped working. He twirled and made some quick adjustments, and the baritone returned. 'Sorry about that. As I was saying, I am V-man,' he repeated and paused for dramatic effect before continuing, 'where V stands for Vigilantism, Vendetta, Victory, Vision, Valour . . . take your pick.'

Sinha gawked at V-man for a few moments, before recovering his composure. 'Actually, there is still a problem. Even if I have all the evidence, what can I do? I am just a . . .'

'. . . caged parrot who speaks in his master's voice,' they both spoke in unison.

'I know what it feels like to be in your shoes,' V-Man said sympathetically. 'Reporting to egoistic, self-absorbed politicians, having to deal with people like Mulayam. But don't fret, I have a plan to set you free.'

Sinha was now close to tears. 'You . . . you can do that? Get me into a position where I can pick and choose my own cases? Be a master of my own destiny?'

'Yes, to some extent, but don't set your hopes too high. Tomorrow night I'll be paying a visit to the judges of the Supreme Court bench monitoring the coal-scam case to apprise them about how your boss, Ashwani Kumar, has been prying into your report and how your office is being abused in general.'

'Oh, V-Man, sir. You are so wonderful. Not only are you brave, but you have also super empathy,' Sinha gushed. 'Could you also help me improve my English? That's another thing some ministers keep bullying me about.'

'Hmm . . . start with mugging up the GRE word list. Then read books by Dr Shashi Tharoor. And if I were you, I would watch Manish Tewari defending his government with his wordplay, rather than *Big Boss* in the evenings.'

Sinha stared at him in puzzlement.

'Look, I need to get going now. Missus will be waking up in an hour or so and I don't want my cover to be blown,'

V-man said, shrugging his shoulders. With that, he whipped out a gadget and shot out a nylon string with a small hook that attached itself to an overhanging branch. And in a flash, he was gone.

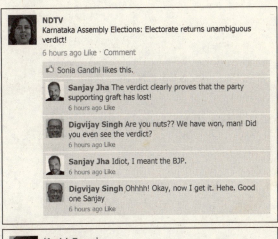

NDTV
Karnataka Assembly Elections: Electorate returns unambiguous verdict!
6 hours ago Like · Comment

👍 Sonia Gandhi likes this.

Sanjay Jha The verdict clearly proves that the party supporting graft has lost!
6 hours ago Like

Digvijay Singh Are you nuts?? We have won, man! Did you even see the verdict?
6 hours ago Like

Sanjay Jha Idiot, I meant the BJP.
6 hours ago Like

Digvijay Singh Ohhhh! Okay, now I get it. Hehe. Good one Sanjay
6 hours ago Like

Manish Tewari
That the BJP could manage only 40 seats clearly proves that Modi magic hasn't worked in Karnataka. I'm confident that BJP will loose in the 2014 elections too
6 hours ago Like · Comment

👍 Sonia Gandhi and 25 others like this.

Ashwani Kumar lose*, not loose.
6 hours ago · 👍 Oxford Dictionary likes this

Manish Tewari Huh? Okay. BJP will lose in 2014. Hppy?
6 hours ago Like

Ashwani Kumar Happy*, not hppy.
6 hours ago · 👍 Wren & Martin likes this

Manish Tewari WTF MAN!!! #$#@$! Correct this you a$$hole -> Our holistic campaign has defenestrated the regnant dispensation and propelled them into a state of discombobulation.
6 hours ago · 👍 Oxford Dictionary, Wren & Martin, GRE, TOEFL like this

Ashwani Kumar Er..
6 hours ago Like

Manish Tewari DO. NOT. MESS. WITH. ME.
6 hours ago Like

SEVEN

The Queen's fury

MAY 2013

A FEW DAYS LATER, the Union railway minister's nephew was arrested for allegedly receiving Rs 90 lakh in part payment through middlemen as part of a larger package of Rs 10 crore in return for securing the bribe-giver a 'lucrative' posting in the railway board. The case, dubbed the Rs 10 crore cash-for-post railway bribery scam by the media, severely dented the government's image. As though that wasn't enough, the Supreme Court also passed scathing comments on Law Minister Ashwani Kumar prying into the CBI's confidential report on irregularities in the allocation of coal blocks by the UPA regime.

It was a double blow to the government, and the continuation of the railway minister and the law minister looked untenable. And when the next day's headlines read 'Sonia unhappy with the conduct of some ministers', pundits reckoned it was a question of when, and not if.

Ahmed Patel made the call that needed to be made to the Prime Minister's Office. The principal secretary picked it up.

'Get me the prime minister,' Patel said in a brusque tone.

'I think the prime minister doesn't exercise authority any longer, sir,' the principal secretary blithely said.

'Yeah, I know that. Look, I don't have time for small talk. Can you pass on the information from 10 Janpath that a couple of . . .'

'No, no, you misunderstand, sir. I don't think he's been in charge for some months now,' the principal secretary interrupted, puzzled by Ahmed Patel's insouciance.

Ahmed Patel was now irked. 'Look, dude, that's been the case for the last four years. Now I really don't have time for chit-chat. Can you please . . .'

'No, you aren't getting what I am trying to imply, sir,' the principal secretary hastened to clarify. 'The prime minister was dropped from the Cabinet as per your instructions.'

'What do you mean?' barked Patel.

'The list of Union ministers that 10 Janpath had forwarded to the PMO six months ago as part of the Cabinet reshuffle did not have Dr Singh's name. So Dr Singh has stopped coming to work since then.'

'Shit, let me check what I sent you,' said Ahmed Patel and hung up. After rummaging through the archives, he found the list of the last Cabinet reshuffle. Dr Singh's name was indeed missing. A genuine oversight because of which India did not have a prime minister for the last six months, and no one had noticed.

Ahmed Patel frantically called up the Cabinet secretary to check whether Dr Singh had been chairing Cabinet meetings.

'We've had over a dozen Cabinet meetings over the last six months,' the Cabinet secretary answered, 'but I can't recall his presence. Actually, you know how it is, *na*? He just merges into the background. Let me check with Chidambaram sir.'

After a few minutes, he called back. 'He also doesn't seem to recall whether the prime minister was there or not. Oh my god, did the prime minister, in keeping with his self-effacing and soft-spoken manner, assume that he has been dropped and has since recused himself?'

'Shit. If this news gets out, it will be a triple whammy for the UPA regime. We need to reinstate him before word leaks out,' cried Ahmed Patel.

In tow with senior officials, Ahmed Patel rushed to 7 Race Course Road, the prime minister's residence. The first lady greeted them warmly and asked them to take a seat in the drawing room.

'*Coffee lenge ki chai*?' she asked.

'Ma'am, there's no time for courtesies. Where is Dr Singh? We must talk to him at once,' the Cabinet secretary cried.

'Oh, he's in his study room. Come to think of it, he seems holed up there most of the time. Come, let me take you to him,' Gursharan Kaur said, leading them past a bookshelf with very intimidating titles, such as *Stochastic Control for Economic Models* and *Downward Wage Rigidity and Labour Mobility*. Dr Singh was deep in study, a number of issues of the *Journal of Economics Perspectives* sprawled over his desk.

'Sir, there has been a mistake. You are still the prime minister of the country,' the red-faced Cabinet secretary said. 'We apologize profusely for the screw-up at our end. Please come back to work, sir!'

Dr Singh looked up from his studies, gazed at the Cabinet secretary without any trace of emotion and nodded imperceptibly.

'And one more thing. Ashwani and Bansal need to be sacked as per instructions from madam. Once you sign off on that, come over to 10 Janpath for an important meeting,' Ahmed Patel said.

'*Theek hai*,' said the scholar-turned-prime-minister, and India got back to having a prime minister once again.

* * *

A few days later, both Ashwani Kumar and Pawan Kumar Bansal were sacked.

A shiver ran down Bansal's spine as he walked past the lawn in 10 Janpath to step into the Congress president's office. Sonia Gandhi's stern visage at the head of a long rectangular table came into view with members of the Congress Working Committee seated along the table's longer edges. Dr Singh was seated to her right, staring back grimly, his lips tightly pursed, faint traces of a furrow discernible on his brow. This, Bansal immediately realized, meant the prime minister was furious. Bansal, after all, had been his hand-picked nominee, his wife's favourite, a member of the so-called Kaur group. The finance minister was seated to the Congress president's left, staring impassively at the draped window opposite him.

His was the look of the priest at the scene of an execution, going over his benedictions in his mind. Rahul, sporting a three-day stubble and seated next to the finance minister, already appeared bored by the proceedings, as he stared vacuously at the ceiling fan.

'And what do you have to say in your defence, Bansal?' Sonia said, peering over her spectacles into the eyes of the trembling railway minister.

'It was my nephew's fault, madam,' stuttered Bansal. 'I didn't know that he was capable of such . . . er . . . mischief.'

'Ever since Suresh Raina blamed his nephew for those Pakistan-bashing tweets, it's become fashionable to blame it all on the nephew, eh, Ahmed?' Sonia chuckled, looking at her secretary.

Under different circumstances, her ministers would have laughed heartily, but now was not the time.

'You have strived to derive pecuniary gain from your position through illegal means,' Sonia continued, 'and in being caught red-handed you have wrought immense damage to my government's standing. Now what does this do to Rahul baba's chances of taking over from Dr Singh, you fool?'

'I am not to blame, madam. All this was done behind my back by that blasted nephew of mine,' Bansal sobbed.

'Even so, as the proverb goes about Caesar's wife . . . er, what exactly is it?'

Ahmed Patel bent over and whispered into Sonia's ears.

'Yes, thank you, Ahmed. Caesar's wife must be above suspicion.'

'Er . . . Madam, you are Caesar's wife, not me,' Bansal retorted reflexively, immediately regretting his words.

'How dare you talk like that? I am madam's foot soldier, a legionary to be precise, and I can shoot you for her sake,' Home Minister Shinde growled. Sonia restrained him.

'I beg your forgiveness, madam. I meant I am Caesar's wife . . . no, I mean . . . I am a Caesarean,' Bansal began to ramble. 'It shall never happen again. I have always abided by the decision of the high command,' Bansal beseeched, sweat streaming down the side of his face.

'Then be prepared to take punishment,' said Sonia. 'Stripping you of your portfolio won't suffice. Your punishment must act as a deterrent to others of your ilk, one that is severely disproportionate to the embarrassment you have caused the party. I command, nay, condemn, you to,' Sonia paused, took a deep breath, and continued, 'book tatkal tickets on the dreaded IRCTC server between 10 a.m. and 11 a.m. for the next two months as a means of atonement for your various sins of commission and omission.'

There was a moment of stunned silence as Bansal's face turned a ghastly white before he shrieked in shock and slumped to the table. Chidambaram looked away from the gruesome scene. Even Dr Singh rolled his eyes in shock. 'Poetic justice indeed. Hoist with his own petard. Those who live by the sword are destined to die by it, as the proverb goes,' whispered a CWC member. 'What makes it worse is that the chap has to log on to that dreaded site during peak travel season,' another senior Congress leader said in a hushed tone.

The uncomfortable silence was pierced by Bansal's plaintive shrieks of mercy as he was led away. They would reverberate through the halls and corridors of 10 Janpath and echo many times over in the minds of those who were witness to the macabre sentencing.

10 Janpath's swift act of retribution took the wind out of the sails of the Opposition baying for Bansal's scalp. 'We just wanted him to be sacked, with prosecution being a distant pipe dream, but, boy, this is way over the top. Now we may have to disrupt Parliament demanding his pardon,' a shocked Sushma Swaraj remarked after hearing about the sentencing.

The party did well not to let the details of Bansal's punishment leak into the public domain. It was one thing to create a strong deterrent effect that would inhibit naughty ministers from malfeasance beyond pilfering the odd stationery item from their office, but quite another to generate a massive sympathy wave for the disgraced ex-minister. Bansal spent the remaining summer of 2013 slouched in front of a desktop in a cubicle in the Congress headquarters labouring through the Herculean task of booking 3000 tatkal tickets. Every time the screen in front of him displayed 'Service unavailable', Bansal would let out a primeval scream of frustration, each exceeding the previous one in its pathos and wretchedness, causing passers-by to shudder.

EIGHT

Unstoppable force vs Immovable object

JUNE 2013

THE SOLE MCDONALD'S IN New Delhi's Khan Market shopping complex is usually not frequented by VVIPs and celebrities who prefer to patronize the more high-end eateries in the vicinity. But that hot summer afternoon in June was an exception. The West Bengal chief minister was seated, observing the surroundings with a sense of bewilderment. It was Mamata's first visit to a McDonald's joint. She had previously thought that the iconic golden arched 'M' emblazoned against a red background stood for Marxism or, even worse, Maoism, and that these ubiquitous Mac joints were communist strongholds. To now learn that McDonald's was the most potent symbol of American capitalism and junk-food globalization came as a pleasant surprise.

Derek O'Brien gingerly placed the tray containing two Maharaja Macs, a packet of French Fries, and two cans of Coke on the table in front of his boss. Derek had not brought his supremo there to familiarize her with fast food. In precisely thirty minutes, as per the plan, Prakash Karat would enter nonchalantly, and Derek would introduce him to his mercurial boss. This could end in disaster. On the other hand, if Mamata and Prakash hit it off, paving the way for a TMC–CPI(M) alliance, hatched in a McDonald's restaurant, history would be made. A Third Front government in the Centre, with the TMC as the anchor, would come into the realm of possibility.

If Derek played his cards right, maybe he could become the PM too. And what a knowledgeable PM he would make. He might not be an expert in any particular field but was second to none in possessing superficial cross-domain knowledge as a good quiz master ought to be.

* * *

Prakash Karat nervously looked at his watch in a bookstore two shops away. Twenty minutes to go before his rendezvous. Would she smile or spring at him like a wild cat? He decided to read some Marx to soothe his frayed nerves.

'Can you give me a copy of *Das Kapital* by the one and only Karl Marx?' he asked the bookstore manager.

'We don't have that in stock, sir,' the manager replied, slightly puzzled.

'What do you mean you don't stock *Das Kapital*?' Karat hollered.

'Er . . . no one orders that any more, sir. Would you want to check out some other books on economics?' the store manager nervously offered.

'I only read Marxist literature. Have you got anything on socialism?' Karat asked.

'Aha,' the manager said. 'I have just the book for you, sir,' he said, and reached for a book from the upper tier. He showed him *Social Networking for Dummies*, with Mark Zuckerberg's smiling visage on the cover.

Karat baulked. Social media was anathema to communists, a sinister capitalist conspiracy to undermine socialism with social networking. But now with even JNU students wasting time on Facebook rather than wasting time agitating against American-style capitalism, it was becoming impossible to ignore it.

And with really not much to do now that the Left was out of power in both Kerala and West Bengal, Karat had occasionally 'hung out' on Facebook. And then the fake positivity began to get to him. College friends he had not been in touch with, posting pictures of their Caribbean cruises, which made him feel bad that he was a communist doing meaningless work rather than an I-banker doing even more meaningless work, but earning a six-figure dollar salary to afford a Caribbean jaunt. And then he discovered Twitter. Since then, life had become more satisfying.

'Er . . . that's not what I was looking for,' Karat said, rejecting the book. 'I need something that derides capitalism. You follow?'

The manager thought hard. 'Um . . . there is this book *The Financial Crisis: Is American Style Capitalism Doomed?* You might like that,' the manager offered.

'Okay, let's see it,' Karat said. Literature on the financial crisis and subsequent American job losses always lifted his spirits, and he had twenty more minutes to kill. He started leafing through the book.

Prakash Karat
My first post on CPI(M) FB page! Comrades, Karl Marx once said Democracy is the road to socialism!
6 hours ago Like · Comment

👍 Brinda Karat likes this.

Lucky Sharma Huh? What's Karl Marx?
6 hours ago Like

Pintu Pandey What's socialism?
6 hours ago Like

Pinky Chaudhry Unliking this dumb page
6 hours ago Like

Munna _|_
6 hours ago Like

Prakash Karat Sniff :(
6 hours ago Like

* * *

'*Ei ki*, Derek?' Mamata asked, pointing to the Maharaja Mac.

'Oh, that's a Maharaja Mac, Didi,' Derek answered, feeling relieved. Answering questions and sharing GK trivia was familiar terrain and also a valuable chance to earn brownie points.

'Did you know that McDonald's is the fourth largest employer in the world, Didi?' Derek continued. 'Even more than the Indian Railways, with over 1.9 million employees worldwide in various franchisees.'

'Wow. That's bery nice,' Mamata said.

'And that's not all, Didi,' Derek said, biting into his burger. 'McDonald's feeds 68 million people per day, that's about 1 per cent of the world's population.'

'Ain?' Mamata said, sounding impressed. This was going well, Derek thought.

'Yes, Didi. The 27 billion dollars in revenue it earns annually make it the 90th largest economy in the world, as big as Mongolia's.'

Mamata looked around in awe, with all the giddy-headedness of a teenager on her first visit to a mall. It was all so exotic.

'And what is that white thing in between the buns, Derek?' she asked.

'Oh, that's mayonnaise, Didi,' Derek remarked, munching his burger.

A shadow passed over Didi's face. 'M . . . mayo . . . what?' she asked.

'Mayonnaise, Didi,' Derek said. He was thinking hard about providing more interesting background information, but somehow he had never bothered googling for mayonnaise.

But Mamata's facial features were undergoing a transformation, her mouth now pursed into a scowl, eyes flared.

'You cheat! You traitor!' she hissed.

Derek dropped his burger. 'Wha . . . What's wrong, Didi?'

'What do you call a person who adds Mayo in between the sandwich?'

'I . . . I don't quite follow, Didi,' Derek mumbled, swallowing the lump in his throat.

'You idiot! What do you call a person who plays the piano?' she said, a steely glint in her eyes.

'Pi . . . Pianist?' Derek mumbled.

'And a person who exorcises?'

'Ex . . . Exorcist?'

'So what would you call a person who prepares Mayo . . . whatever?' she screeched.

And then the ball dropped. A trembling Derek gasped, 'Mayo . . . ist! Shit!'

At exactly that moment, Karat made an appearance at the entrance. Just as he began to raise his arm in a greeting, Mamata let out a blood-curdling, eardrum-shattering scream that nearly knocked Derek cold.

Karat immediately vamoosed.

'I just saw that Maoist, no Marxist, Karat at the entrance!' Didi thundered.

'Must be a mistake, Didi,' Derek tried to pacify his enraged boss.

'No, it was him! You idiot, you brought me to a Maoist restaurant?! You have disgraced me and the party, Derek, and for this you will be expelled,' she thundered, and stormed out of the restaurant, while Derek stared after her, dumbstruck, his dreams shattered.

Hiding behind a parked Land Rover a few metres outside McDonald's, Karat heaved a sigh of relief. It was the first and last time he would attempt to make contact with the TMC supremo.

Iron Man
Hey dude, Superman, why aren't you wearing your trademark red underwear anymore?

6 hours ago · Like · Comment

👍 Lois Lane and 554,344 others like this.

Superman I am. Just that I wear it inside now.
6 hours ago · Like

Iron Man LOL! Took you long enough to learn the right way. Why the sudden change though?
6 hours ago · Like

Superman Long story man... I was flying over West Bengal and decided to stop for a roshogulla in Kolkata, when all of a sudden, a bunch of chaps started bashing me up, while a lady stood there pointing at my red underwear and screaming...
6 hours ago · Like

Mamata Banerjee YOU MAOIST SUPERHERO!!!
6 hours ago · 👍 Derek O'Brien likes this

Superman Jeez, here too!? I'm flying off to Google Plus. Bye!
6 hours ago · 👍 Larry Page likes this

Iron Man Uh-oh. Jarvis, cancel the bright red rendering of my suit. Make it blue instead.
6 hours ago · Like

Jarvis Already done, sir.
6 hours ago · 👍 Mamata Banerjee likes this

NINE

The masked vigilante

JULY 2013

IT WAS RAINING HARD in Mumbai. V-man was hunched under his cape at the roadside shack in one of the shanties nestled amidst high-rise buildings in South Mumbai. With the cape serving as a raincoat and covering his hood and upper torso, he could have passed off for another one of Mumbai's underprivileged denizens. But V-man was feeling truly chuffed as he took another deep drag of the cigarette and let out a curl of smoke that soon dissipated in the drench of the ongoing monsoon.

He had just climbed fifteen floors up the building in front of him, courtesy the suction devices he had added to his gadgetry, stared down Arnab Goswami, and passed on an important piece of information: files pertaining to the allocation of coal blocks under the ad hoc allocation policy had gone missing.

The meeting itself had been dramatic with V-man neatly synchronizing his introduction to the crack of thunder, just after a flash of lightning lit up his silhouette against Arnab's window. Arnab was for once lost for words and allowed V-man to do all the talking.

Over three months had passed since the dramatic resignations of Pawan Kumar Bansal and Ashwani Kumar, and there had been a drought of new scams. Even Arnab was finding it difficult to find themes to outrage over, having to make do with complex, nuanced issues with little scope of grandstanding such as the slowing of GDP growth and the widening current account deficit. Along with the slowing down of the economy, the business of outraging was in recession until V-man's stunning tip-off.

V-man could have avoided the trip to Mumbai, and instead tipped off Delhi-based news anchors such as Barkha or Rajdeep. But given his exacting standard, V-man wanted the best. In any case, if Arnab broke the story, the rest would follow suit.

'The Nation demands an answer, Mr V-Man. Who are you?' a grateful Arnab had managed to stammer as V-man was about to depart.

'Oh, save your questions for Mr Jha, Arnab. And you know, quite frankly, The Nation doesn't care a damn,' shot back V-man, before swinging away.

The downpour had now subsided. A lathi-wielding constable was on his beat and heading towards V-man's shack. V-man was a bit of a social media celebrity, but he didn't expect the policeman to recognize him. Ever since Ranjit Sinha had credited the caped crusader for his breakthrough in the Cash for Railway Post scam, V-man's Twitter handle, @VManBegins, had acquired over 30K followers and was fast growing, the growth fuelled by V-man's acerbic tweets targeting the UPA dispensation, never missing a chance to crack a Rahul Gandhi joke whenever #pappu trended. He particularly enjoyed taking a swing at the Nehru–Gandhi scion. Tweeting was almost as satisfying as being a superhero. Twitter had even verified his account.

The constable was now close. V-man decided it was time to make himself scarce and disappear into the night.

TEN

The Singham's roar

AUGUST 2013

'AS PER THE CENTRAL Statistics Office, the Indian economy grew by 4.8 per cent this fiscal, the slowest in a decade. Meanwhile, inflation as measured by the Consumer Price Index continued to remain in double digits with food inflation at a whopping 20 per cent,' a glum-faced Chidambaram read out at the UPA's Cabinet meeting held to take stock of the economy.

'What does this mean for us?' Sonia asked.

'It means we are screwed, madam,' Chidambaram answered in an earnest tone. The Cabinet collectively gasped.

'I see growth bottoming out—that is good news because it means we could yet get back to a high-growth trajectory,' interjected Montek Singh Ahluwalia, the deputy chairman of the Planning Commission.

'*Abey chup!*' snapped Mani Shankar Aiyar, special invitee to the Cabinet meeting. 'You have been parroting this "growth bottoming out" for the last five years. Every time you say it, the economy assumes an even lower bottom. The time has come, madam, for a dash of Nehruvian socialism to shore up our electoral fortunes.'

'Not unless we unleash more economic reforms,' Dr Manmohan Singh said, entering the room, with the minister of state in the PMO, Mr Narayanasamy, scurrying behind him with a stack of files. The ministers looked up in awe as Dr Singh smartly proceeded to his chair, looking straight ahead, making eye contact with none.

'Oh, you and your sad devotion to that dogma called reforms, Dr Singh,' scoffed Mani Shankar Aiyar. 'What good has it done the country for the last four years? Job creation is zilch, economic inequality is increasing, the current account deficit continues to widen, prices of onions and vegetables have shot through the roof. So much so that the onion is considered a woman's best friend now . . .'

'Don't be so dismissive of the power of free market reforms, *former* panchayati raj minister,' Dr Singh said, emphasizing the word 'former' as he stood up.

'Your economic mumbo jumbo doesn't impress me, Dr Singh,' Mani continued in a voice dripping with sarcasm. 'Take the case of FDI in retail. Has it made any difference? Wal-mart hasn't even invested a single dollar in the Indian market despite all the hype you and your cronies tried to generate about it being a game changer.'

Dr Singh turned in Mani's direction and raised his hand towards him, thumb and fingers curled in a pinching gesture.

Suddenly, Mani felt a choking sensation as though an invisible hand had gripped his throat. His eyes began to bulge out and he began to spatter.

'Your lack of faith in free market reforms is disturbing, Mr Aiyar,' Dr Singh rumbled, eyes fixed on his tormentor.

It was never a good idea to cross Dr Singh, especially when it came to economic policy.

'Dr Singh, enough of this. Release poor Mani!' beseeched Sonia.

The other Cabinet ministers watched in horror as Mani began making gagging sounds.

'Enough! Enough!' Sonia shouted, but her voice was suddenly distant.

Dr Singh woke up with a start from his dream, Sonia's voice echoing in her head.

'Mannu, what's wrong? Was it a bad dream?' Gursharan asked, her tone suffused with concern.

'Er . . . yes. I had the weirdest of dreams. I was death-choking Mani Shankar Aiyar just like Darth Vader.'

'Don't be silly, dear,' Gursharan chided. 'You could never have dreamt of such a thing. Are you sure, darling?'

Dr Singh looked indignant. 'What do you mean I can't dream of being Darth Vader? Of course I did!' he roared.

Gursharan flinched, taken aback by her husband's unusually fierce reaction. She stared at her husband, his face distorted with indignant anger, when suddenly his features began to blur with the rest of the room.

Gursharan woke with a start, finding herself in the familiar environs of their bedroom. It was 4 a.m. Except for the chirping of crickets and the metronomic ticking of the clock, there was all-round silence. Dr Singh began to stir.

'No wonder,' she muttered.

What an unsettling dream within a dream that was and how far removed from reality. To dream that Manmohan was dreaming that he was this alpha male of a character domineering over his Cabinet. The absurdity of it all.

The yelping of a stray dog from the servant quarters jolted Gursharan back to the dullness of the present and its bitter reality. Dr Singh was now the butt of ridicule, an object of derision across the polity and media, putty in the hands of satirists, a football to be kicked by columnists wanting to take a break from penning ponderous, preachy editorials. Dr Singh's persona lent itself to various genres of humour, from sophisticated wit at the expense of his geeky personality to the more slapstick, ribald variety directed at his reticent demeanour.

How had things come to such a pass? From the heady days of the early '90s when Dr Singh had been hailed as the father of economic reforms, his fall from grace had been precipitous. Was this also a dream, a particularly bad one? There was only one way to find out. She picked up the totem from her bedside drawer table and spun it.

'*Sab theek hai*?' a bleary-eyed Dr Singh mumbled beside her.

'No, it's not,' she snapped, and glared at her husband. Then her features transformed, anger giving way to anguish. 'Why are you putting up with this crap, Mannu?' she pleaded, her eyes welling up with tears. 'You know what they call you now? An overrated economist and an underrated politician. It hurts so much!'

'Half true,' Dr Singh murmured.

Gursharan despaired. 'Why don't you just quit then? Is it worth being pilloried like this? The latest joke going around is that you were accidentally dropped from the Cabinet and no one even noticed!'

Dr Singh blinked.

Gursharan's mouth dropped open. 'That wasn't a joke?'

For a while, Gursharan gaped at Dr Singh, who stared back impassively, until the totem that Gursharan had set spinning earlier tottered and fell off the table, snapping her out of her daze. The chirping of birds wafted through the window, heralding the breaking of dawn. She sighed deeply.

'I'll get the morning papers and make some tea,' she said, and went out of the room.

A minute later, she stormed back, and flung the day's *Times of India* at him. 'Congrats, Dr Singh,' she said sarcastically. 'As if epithets like *nikamma*, underachiever, pet poodle, lame duck were not enough, they are now calling you a *chor*!'

'COAL FILES GO MISSING FROM COAL MINISTRY; PM IS A CHOR, CRIES OPPOSITION,' screamed the main headline.

Dr Singh's eyes widened ever so slightly.

* * *

The news of the missing coal files sent the government into a tizzy. Top babus of the ministries of coal, power and finance spent the first half of the day actually doing tangible work: rummaging through desk shelves, peering under carpets, and cushions of sofas, and sniffing behind window curtains, all in a vain attempt to locate the missing coal files. The morning session of Parliament witnessed stormy scenes with members of the Opposition baying for blood. An ashen-faced Coal Minister Sriprakash Jaiswal got up to address the House.

'We have searched everywhere, but the coal files are missing,' he said with trepidation. 'Even a Google search has failed to throw up leads. CBI Director Ranjit Sinha and I personally stayed up till the wee hours of morning, going all the way to the 350th page link to the search query "Where the hell have the missing coal files disappeared?"

'We came across a lot of jokes on the coal scam such as "After thorium, iron ore mining and coal scams, Periodic Table to be rearranged based on size of corresponding scam", "Dr Manmohan Singh to star as the mute hero in Rakesh Roshan's sequel to *Koyla*", but there was no useful information about the missing coal files,' disclosed Jaiswal.

Bedlam ensued as soon as the coal minister finished his statement. Opposition members flooded the well of the House, insisting that the prime minister make a statement in Parliament on the issue. After all, the missing coal files pertained to the period when the coal ministry was under him.

'Leave the poor man alone, *na*?' Parliamentary Affairs Minister Rajiv Shukla pleaded with the leader of the Opposition, Sushma Swaraj. 'Why insist that he e-speak? What's he got to do with all this, e-Sushmaji?'

'Grr, we don't care! He is the prime minister!' Sushma replied. 'We want to hear his voice. Moreover, it has been over two years since he has spoken on the floor of the House. I believe that there is even an RTI application pending on wanting to have a sample of the prime minister's voice which the government is trying to evade. *YEH KAISE CHALEGAAAA!?'*

Rajiv Shukla slipped his noise-cancelling headphones on before Sushma's eardrum-shattering scream could do any further damage. It looked like the PM would have to exercise his vocal chords to save the monsoon session.

* * *

Dr Singh was in his office working on the 12th Five Year Plan when the call came from 10 Janpath.

'Hello, Dr Singh. How are you doing?' Ahmed Patel said. Dr Singh nodded in silence.

'Um, Dr Singh,' Ahmed Patel continued, 'the Opposition is insisting that you make a statement on the floor of the House on the missing coal files this afternoon. If not, they have threatened to stall House proceedings indefinitely.'

Ahmed waited for a response from the other end. When none came, he continued, 'I know you have had nothing to do with the whole affair, save for signing off on the files which have since gone missing, but still, can you say a few insipid lines about it and round it off with a nice Urdu couplet. They have a disarming effect on women, and Sushma will go easy on you after that. That's fine, no? Don't worry if the Opposition heckles you too much; we will let Mani Shankar Aiyar loose on them.'

Ahmed paused again, craning his neck to hear Dr Singh's reply or even the sound of his breathing. He couldn't hear a thing. 'Uh, okay then. Madam will see you as usual this

Friday for the weekly briefing,' he said, and disconnected.

Dr Singh replaced the receiver, and sat quietly, staring at a spot on the wall.

Moments later, he picked up his files, locked his office and got into his official Ambassador to leave for the Parliament.

The chauffeur flicked on the music player. Starting with the peppy beats of a *Dhoom 2* number, a series of songs resounded in the closed environs of the Ambassador.

Chori chori kiya re, dil de dil diya re . . .

Chura liya hai maine tere . . .

Chori pe chori, chori pe chori haath pakarke ungalii marori . . .

By the time the car pulled into the space outside the Parliament's entrance, the faintest hint of a scowl had appeared on Dr Singh's face.

The Opposition benches began to boo him the moment he entered the House. Rajiv Shukla stepped to his side, and took his hand. 'Good morning, e-sir,' he snivelled, and added with exaggerated concern, 'why is your hand so hot, e-sir? Are you feverish? Don't worry e-sir, you'll e-steal the thunder today,' he flashed a toothy grin.

Dr Singh eyed Shukla for a fleeting instant, and then walked over to his seat.

'*Baith jayiye, shaant ho jaiye,*' the Speaker cooed. 'Dr Singh will address the House.'

The heckling only grew louder. Undeterred, Dr Singh picked up a copy of his speech. Those on the treasury benches slipped on their headphones, including the MPs sitting right next to him.

'Madam Speaker,' he mumbled, 'with your permission

I would like to set the record straight on a matter that has seized the attention of the House . . .'

The booing grew louder. Someone shouted, '*PM chor hai!*' and the boos changed to chants of '*PM chor hai! PM chor hai!*'

For a few minutes, Dr Singh continued to read, but the jeering continued unabated. Suddenly, a wisp of smoke rose from his right shoulder. His frame then began to tremble, imperceptibly at first and then violently. His left fist curled around the paperweight on his desk and shattered it into pieces. The members sitting around him backed away in panic, as the fabric on his arms and shoulders suddenly caught fire. Dr Singh brought down his palm on the desk, shattering it.

Silence befell the House instantly. Shell-shocked members across party lines stared at the avenging apparition they once knew as the prime minister.

'IS THIS HOW ONE BEHAVES IN THE TEMPLE OF DEMOCRACY? HAS ANY OTHER NATION CALLED THEIR PRIME MINISTER A CHOR? YOU GUYS STALL PARLIAMENT PROCEEDINGS AND BLAME US FOR GOVERNANCE? I AM NOT THE CUSTODIAN OF THE COAL FILES. TO HELL WITH YOU . . .'

For five minutes, fire poured out of Dr Singh as it would from a flamethrower, scorching everything in its path. MPs near the well of the House cowered under the desks, whereas those in the backbenches withdrew to the far end of the House. When he was done, those Opposition MPs who were still standing looked at each other desperately and, finding no traces of resilience, fled out of the House. It would be hours before they would recover and term their flight as an indignant walkout.

Back in the House, there was still pin-drop silence, as trembling MPs in the treasury benches cautiously watched Dr Singh rearrange his notes neatly on his desk, and resume his meditative pose.

* * *

That night, as Gursharan watched the recap of the day's events in the Parliament on primetime news with growing disbelief, Dr Singh calmly walked in, his safari suit torn and frayed at various spots. He left his shoes near the entrance and put aside his briefcase. Then, with an open-mouthed Gursharan gaping at him in astonishment, he walked into the closet and shut himself in.

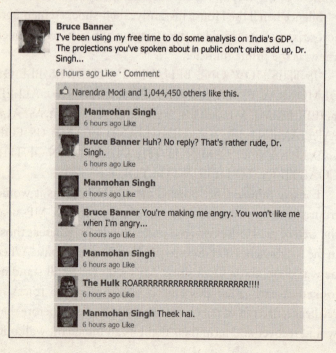

Bruce Banner
I've been using my free time to do some analysis on India's GDP. The projections you've spoken about in public don't quite add up, Dr. Singh...
6 hours ago Like · Comment

👍 Narendra Modi and 1,044,450 others like this.

Manmohan Singh
6 hours ago Like

Bruce Banner Huh? No reply? That's rather rude, Dr. Singh.
6 hours ago Like

Manmohan Singh
6 hours ago Like

Bruce Banner You're making me angry. You won't like me when I'm angry...
6 hours ago Like

Manmohan Singh
6 hours ago Like

The Hulk ROARRRRRRRRRRRRRRRRRRRRRRRR!!!!
6 hours ago Like

Manmohan Singh Theek hai.
6 hours ago Like

ELEVEN

The rise of the Gujarat lion

SEPTEMBER 2013

'GET UP!'

'Mmm . . . five more minutes . . . I just went to sleep . . .'

'It's 6.30 already! Get up!'

Rajnath Singh woke with a groan and peered at his wife, dark circles exaggerating his sunken eyes.

'You look like shit,' she said matter-of-factly.

It was the 245th night-out Rajnath Singh had put since taking over as BJP president. The endless meetings over chai, pakodas, and jalebis stretching well into the night with various factions in the Sangh Parivar to engender consensus over the party's prime ministerial candidate over the last six months were beginning to take a toll on the BJP president's health, and it was not just because of the high sugar intake.

Rajnath was already bald and did not have any more hair to lose, so that was one less thing to worry about.

After Narendra Modi's thumping victory in the Gujarat Assembly polls, although the cadre and the RSS were in favour of declaring Narendra Modi as the prime ministerial candidate, there remained the small matter of persuading the members of the party's highest decision-making body.

The BJP, to its credit, prided itself on placing merit over lineage in deciding succession issues. But the reality was that the saffron party had been no different from others. After all, to decide leaders by the simple expedient of holding elections rather than through Byzantine intrigue and Machiavellian wheeling and dealing was to strip party politics of its very soul. It would cease to be the higher calling that attracted the shrewdest and the best in the country. And so, politicians, ever mindful of its dangers, had ring-fenced their craft from the insidious idea of inner-party democracy.

Under Rajnath's watch, the race for becoming the BJP's PM candidate was beginning to resemble an Agatha Christie plot with its meandering, slow-paced narrative, occasional twists, multiple suspects, needless red herrings and no clarity until the final chapter. New names for the PM candidate would pop up at regular intervals; each time Advani praised a leader it would trigger speculation and frenzied activity, with leaders visiting each other for another round of discussions over chai and pakoda; and just when Rajnath thought he had won over a leader to the NaMo camp, the said leader would turn around and shower effusive praise on Advani, taking negotiations back to square one. Thus the process had been dragging on for four months.

In his extreme moments of frustration, Rajnath had even wished that the party had been a bit more like the Congress, and simply declared Vajpayee's foster son-in-law as the PM candidate. On other occasions, he had come close to writing to the Election Commission to put off the General Elections by another five years, preferably even indefinitely, to give him sufficient time to build consensus. Indeed, many MPs would have supported him wholeheartedly had he done so. After nine years of enjoying not being in government, the prospect of coming back to power and trying to do something useful such as running the country as opposed to staging walkouts after rushing to the well of the House haunted many BJP MPs. A British peer has said that power corrupts and absolute power corrupts absolutely, but in this case it might seem that absolutely no power could corrupt just as absolutely as well.

Finally, after the 1234th round of confabulations, only one pocket of resistance stood between Narendra Modi and the PM candidature: the party patriarch, L.K. Advani, and his protégé, Sushma Swaraj. Rajnath was determined to persuade the Bheeshma Pitamah one way or the other. The day of reckoning had arrived.

'And if you can't achieve your goal today also, don't bother coming back home,' Mrs Rajnath Singh said sternly, after placing a cup of tea on the desk.

'Don't worry, darling. It will be done today,' he assured her, keeping his fingers crossed.

Smriti Irani was already on her way to Sushma Swaraj's residence. Their confrontation would not be about the PM candidate, but also the clash over who would take over in the BJP as the epitome of the traditional Hindu, sindhoor-sporting, kohl-lined *pavitra* Bhartiya *nari*. If Swaraj could disarm opponents with her emotion-laced shrill oratory, Smriti was second to none in inducing pangs of guilt with dialogue delivery honed on the sets of various daily soaps. If Sushma could shake her leg to patriotic songs set to vigorous Punjabi beats, Smriti was second to none in Antakshari.

And then he received this message from Advani that turned his sallow, haggard face pallid:

Dear Raj,
To say that I am pissed with your style of functioning would be an understatement. I told you let's put off the decision over the party's PM candidate till at least the results of the Assembly elections, but you did not heed my sagacious advice. What is the hurry in announcing a PM candidate? Isn't it enough that the Congress is being led by Shri Rahul Gandhi?
* I will not be coming for today's meeting of the Parliamentary Board. Instead, I'm going to ponder over where we are heading as a party. Please don't call me.*

Yours poutingly,
Lal

PS: All other office-bearers have been CC'D.

* * *

Nine hundred kilometres south-west of Delhi, sitting in his spartan office, the Gujarat CM was staring into his computer, lost deep in thought. He had finished playing solitaire for the fifteenth time. He was supposed to hear from Rajnath the previous night, but the call still hadn't come. His Gmail status message was also not comforting. 'One of those f***ed up days,' it read.

Should he call up Rajnath or wait for another twenty minutes? He decided to play another round of solitaire.

Amit Shah barged in to interrupt his boss's line of thought.

'Saheb, quarry has now gone into Haldiram's. Ordering a dhokla and one cup of tea, as we speak.'

'Not today, Amit. I'm preoccupied with other things,' Modi said, waving him away.

'Jee, saheb,' Shah said, and went out of the room.

Modi couldn't take it any more and decided to call up the BJP president.

'Vande Mataram, Rajnathji. *Aa jaon kya?*' he asked.

'Jai Shri Ram, Modibhai. Things are a bit messed up right now . . . I'll call you back,' Rajnath replied. Modi could hear the unmistakable din of traffic in the background.

'Rajnathji, where are you?'

'I was on the way to Jaitley's house, but it turned out he was on the way to my house. Now we have decided to meet at Andhra Bhavan for breakfast,' gibbered Rajnath.

'Arre bhai, I told you to get more tech-savvy and install WhatsApp to avoid such snafus. Anyway, what's the hungama about?'

'Advaniji has refused to attend the Parliamentary Board meeting. No one knows what he's thinking. Everyone's in a state of panic. Listen, I'll call you back in a while . . . or maybe not. Hai Bhagwan, I hate my job,' Rajnath whined, and disconnected.

Modi slouched back on his swivel chair and began to stroke his beard, wondering what was going through Advani's mind.

A minute later, he straightened and pulled his laptop closer. He opened a secure shell console, and began typing furiously. As his fingers flew across the keyboard, a mass of text, numerals and special characters scrolled up the screen at a dizzying speed, too fast for anyone to follow. Modi himself barely looked at the screen or the keyboard. At one point, he yawned, and nonchalantly took his right hand off the keyboard to take a sip of masala chai he'd made himself, without any let-up in the typing speed, and seamlessly put it back on the keyboard a moment later. After a few minutes of work, he sat back, exhaled, and with a smile of satisfaction, slammed the return key.

The screen split into four panels, each panel featuring a different image. The first panel contained a mirror, the second a bed that seemed to be occupied, the third a dining table and the fourth a computer. The panels were titled Camera 1, Camera 2, Camera 3 and Camera 4. For a few minutes, Modi slouched in his chair and watched the screen, munching on a bag of *thepla*s. The screen remained unchanged while the digital clock on the bottom right of the screen ticked by. When the theplas and his patience ran out, he leaned forward and pressed a function key.

A rooster crowed. Modi pressed the key again. The rooster crowed again. The sheets on the bed in the second panel stirred and, a moment later, L.K. Advani rose from his bed, yawning and stretching. Modi watched with interest, as Advani moved from the second panel to the first and began brushing his teeth vigorously. Moments later, he appeared in the third panel to make himself a sandwich, and then eventually settled in panel four in front of the computer.

Modi switched to the console, and typed a few more lines of gibberish. The camera feeds were promptly replaced by a Windows desktop screen, but it wasn't Modi's. Modi took another sip of his tea, and watched as the mouse pointer twitched and began to make an agonizingly slow journey towards the Chrome icon on the left end of the screen.

'Come on, come on, come on,' muttered Modi.

The browser opened with Blogger.com's login screen. Then in slow motion, the username 'Lal' and a four-letter password appeared letter by letter in the login fields. A moment later, Blogger's dashboard opened. The mouse then moved upwards and homed in on the 'New post' link. Modi leaned closer to the screen as letters began to appear in the title field of the form that followed.

'Why . . . Narendra . . . Modi . . . will . . . make . . . a . . . disastrous . . . PM . . .' he read it aloud slowly.

'*Maa Jagdamba!*' Modi cried.

* * *

Back in Delhi, Advani's message and Modi's snapshot of his draft blog post had sown the seeds of confusion and chaos. Leaders wasted no time in dashing to each other's houses for yet another round of meetings. With all the central BJP leaders in Delhi and their respective retinues hitting the roads simultaneously, and working their mobiles, traffic jams began to get reported from different parts of the city and cellular lines began to clog up.

Amidst the chaos, Sushma Swaraj was facing off with Smriti Irani in one of the most riveting dramas in modern India's political history. Only the maudlin background score and commercial breaks were missing. Both the ladies were decked in full battle gear: large vermilion bindis adorning their foreheads, *maang* filled with sindhoor, eyes lined with kohl, and draped in crimson-red saris.

'Grr . . . you have such a foreign-sounding surname! And you know how much I detest foreigners,' shrieked Sushma, firing the first salvo in what political scientists would dub as 'the great Swaraj vs Irani debate'.

'You know that's not true, Sushmaji. My surname might be Irani, but I am half-Bong and half-Punjabi. I am true to my character Tulsi,' was Smriti's pat rejoinder.

'Tell me one good reason why I should make way for you?' queried the older woman.

Smriti paused and turned towards Sushma in super slow motion three times in succession. And then in a soft voice full of pathos, she delivered the killer lines: '*Kyon ki saas bhi kabhi bahu thi, Sushmaji*,' and batted her eyelids to rub it in.

And at that moment, staring back at her younger version, slack-jawed, Sushma knew that she had been bested, the generational change had been effected.

* * *

Back in Gandhinagar, Modi paced his office floor restlessly. The danger for now had been contained. He'd acted quickly,

and got the BJP IT cell to lean on Advani's ISP to block access
to his blog for the day. Thankfully, Advani detested both
Facebook and Twitter, so the chances of his taking to the
social media to vent his frustration were remote.

But he had had enough. This nonsense of brinkmanship
had been going on for too long. If Rajnath Singh did not bring
Advani around today, the decision would undoubtedly be
postponed to another day. And then to another day. And to
another. Until one day when they'd not need a PM candidate,
but a Leader of the Opposition.

It was then that Rajnath Singh called, and said in a
resigned tone that the problem was beyond him.

'He won't even talk to me, Modibhai. I don't know what
to do,' he said helplessly. 'It's up to you, Modibhai. Please
find a common ground with Advaniji.'

Modi froze, and stood staring at the phone well after
Rajnath had disconnected. Then, in slow motion, he walked
across the room and came to a halt near the Sardar Patel
portrait on the wall facing his desk. For a long time, he stood
gazing at his idol. And then Modi came to a decision.

* * *

Two hours before the Parliamentary Board meeting, Advani
sat in his home with a sullen expression on his face.

His Internet connection had conked off in the morning
just when he was about to publish his blog post. Robbed of
his morning activity, Advani had picked up the newspaper
only to find Modi's face splashed all over the front page.
He'd promptly tossed it into the bin. He'd then switched on

the TV and found every news channel reporting on NaMo's possible elevation. Frustrated, he'd sworn off news for the day and, instead, turned to HBO. When he saw *Finding Nemo* playing, he'd uttered a plaintive cry, yanked the TV's power plug out of its socket, and resigned himself to simply sitting on his couch.

Several hours later, Advani was still sitting on the couch in his living room, bored out of his wits, having done nothing apart from screaming at Rajnath the few times he'd called since morning, when the phone rang once again.

'Hello, Advaniji?'

'I TOLD YOU I DON'T WANT TO TALK TO YOU . . .'

'It's me, Narendra . . .'

Advani was quiet for a few moments. Then he said, 'Why, Narendra, why? I sportingly made way for Vajpayeeji. Why can't you be large-hearted enough to step aside for me?'

'Advaniji, please listen . . .'

'No, you listen, Narendra. You kids are so impatient, I tell you. You are only sixty-three, in the blossom of your political career. Why this unseemly hurry to get to the top?' Advani railed.

There was now a pause at the other end. Then Modi said, 'Ding dong!'

'What?'

'Someone's at your door.'

At that moment, the doorbell rang. Advani looked flabbergasted. 'How did you . . . ?'

'I've sent you something. Please have a look at it,' interrupted Modi. 'I'll stay on the line.'

Five minutes later, when Advani had seen what Modi

meant him to see, he was sobbing like a child. With a trembling hand, he picked up the receiver.

'I am sorry, Narendra. I . . . I . . . didn't know . . .' he choked.

'You don't have to be sorry about anything, Advaniji,' said Modi kindly.

The two then spoke for a long time, rekindling their relationship of a mentor and his protégé, making up for all those years when they didn't see eye to eye on anything. When an hour had passed, Modi said, 'I take it you are no longer opposed to my candidature?'

'Of course not, beta. You have my blessings, now,' Advani said, a lump forming in his throat.

'Will you hug me wholeheartedly when I feign to touch your feet, and accept my bouquet of flowers lovingly?'

'Yes, *mere lal.*'

'Will you feed your bhakt a ladoo with your own hands?'

'Of course, with full enthusiasm.'

'All right. Let me warm you up. Vande!'

'Mataram,' whined Advani.

'No, no. Let's do it again. Vande!'

'Mataram!' uttered Advani, with a little more effort.

'Ah, that's better. All right, I'm now on my way to Delhi to accept the nomination to become the BJP PM candidate.'

* * *

Later, after the customary pose with hands-raised photo op, feeding of ladoos, and acceptance speech, all the leaders were resting in the side-room. 'Tea, sir,' the tea-boy asked, holding a tray of half-filled plastic cups.

'No more caffeine for me,' said Rajnath, his eyes sunken but relief writ large on his face. 'Off to Hrishikesh for a week-long camp of meditation to recover my health. Whew!'

Rajnath then turned to Modi. 'But tell me, Modibhai, what exactly did you say to Advaniji that made him do a U-turn? Now he can't stop singing your praises!'

Narendra Modi smiled enigmatically.

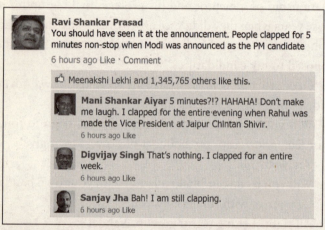

Ravi Shankar Prasad
You should have seen it at the announcement. People clapped for 5 minutes non-stop when Modi was announced as the PM candidate
6 hours ago Like · Comment

👍 Meenakshi Lekhi and 1,345,765 others like this.

Mani Shankar Aiyar 5 minutes?!? HAHAHA! Don't make me laugh. I clapped for the entire evening when Rahul was made the Vice President at Jaipur Chintan Shivir.
6 hours ago Like

Digvijay Singh That's nothing. I clapped for an entire week.
6 hours ago Like

Sanjay Jha Bah! I am still clapping.
6 hours ago Like

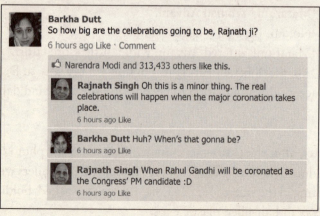

Barkha Dutt
So how big are the celebrations going to be, Rajnath ji?
6 hours ago Like · Comment

👍 Narendra Modi and 313,433 others like this.

Rajnath Singh Oh this is a minor thing. The real celebrations will happen when the major coronation takes place.
6 hours ago Like

Barkha Dutt Huh? When's that gonna be?
6 hours ago Like

Rajnath Singh When Rahul Gandhi will be coronated as the Congress' PM candidate :D
6 hours ago Like

LK Advani
Blog update: How 'Man of Steel' Superman trumps the Avengers in every aspect

6 hours ago Like · Comment

👍 Superman, Batman, DC comics like this.

Superman HAHAHAHAHA! Up yours, Avengers!!!!
6 hours ago · 👍 Batman likes this

Nick Fury This is not on, boys. Show him who we are!
6 hours ago Like

Iron Man Advani ji, we are a team of superheroes, earth's mightiest warriors, and you, sir, have pissed off every one of them!
6 hours ago · 👍 Captain America and 4 others like this

LK Advani So what? I have Sushma ji, Uma ji, Nitish ji, and an army of communal-turned-secular fans.
6 hours ago · 👍 Nitish Kumar and 5 others like this

Iron Man We have the Hulk.
6 hours ago · 👍 Hawk-Eye and 4 others like this

LK Advani I have the Bulk.
6 hours ago · 👍 Sushma Swaraj and 5 others like this

Nitin Gadkari Hello boys! *chomp chomp*
6 hours ago Like

Thor HEY! HE ATE MY HAMMER!!!
6 hours ago · 👍 LK Advani and 6 others like this

MIDDLE OVERS

'Important phase of play for both the teams. Just get the feeling that something's gotta give, Chappelli.'

—Ravi Shastri

TWELVE

The family's war room

'*LO JI, MADAM, AA GAYA*,' announced the autorickshaw driver.

Alka gazed at the quaint-looking estate that wore the understated look of a typical Lutyens bungalow. Inside the sprawling grounds, however, serious activity was underfoot. It was here at 15 Gurdwara Rakabganj Road that the grand old party of India conceptualized, tested and set in motion its election strategies, and it is here that history would be made in 2014. And Alka was determined to be a part of that.

A week after she had filled in an online application, uploaded scanned copies of her college grade sheets along with a 5000-word essay on 'Why Rahul Gandhi should be the country's PM', she had received an email from the man who was in charge of recruitment, Shri Digvijaya Singh himself.

She had been shortlisted, and was required to appear for an interview.

'This way, please,' said the lady security guard at the gate, guiding her into a mini booth. She then subjected her to a thorough frisking, and when she was satisfied, she overturned the contents of Alka's handbag on to her desk, and flung the empty handbag into the trash can.

'Hey! What the hell!'

'We do not allow anything that may have an RSS connection into this building,' the guard replied tersely.

'How is my handbag connected to the RSS?' demanded Alka.

'It's saffron in colour.'

'No, it's not! That's yellow!'

'Close enough,' she said, and brusquely pushed Alka through. 'You are cleared. Reception is down the path and to the right.'

Furious, but left with no option, Alka picked up the contents of her handbag, dropped them into a plastic cover and walked towards the reception.

Everywhere she looked, portraits of the Nehru–Gandhis adorned the walls. Scores of Pandit Jawaharlal Nehrus, Indira Gandhis, Rajiv Gandhis and Rahul Gandhis stared down at her from the walls, sporting a bevy of expressions: smiling benevolence, quiet confidence, stern resolve, controlled fury. She scanned the length and breadth of the wall and spotted a small rectangle at the top right corner that had been left uncovered.

Just when she was wondering if it was intentional, the receptionist followed her line of sight, and muttered a curse. She snapped her fingers, and out of nowhere two men appeared, placed a ladder under the spot, and carefully installed Rajiv Gandhi's portrait in the uncovered area.

Moments later, she was at the waiting room. Two young men in rather strange attire looked up.

'Uh, you guys waiting for the interview?' she asked.

They nodded.

'Why are you, uh, topless?' she asked the first one.

'Orange shirt,' he explained, shivering under the onslaught of the AC.

The second guy avoided her eyes, and tugged at his shirt in an attempt to pull them over his bare thighs. 'Khaki trousers,' he mumbled, staring at his feet.

She shook her head and strolled out of the room, looking around to familiarize herself with the surroundings, hoping to soothe her frayed nerves. The place was positively buzzing with activity. Through the windows in the corridor, she could get a glimpse of several rooms in the building.

A lecture session seemed to be under way in one of the rooms. A figure was written on the whiteboard in big bold letters: 2002.

'2002 was the worst year in the history of independent India because of what happened in Gujarat,' the lecturer intoned. 'As patriotic and secular denizens of this country, it is our solemn duty to bring it up every time a camera is thrust upon us and—'

'But what if the BJP spokesperson counters with 1984?' someone interrupted. The lecturer flung the duster in the direction of the question. 'Then you say two wrongs don't make a right, idiot!'

Another room seemed to be reserved for recreational activity. A bunch of young men and women threw darts at a large poster of Narendra Modi. As she watched, one of the darts landed on Modi's mouth, leading to whoops, high-fives and screams of 'bull's eye!'

She heard a man's high-pitched voice emanating from the room down the corridor. She tiptoed up to the window to take a peek. It seemed to be a social media tutorial for eNREGA activists. A projector was beaming images of a PPT presentation on the screen. About thirty students, all of them male, but with misleading female name tags such as @radhikalamba, @priyankajames, @saniahayat, were paying rapt attention to Ajay Maken's lecture.

'You idiots, the hashtag Pappu and its variants are insults,' Maken screamed. 'Any of you bozos found using such vile hashtags will be summarily suspended from the programme.'

The Congress had been slow to embrace social media, but was now quickly trying to catch up. Their first coordinated intervention had been to post tweets praising Rahul Gandhi on his birthday, but there had been a screw-up: eNREGA activists had unwittingly helped their opponents by appending #PappuDiwas to their tweets in praise of Rahul.

Maken switched to the next slide. 'Memorize these by heart and plug them as often as you can,' he said. The whiteboard flashed the words #YouthIcon, #PrinceCharming, #HeirApparent, #Number2 in a large font.

'And don't go overboard in your praise of Rahul lest it be construed as sarcasm,' Maken warned. 'Tweets praising Rahul must be heartfelt and simple. No fancy adjectives. No hyperbole. Here is a model tweet by Diggy sir.'

The projector beamed a snapshot of Digvijaya Singh's tweet:

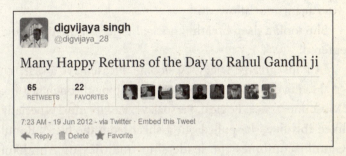

'See how crisp and to the point it is. Doesn't it have a ring of credibility to it?' he said.

The students nodded.

'And make sure to tag Shashi sir with a "Sir, please RT" if you want your labour of composition to be read by millions rather than getting lost in the churn,' Maken added.

'Sir, what if we can't think of anything nice to tweet about Rahulji?' a student asked tremulously.

'Then tweet something nasty about Modi,' Maken replied curtly. 'And make sure you append #MajorBlowToModi and tag NDTV. If it's your lucky day, they might even blow it up into a news story.'

Presently, a lady with a writing pad in her hand came over to her.

'Ms Chaturvedi?' she asked.

'Yeah, that's me.'

'Sir will interview you now. Follow me,' she beckoned, and led her through another corridor, left her in front of an imposing door, and disappeared along the way they'd come.

The label on the door read 'Digvijaya Singh, General Secretary, Indian National Congress (with the blessings of Soniaji)' and under that, in bold-red letters, were the words, 'RSS agents not allowed'.

She took a deep breath, knocked twice on the door, and entered.

'Alkaji!' greeted Diggy. 'Welcome. Please have a seat.'

'I read your essay,' he continued, flipping through her file. 'Most impressive. Logical. Persuasive. Passionate. I especially liked this line,' he pulled out a sheet from the file: '"Rahul Gandhi combines the leadership qualities of Abraham Lincoln, the energy of Winston Churchill and the compassion of Martin Luther King." Brilliant!'

'Thank you, sir,' said Alka, blushing.

'You will be happy to know that we are getting this line engraved in granite slabs and sending it to our offices across the country,' smiled Diggy.

'I am . . . overwhelmed, sir,' she said, visibly stunned.

Diggy eased back in his chair, resting his left elbow on its armrest. 'So what are your SAT scores?'

'SAT, sir?' she said, confused. 'I didn't know I was required to take SAT to qualify for this position.'

Diggy's smile faded.

'Look over there,' he said, nodding with his chin towards the glass partition on his right. 'You see the people over there? Every single one of them has perfect SAT scores.'

Outside the glass partition of Diggy's chamber, across the corridor, Alka saw a group of unshaven boys sitting around a table, passing around a joint and giggling wildly.

'A perfect SAT score isn't yet a mandatory requirement

for the Congress war room, but given the kind of people we are naturally attracting, we are seriously contemplating making it one,' Diggy added. 'And here you are telling me that you haven't even taken the test. How were you able to apply without having filled the test by the way?'

'Wait a second, sir. You are not talking about the Scholastic Aptitude Test, are you?'

Diggy stared at her in disbelief. 'Are you pulling my leg? Why would I talk about the Scholastic Aptitude Test? I'm talking about the quiz you took during your online application.'

'Oh, the bunch of questions all of whose answers were Rahul Gandhi,' she remarked in relief. 'Of course I took the Syco . . er . . . SAT and got a perfect score too.'

Diggy exhaled. 'Phew. For a second I thought we had a bug in our screening process. Imagine the consequences,' he said, shaking his head. 'Well, anyway, let's start the interview with the usual first question. Tell me about Rahul.'

Alka's nerves eased, and she smiled. This part of the interview she was comfortable with, having rehearsed her answer ad nauseam.

Diggy appeared satisfied with her answer, and smoothly moved to the standard follow-up question.

'Where do you see Rahul after five years?' asked Diggy.

'As India's prime minister, of course!' she shot back without a second's hesitation.

After a few more questions that Alka answered adequately, Diggy swung his laptop around towards her.

'Okay, now let's test your observation skills,' he said. 'This is a video clipping of a speech Modi gave at Fergusson

College in Pune recently. Listen to this speech carefully and identify points that we can attack him on.'

Saying thus, Diggy left the room. When he returned half an hour later, Alka smiled at him triumphantly.

'Got it, sir! Listen to this part,' she said, and turned the screen back towards Diggy. 'Modi says that China spent 20 per cent on its education. This is incorrect. According to Xinhua, China's official news agency, China spends only 4 per cent of its GDP on education.'

'Wow. Really? The bugger had me convinced about that!' exclaimed an incredulous Diggy. 'In fact, ever since he said this, I've been giving the same gyan in every conference that we have to spend 20 per cent on education!' he added, shaking his head.

'This is good stuff,' he murmured to himself, and then began typing furiously on the laptop. 'Let me shoot a quick email to Shashiji to rake it up on Twitter . . . and a quick email to Kanishka to remove this idea from Rahul's next speech . . . and an email to our friends in the media . . . and done!'

The interview resumed. Back and forth, the two went on. For each of Diggy's questions, Alka had a quick answer that she delivered eloquently without hesitation. An hour later, Diggy closed the file in front of him and pushed it aside.

'Okay, we are down to the last question. If you get this, you are in,' said Diggy.

'It is the luckiest day of your life. Rahul Gandhi calls you for a chat. Your immediate reaction, of course, is to swoon and collapse on the floor. When you recover and go over to his chamber, you find him in a pensive mood. He tells you that he may have been wrong about a decision he took earlier. He then turns to you and asks you if you think this assessment about his decision is correct. What would be your response?'

'That's easy. Rahul Gandhi's assessment, of course, cannot be wrong. I will tell him . . . ohh!' she trailed off as the full import of the question hit her.

Diggy grinned. 'Choose your next few words carefully, Alkaji. This is a trick question.'

Right, she thought. She tried to work it out in her head. Rahul Gandhi can never be wrong. That much she knew. Now if she agrees with Rahul's assessment, she would, in effect, be saying that he was wrong earlier, which is anathema even if Rahul himself may have suggested it. Whereas, if she doesn't agree with his assessment, she would end up telling him that he is wrong now. Heads I lose, tails you win. She shifted nervously in her seat.

'Think,' said Diggy with a patronizing smile. 'Not for nothing have we ruled over this country for sixty years.'

Alka rubbed her forehead, willing her mind to come up with the solution.

'If it were that easy to get into the Congress, the likes of Ravi Shankar Prasad and Piyush Goyal wouldn't be moping around in third-rate parties,' Diggy added pointedly.

As hard as she tried, the answer did not come to Alka. Tears sprung to her eyes, as she felt her dream slipping away.

'I don't know, sir,' she despaired. 'I really don't. This is like a no-win situation! I may not know all the answers, but I know that I want to work for the Congress and for Soniaji and for Rahulji, and I will do anything to work for them. I just want one chance! Please! Please give me one chance!' she cried, and burst out sobbing.

Diggy looked visibly moved. He stood up hastily and walked around the table to comfort the distressed young lady.

'Hey, it's okay, we didn't expect you to get this one,' he said, handing her a tissue. 'Everyone gets confused here. It's more of an eliminator actually, meant to chuck those idiots who are dumb enough to ask what Rahul's original decision was.'

Alka calmed down a little, and blew into the tissue loudly.

'In fact, there has only been one person in the history of the Congress who has been able to answer that.'

'Really? Who?' she sniffled.

'Sanjay Jha.'

'What did he say?'

'That's just it,' replied Diggy. 'No one knows what he meant by whatever he said. Or even what he said. By the time he finished his reply, his interviewer had leapt out of the seventh-floor window and fallen to his death all the way down to the pavement below.'

Diggy crossed himself, looking a bit shaken by the memory. Alka wiped her tears. Moments later, Diggy shook himself out of his thoughts and turned to her.

'Well,' he smiled, and extended an envelope. 'You are hired. Here's your appointment letter.'

Later, when the formalities were completed, Alka found herself standing outside, envelope in hand, feeling a mixture of shock, relief and euphoria. She was in! It was yet to sink in fully though. Diggy had been such a gentleman, everything an interviewer should be—intelligent, sensitive and accommodating.

Wonder why people call him weird, she thought.

She opened the envelope, unfolded the two-page letter and on the first page found a full-length photo of Diggy pointing a forefinger at her, grinning his familiar chipped-tooth grin. A welcome message was printed at the bottom:

'Congratulations! You are *sau taka tunch maal!*'

THIRTEEN

The challenger's war room

OCTOBER 2013

'S . . . S . . . SORRY, SIR.'

'Hmm,' said Modi. '*Sorry se kaam nahi chalega, bhai.*'

'Sir?' the young speech-writer trembled.

'*Murga ban.*'

Shaking like a leaf, the young man slowly descended to a squatting position, put his arms through his legs and held his ears.

'Now repeat one hundred times: China spent 4 per cent and not 20 per cent on education.'

'China spent 4 per cent and not 20 per cent on education. China spent 4 per cent and not 20 per cent on education. China . . .' echoed the hapless speech-writer, with Modi tapping his foot on the floor to keep count, while Amit Shah stood by his side.

When the human rooster completed his imposition, and Modi sat back satisfied in his chair, Amit Shah cleared his throat and leaned towards his superior.

'The damage is already done, Modibhai,' whispered Amit Shah with a worried expression.

Modi ignored the suggestion. 'Are the candidates here?' he asked instead.

'Yes,' said Shah, and nodded at a young man standing a step behind him. 'He's the first one.' The boy stepped forward, stuck his chest out, and said with pride, 'Ramachandran Gopal, sir.'

Modi scratched his beard, and ran an appraising eye over him. 'That may have been enough to get into my team some time back, but not any more,' he said, at which Gopal's chest deflated as if somebody had stuck a pin into it.

Modi stood up, folded his hands behind his back and made for the door. 'Walk with me,' he said, prompting Amit Shah to fall in line behind him with young Ramachandran a step behind.

'eNREGA chaps are trending #Feku on Twitter, Modibhai,' said Shah.

Modi turned towards a long corridor with bright sunlight at the end of it. Their footsteps echoed in the silence as they walked towards the light.

'It's the top trend right now,' whimpered Shah.

'If we get our guys to tweet with a pro-Modi hashtag, their trend will fall,' replied Modi, without turning. Amit Shah scurried to his side.

'But even if we begin tweeting a pro-Modi hashtag, it will take a number beyond reckoning, thousands to make it trend!'

'Tens of thousands.'

'But Modibhai, there is no such force,' protested Shah, just as they stepped into the sunlight on the balcony.

And then a thunderous roar greeted them from the vast grounds far below the narrow balcony they stood upon. A shocked gasp escaped Amit Shah's lips, and he reached for the railing to steady himself at the surreal sight that greeted him—rows and rows and rows of swayamsevaks in khaki shorts stretching to miles in every direction, standing with outstretched fists in a perfect forward stance, roaring their war cry at the sight of their redeemer.

Modi raised a hand.

'A new power is rising. Its victory is at hand!' thundered Modi. 'This night, Twitter will be stained with the blood of eNREGA tweets. March to your workstations. Spare no one!'

The army's roar threatened to bring the skies down.

'To war!'

A tear ran down Amit Shah's cheek as he gaped at the bloodthirsty cyber warriors departing from the grounds in vast hordes, their cries renting the air.

'There will be no dawn for eNREGA's trend,' declared Modi.

Behind him, Ramachandran cleared his throat and leaned towards Modi. 'Saruman from *Lord of the Rings*, sir?' he asked politely.

Modi grinned. 'Nice, no?'

'Awe-inspiring, sir.'

'Come, let's begin your interview,' Modi put an arm on the young man's shoulder and led him back into the heart of his sprawling war-room complex in Gandhinagar.

'It is good to see youngsters such as yourself wanting to be part of my team. We do some very exciting work here. There will be plenty of opportunities for you to grow as a professional, hone your skills, and develop a well-rounded personality. And if you are really good, and if you have what it takes, who knows, in due course, you may reach the very pinnacle in this field.' He glanced at Ramachandran over his glasses. 'You could be my Ahmed Patel.'

Ramachandran gulped.

'Ready?'

'Yes, sir.'

Modi spun on his heel, and marched ahead.

'Who is the best prime minister to have led India?' he barked.

'Atal Bihari Vajpayee, sir,' shot back Ramachandran, scampering to his side.

'Who is the best prime minister to not have led India?'

'Sardar Patel.'

'Who is the current prime minister of India?'

'No one, sir.'

Modi cast a sideways glance at Ramachandran and nodded appreciatively.

The two turned into a narrow corridor flanked by full-length glass panes on either side. Beyond the glass walls, hundreds of young men and women were hard at work.

The first room housed an array of technicians, young and old, in white lab coats, poring over what appeared to be reams and reams of data. A large map of Gujarat hung on one of the walls, while a whiteboard with stray numbers, bell curves, integral symbols and Greek letters scribbled all over it covered another. What Ramachandran was looking at was Modi's Gujarat Analytics and Statistics (GAS) unit, whose members worked 24×7 slicing and dicing Gujarat's data, extracting insights that they would channel to the PR team down the corridor, who would in turn convert them into catchy headlines, supplement them with appropriate photographs of Modi sourced from another team in the complex, and release the finished articles in a gamut of mainstream media publications carefully chosen by a team of IIM-A-educated segmentation experts.

In the second room, he saw scores of young men and women furiously tapping away on their computers. Every now and then someone burst out laughing, and the number on a large ticker installed in the far end of the room went up by one. This was the world's largest repository of jokes on Rahul Gandhi, Sonia Gandhi, Manmohan Singh and Robert Vadra. A giant electronic board high up a wall listed the top five gags in three columns titled 'Popular this week', 'Popular this month' and 'Best ever'.

The next room accommodated a variety of mini assembly lines, job shops and manufacturing units populated by numerous workers, producing an assortment of paraphernalia, including Modi T-shirts, Modi smartphones, Modi teddy bears, Modi fairness creams, Modi deo-sticks, Modi dog collars and so on.

'Next round,' said Modi, snapping Ramachandran out of his slack-jawed stare. 'I'll say a word, and you have to respond with the first word that comes to your mind. Rajiv Gandhi.'

'Bofors.'

'Rahul Gandhi.'

'Pappu.'

'Robert Vadra.'

'Shark.'

'Pakistan.'

'Hai hai.'

'That's two words, but I'll give it to you.'

At this point, Modi stopped abruptly, and fixed Ramachandran with a penetrating stare. 'What happens when a puppy comes under the wheel of a car?'

Ramachandran paused.

'It gets hurt, sir,' he said quietly.

Modi stepped forward, grabbed Ramachandran's face with both hands, and scrutinized his expression. Ramachandran looked back dolefully, his eyes a cesspool of sadness. 'That's good,' Modi said, and let him go.

They resumed their walk down the corridor and presently came to a door sporting a large sign with Niticentral written on it. The room's layout resembled a regular office with desks, computers and cubicles, occupied by a dozen people tapping away at their keyboards. One of them, a bespectacled middle-aged man in a crumpled kurta, spotted Modi, snuffed out the large pipe he was smoking and hurried out of the door.

'Modibhai!' said Kanchan Gupta. 'Just a word!'

'We are working on this new photo series,' he said excitedly. 'Imagine this size 72 headline on Niticentral's home page: "The unseen pics of Narendra Modi!"' He spread his palms apart in the air like a wannabe movie director, and paused for dramatic effect. 'We could have pics of you brushing your teeth, flossing your gums, rinsing your face, drinking a glass of Gujarat's milk, gargling after breakfast, scratching your beard, sniffing a flower in the garden, pulling ticks out of your dog's hide . . . the possibilities are endless! It would be an absolute superhit!' he cried in delight.

'Let me think about that, Kanchanji,' said Modi. Gupta returned to his pipe, while Modi resumed his walk down the corridor.

A few minutes later, they pushed a door and entered a dimly lit section of the corridor. Modi pulled a pair of earmuffs off a hook behind the door and handed it to Ramachandran.

'Put these on.'

Ramachandran looked puzzled, but did as he was told. A minute later, the purpose of the earmuffs became clear as a volley of invectives, shouts and catcalls stung his ears despite the protection.

'Bencho! Paid media!'

'How much did the Congress pay you to post this, you a$$hole?'

'*Congress ke bhadwe, kitne paise milein*?'

Across the glass partition, in a room adorned with posters of Virat Kohli, Raghu Ram, Jackie Shroff, and characters from the cult Bollywood movie *Gunda*, a bunch of agitated guys were hunched over their Twitter stations.

Ramachandran quickened his pace.

The door at the end of the corridor opened into a small room with a sparse desk and a massive sofa.

'So, here's your last question,' said Modi, sinking into the sofa. 'If you get this, you are in.'

'Yes, sir!' Ramachandran stiffened.

'Tell me a Pappu joke.'

For a second, Ramachandran was thrown off guard, but he immediately recovered and launched into his reply with confidence.

'Dhoni, Mukesh Ambani, Pappu, Modibhai and a schoolgirl are on a plane. Suddenly the pilot gets a heart attack and drops dead. The plane is rapidly plummeting when the passengers realize that there are only four parachutes. Dhoni says Team India needs him, picks a parachute and jumps off. Ambani says that the entire Indian economy counts on him, picks another and jumps off. Pappu says he deserves a parachute because his last name is Gandhi and jumps off. Realizing that there is only one parachute left, Modi tells the schoolgirl, "Beti, you are India's future, you take the last parachute and jump", upon which the schoolgirl tells him, "You can also come, Modi Uncle, there are actually two parachutes left. Pappu genius grabbed my schoolbag and jumped off,"' he said, and burst out tittering.

Modi stared at him poker-faced, and Ramachandran's laughter promptly fizzled out.

'Ha ha,' Modi deadpanned. 'Everybody knows that joke.'

Ramachandran looked mortified.

'Try again.'

Ramachandran racked his brains, trying hard to recollect a good Pappu joke or trying to invent a decent one on the spot, but under pressure, his mind and memory betrayed him, and he could come up with nothing.

After five minutes, Modi's patience ran out. 'I'm sorry, Ram. I like you but I cannot change our recruitment policy for you. A Pappu joke is an absolute must,' he said apologetically, and stood up.

Ramachandran looked upset. 'Might as well go to Rakabganj Road and lick Shahzada's boot now,' he muttered under his breath.

'What did you just say?'

'Umm . . . boot?'

'No, before that.'

'Er . . . Shahzada?'

'Shahzada,' murmured Modi, his eyes twinkling. A ghost of a smile tugged at the corners of his mouth. He started for the door.

'The work hours are 10 to 6. Contact Amit Shah for your appointment letter.'

Ramachandran gawked stupidly at the departing leader.

'Shahzada!' giggled Modi.

Sanjay Jha
Madam! Madam! We did it! Made #Feku the top trend on Twitter! Woohoo!
6 hours ago Like · Comment

👍 eNREGA likes this.

Sonia Gandhi Idiot, I pay you to praise Rahul, not mock him!
6 hours ago Like

Sanjay Jha No no, madam, #Feku refers to NaMo and mocks his FICCI speech to women entrepreneurs.
6 hours ago Like

Sonia Gandhi Then how come all the top tweets are jokes on Rahul????
6 hours ago · 👍 1,304,540 people like this

Sanjay Jha Um...
6 hours ago · 👍 1,124,542 people like this

Sonia Gandhi You are fired. And no, you won't even get paid under eNREGA.
6 hours ago Like

Sanjay Jha NaMo sir. Forwarding my resume to you for PR work..
6 hours ago Like

Narendra Modi Thank you Sanjay bhai, but you can best serve me by doing PR work for Pappu :)
6 hours ago · 👍 1,224,124 people like this

Rahul Gandhi
Mr Modi, what is so special about your oratory abilities that I don't have?

6 hours ago Like · Comment

👍 Digvijay Singh and 340 others like this.

Narendra Modi I can speak extempore.
6 hours ago Like

Rahul Gandhi I can speak Italian.
6 hours ago · 👍 Sonia Gandhi likes this

Narendra Modi My audience claps whenever I said awesome stuff. Like in SRCC.
6 hours ago Like

Rahul Gandhi My audience claps even if I say super dumb things. Like in Jaipur Chintan Shivir.
6 hours ago · 👍 Mani Shankar Aiyar likes this

Narendra Modi I talk about development at the grassroots.
6 hours ago Like

Rahul Gandhi I actually walk all the way to the grassroots and do development myself at their houses.
6 hours ago · 👍 Sushil Kumar Shinde likes this

Narendra Modi I tell farmers how they can get more milk from their cows.
6 hours ago Like

Rahul Gandhi I milk their cows myself, and their bulls too.
6 hours ago · 👍 Digvijay Singh likes this

Sonia Gandhi Son, please get off Facebook before we lose all of our middle class supporters.
6 hours ago · 👍 Manmohan Singh and 9400 others like this

FOURTEEN

The Social Engineer

OCTOBER 2013

BIHAR CM NITISH KUMAR was ensconced in his swivel chair at the state secretariat, gazing pensively out of his window. The broad channel of the Ganga was visible over the horizon, the azure, cloudless sky reflected in her placid waters. It had been three months since the JD(U), at his behest, had snapped ties with the NDA over Modi's elevation, bringing to an abrupt end the seventeen-year-old electorally successful social and political coalition of the forward castes and non-Yadav backward castes.

Would the Muslims now veer towards Nitish, thereby augmenting his non-Yadav OBC plus Mahadalit vote bank to give him an edge at the hustings? Or would Modi attract enough voters across social strata, including the Yadavs, to let the BJP overcome the loss of its alliance partner? Or would Lalu benefit from the fragmentation, with Yadavs and Muslims remaining loyal to him? In a state where winning power is all about getting the caste arithmetic right, it seemed that the Bihar CM had forced a game of Russian roulette on the main players.

But what seemed like recklessness, even political suicide, to political analysts and leaders, was to Nitish a well-thought-out move based on rigorous socio-economic segmentation analysis. Although an electrical engineer by training, Social Engineering was his true calling. As a first-year student at the National Institute of Technology, he had displayed his precocity for the esoteric discipline by mapping out his entire batch into segments based on income and caste, and proposing differential marking to ensure equity in grading. His professors then knew that the boy was destined for greatness.

Immediately after becoming Bihar CM, he had burned the midnight oil, poring over reams of socio-economic data gleaned from various household surveys and multiple statistical tests. And then he made his moves: Mahadalits, a grouping of the twenty-odd poorest sub castes, were carved out from the Dalits and Extremely Backward Castes (EBCs) hived off from Other Backward Castes (OBCs) for differential treatment. This nifty piece of social engineering had expanded JDU's social base by eating into the vote banks of his two rivals, Lalu Prasad Yadav and Ram Vilas Paswan.

Now with Modi's elevation as the BJP's PM candidate imminent, Nitish once again spotted an opportunity where others only saw risk. Modi was the antithesis of Nitish. The Gujarat CM showcased Gujarat as a developed state, a haven for investment. In contrast, the Bihar CM marketed Bihar's poverty to attract aid. Modi believed in broad-based growth that benefited all. Nitish preferred tailoring welfare schemes for specific communities based on micro segmentation. And when his social engineering team, after doing the hard maths, had assured him that if he split with the BJP over NaMo's elevation, a large fraction of socially backward Muslims would align with his party, Nitish grabbed the opportunity.

Since the split, the Congress had been desperately trying to woo him. Unfortunately for the Congress, Nitish, like Mamata, was not corrupt. The CBI had no role to play in alliance negotiation. Nitish had begun playing the UPA to grant a special financial package for Bihar. Karat had also called to invite him for the Third Front conclave. He would have attended. These Third Front conclaves were meaningless but made for good optics, a means to signal that he was neutral for the time being. But when he was informed that Lalu would be attending too if he managed to get bail, Nitish declined. He was the unrivalled satrap in Bihar and did not need to be seen in cahoots with Lalu.

The principal secretary stormed in, interrupting Nitish's train of thoughts.

'Sir, good news and bad news,' he announced breathlessly.

'Okay, the good news first,' Nitish said.

'Sir, the latest NSSO estimates are out. Poverty in Bihar has dramatically declined from 45 per cent to 32 per cent,' he said.

Nitish's face turned red. 'You fool. You call that good news?' he hollered. '*Poora mood kharab kar diya!*'

Just a few months earlier, Nitish had made a stirring pitch for conferring 'special status' on Bihar, and eloquently showcased its backwardness at the Adhikar Rally in New Delhi's Ramlila Maidan. Buoyed by the feedback, Nitish was now all set to demand special status for his state not just from the Centre, but from the West as well. Rallies in London's Trafalgar Square and New York's Central Park had been planned along with the pitch to the House of Saud for a share of Saudi Arabia's petrodollar income. And here was his principal secretary glibly informing him that Bihar was not that poor any more.

'What's the bad news now?' he asked sullenly. 'Not that anything can be worse than what you just told me.'

'Er . . . flash floods in the Kosi basin have rendered people homeless, sir. Purnea is the worst affected,' the principal secretary ventured, unsure of himself.

'Woohoo!' Nitish whooped, the smile returning. 'That's great news, my friend! It's depressing, yes, but in a happy sort of way, if you know what I mean.'

'Er . . . yes, sir. Sorry for getting the good news and bad news mixed up.'

'That's okay. You will learn. I'll ask my right-hand man, N.K. Singh, to make a slick presentation, demanding a special flood relief package from the Centre. Now we are back in business, my friend,' he said, verve in his voice, a sparkle in his eyes.

'One more thing, sir,' the principal secretary said. 'For the inauguration of the new anganwadi kendra in Kishanganj tomorrow afternoon, will it be a skullcap with shawl or kurta–pajama without any headgear?'

'The former, of course,' Nitish snapped. 'And make sure the front-page news carries photos of me hugging the local maulvi.' Nitish felt his four-day stubble. Usually he trimmed it on the fourth day to maintain that neither here-nor-there look to advertise his secularism: not quite clean shaven but not a goatee either. But he would let it grow overnight for the public engagement. One had to calibrate one's image in keeping with one's audience.

Nitish waved him away and ambled through the betel-juice-stained corridor to the last room on the floor. A bunch of kurta-clad, twenty-something interns were hunched over desktop computers. It was the JD(U)'s war room peopled by fresh graduates from Patna University.

'Any luck?' Nitish asked, peering over the shoulders of the head of the segmentation analytics, Satish Kumar. A fellow Kurmi and protégé, Satish was overseeing efforts to provide the next breakthrough: segmentation of the Yadav community into Yadavs and Maha Yadavs, which would help Nitish make inroads into a group whose loyalty to Lalu had been hitherto unwavering. But unlike Dalits and OBCs, the Yadav community was frustratingly homogeneous in every respect, a social engineer's nightmare. But Satish Kumar's team was slogging away, dissecting the socio-economic and demographic data of the most comprehensive household-level database of the Bihari populace.

There had been a glimmer of hope: the community was split 50–50 into SRK and Salman fans. Nitish had been tempted to side with one group, the Salman-loving Yadavs, and had mulled announcing tax relief for Sallu starrers, but that would have alienated the Muslim fans of SRK. So he had desisted.

'Still at it, sir,' Satish Kumar answered. 'We're running tests for the question: Who do you consider to be more annoying:

Yogendra Yadav or Kumar Vishwas? Based on that, we could attempt a segmentation.'

'OK,' Nitish said. 'Be sure to run the Chi Square test for statistical significance. And set the confidence level at 99 per cent. Don't want a false positive.'

'Will do, sir,' Satish Kumar answered.

If Satish was successful in segmenting Yadavs, his team would embark on the next big challenge: dividing the Mahadalits into Super and Hyper Mahadalits. There had been reports that the Mahadalits were not satisfied with the schemes Nitish had launched exclusively for them. Apparently, most of them existed only on paper with no tangible benefits accruing to the target beneficiaries. So another round of social engineering was due to consolidate his shaky hold on the poorest of the Scheduled Castes.

'Oh fuck!' Satish screamed suddenly, his face turning a deathly white.

'What's the matter, *sasura*?' Nitish asked.

'There's been a fuck-up, sir. Actually, it's not any fuck-up. It's a maha fuck-up! The mother of all Excel summation errors. The number of Muslims allied with you in the wake of your exit from the NDA camp is far less than what we had originally estimated,' Satish answered.

'Oh, check again. I'm sure you missed something,' Nitish said calmly.

Satish checked and rechecked. He rebooted and pressed some buttons again.

'Just did the numbers again,' Satish said, and hesitated.

'And?' Nitish demanded.

'If an election is held right now,' said Satish in a low voice, 'it will be a two-way contest between NaMo and Lalu. You are, uh, nowhere in the picture.'

The most advanced social engineering team in the world had committed an Excel error due to which the entire political landscape of Bihar had been upended. It was the equivalent of NASA's Mars Orbiter crashing in the 1990s because the NASA engineers had forgotten to convert to metric measurements.

Nitish stared back, slack-jawed and eyes wide as saucers, too shocked to react.

Then, with a trembling hand, he reached for the phone, speed-dialled a number, and timidly said, 'Hello, Karatwa?'

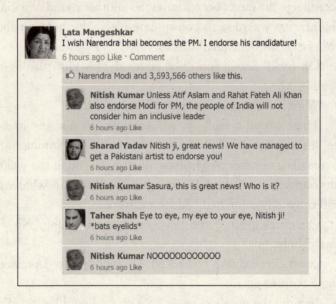

Lata Mangeshkar
I wish Narendra bhai becomes the PM. I endorse his candidature!
6 hours ago Like · Comment

👍 Narendra Modi and 3,593,566 others like this.

Nitish Kumar Unless Atif Aslam and Rahat Fateh Ali Khan also endorse Modi for PM, the people of India will not consider him an inclusive leader
6 hours ago Like

Sharad Yadav Nitish ji, great news! We have managed to get a Pakistani artist to endorse you!
6 hours ago Like

Nitish Kumar Sasura, this is great news! Who is it?
6 hours ago Like

Taher Shah Eye to eye, my eye to your eye, Nitish ji! *bats eyelids*
6 hours ago Like

Nitish Kumar NOOOOOOOOOOOOO
6 hours ago Like

Salman Khan
SHAH RUKHHHHH!!!!
6 hours ago Like · Comment

👍 Farah Khan and 1,240,403 others like this.

Shah Rukh Khan SALMANNNNN!!!!!!! *hug*
6 hours ago · 👍 Farah Khan and 1,240,403 others like this

Salman Khan *hug*
6 hours ago · 👍 Karan Johar and 2,480,806 others like this

Rakhee Mere do anmol ratan... mere Karan Arjun aa gaye!
sniff
6 hours ago · 👍 Baba Siddique likes this

Nitish Kumar We welcome the patch up between Salman
Khan and Shah Rukh Khan. Secular forces must unite to
take on communal Modi.
6 hours ago · 👍 Sharad Yadav likes this

Zoom TV Salman and SRK have buried the hatchet and
become friends. Who's next?
6 hours ago Like

Karunanidhi AMMAAAAAAAAAAA!!!!
6 hours ago · 👍 Stalin, Alagiri like this

Jayalalithaa Stay away from me old man, or I'll put you in
jail.
6 hours ago · 👍 Sasikala likes this

Karunanidhi :(
6 hours ago Like

FIFTEEN

Lion on the prowl

NOVEMBER 2013

DEMOCRACY WAS IN THE air. Politicians suddenly turned sympathetic towards the general public. MPs skipped their trips to Europe and faithfully returned to their constituencies when Parliament wasn't in session. Governments opened their coffers to the ordinary folks.

Election season had well and truly settled in.

Invigorated by his elevation as the BJP's PM candidate, Modi embarked on the campaign trail with guns blazing. On the face of it, he seemed to target the Assembly polls in Delhi, Chhattisgarh, Madhya Pradesh and Rajasthan, but with rallies scheduled in Bihar, Uttar Pradesh and various other states, it was clear that Modi was eyeing the General Elections.

'There are three kinds of sarkar in Delhi,' he thundered in BJP's biggest ever rally in the national capital. '*Maa ki sarkar, bete ki sarkar and damaad ki sarkar!*' Over 400,000 people burst out laughing and cheered wildly.

'A for Adarsh, B for Bofors, C for CWG, D for *Damaad ka karobar!*' he recited in Bhopal. The crowd nodded and clapped heartily.

Everywhere he went, hundreds of thousands of people turned up to catch a glimpse of the Gujarat strongman, and listen to his famed oratory. And Modi never disappointed. With precise voice modulation, well-timed pauses and spicy rhetoric, Modi worked the crowds like none other. The best applause, however, was reserved for the Shahzada barbs.

'*Mitron, aap yakeen nahi karoge, Shahzada ne kaha,* poverty is a state of mind,' he said, in an affected voice, and instantly had his crowd in splits.

After a point, Modi did not even have to narrate a Shahzada wisecrack. He'd simply smile and begin to mouth the word Shahzada, and people would respond with uproarious laughter. The epithet made for an incredibly effective tactic, but its true genius lay in the fact that the Congress leaders were left completely befuddled as to how to respond to it.

'How dare Modi call Rahul nasty names such as Shahzada?' demanded Sibal after a Modi rally, shaking his fist at a bunch of reporters. An hour later, Sibal was summoned to 10 Janpath and pointedly asked if he thought Rahul ought not be called the crown prince. After that, no Congress leader in his or her right mind would be seen publicly disapproving the use of Shahzada.

Unchecked, Modi went on a rampage. He wooed UP-ites

in Kanpur. He struck a chord with ex-servicemen at Rewari in Haryana. He dazzled lakhs and lakhs of Biharis in Patna with sizzling rhetoric, powerful oratory and creative interpretation of historical facts.

But it was only when he left the Hindi heartland, travelled all the way down to Trichy in Tamil Nadu, and still attracted a massive crowd that the alarm bells well and truly began to ring in 10 Janpath.

'Madam, his speech has just begun,' said Ahmed in a low voice, at the hastily arranged meeting in the Congress war room that afternoon. 'There are at least, uh, five lakh people.'

Jairam Ramesh gasped, but expertly converted it into a cough before Sonia's glare fell on him.

Sonia pursed her lips. 'Did he speak any Tamil?'

'A little bit at the start. It was atrocious,' replied Ahmed. 'But people are still cheering for him.'

Sonia clenched her jaw. 'That's OK. We'll do better, because I will speak entirely in Tamil and far better than him. Arrange for a Tamil speech written in Roman script ASAP.'

'Madam . . . that is not all,' said Ahmed in a hoarse whisper. 'They expect Rajinikanth to join him on stage.'

This time no one tried to mask his or her reaction. The entire room gasped in unison. The colour drained from Sonia's face. It was a full minute before she recovered.

'It . . . it's OK. We can counter this. We just have to get someone bigger to share the stage with Rahul,' she said weakly. 'Who's bigger than Rajinikanth?'

Ahmed looked utterly dazed. 'Uh, God?'

Sonia's shoulders slumped as she resigned to the reality. 'Yeah, we can't beat this.'

Narendra Modi
So my Tamil bhaiyon behnon of Trichy! How was the speech? The punch was kinda lost in Tamil translation. Did you get any of my Hindi lines?

6 hours ago Like · Comment

👍 Nirmala Hariharan and 333,113 others like this.

Madasamy No, saar.
6 hours ago Like

Narendra Modi You don't know any Hindi?
6 hours ago Like

Palaniappan Only 2 words, saar!
6 hours ago Like

Narendra Modi What words?
6 hours ago Like

Madasamy "Theek hai"
6 hours ago Like

Narendra Modi ?!?!?!???
6 hours ago Like

Manmohan Singh
6 hours ago Like

Pankaj Pachauri Prime Minister says ROFLMAO.
6 hours ago Like

Meanwhile, Rahul's campaign was like a grounded Kingfisher jumbo jet. He tried every trick to establish a connect with the people, starting with maudlin sentimentality.

'*Mummy ne kaha*,' Rahul grated at one venue in Madhya Pradesh, referring to the day the Food Security Bill was up for vote in the Lok Sabha. '*Rahul, mein button daba ke rahungi chahe kuch bhi ho jaye.*' It evoked titters from the sparse crowd.

Then he tried to market his family's tragic history, narrating a long-winded story from his childhood.

'They killed my grandmother, they killed my father, and they might kill me too!' he declared, eyes blazing. The numbed crowd listened in stony silence. A few in the back rows stifled yawns.

Soon it became difficult to even rent crowds for his rallies. As a desperate measure to boost attendance, sitting through a Rahul rally was also included as approved work under MNREGA. Initially, labourers readily agreed to participate, considering the similarities between approved works such as digging and filling trenches and attending a Rahul Gandhi rally: both were mind-numbing, pointless, and ultimately did not produce any assets for the economy. But after attending a few rallies, the labourers baulked and demanded a 1000 per cent mark-up over the prevailing MNREGA wages.

* * *

'I just don't get it,' Sonia shrieked, in another war-room meeting. 'Modi's rallies attract people in lakhs while empty stands greet Rahul. What are you chaps doing?' she demanded, glowering at the people sitting around the long table.

'If Yash Raj can make a hit out of the *Dhoom* franchise despite it featuring a mediocrity like Abhishek Bachchan, then why can't you bozos do the same for my government?' she hissed, glowering at the attendees. 'We just passed the Food Security Bill, didn't we? Then what is the problem?'

'Uh, PDS grain is indeed cheaper, madam,' Union Finance Minister Chidambaram said, 'but prices of everything else are going through the roof, especially onions.'

At Rs 100 a kilo, onion had become so expensive that it was now perceived as a luxury good, a symbol of wealth and affluence. Boyfriends were gifting onion rings to their girlfriends. Even Apple was mulling rebranding itself as Onion to preserve its image as a premier brand for the lucrative Indian market and stay ahead of the Samsungs and Nokias.

'Then let's pass a right to free onion bill,' snapped Sonia, turning to Dr Manmohan Singh. The scholar-turned-prime-minister was about to meekly nod when Chidambaram hastened to interrupt.

'Er . . . Soniaji, we don't have any money left for funding more freebies,' he said, 'after allocating an additional Rs 50,000 crore for the Food Security Bill. Perhaps we could go in for a rights-based legislation that doesn't entail budgetary backing. Such as Right to happiness or Right to 8 per cent GDP growth.'

Sonia's eyes lit up. 'Right to 8 per cent growth bill sounds fantastic!' she exclaimed. 'Why didn't we think of it before to get the economy back on track?'

Sonia's conception of economics, thanks in large measure to her sessions with the National Advisory Council (NAC), was that by merely enacting legislation conferring a right magically made that right a reality.

'Um . . . it won't guarantee anything,' Chidambaram said. 'Truth is no one can guarantee anything about economic growth, least of all economists. But it's difficult to fix accountability for it. Very easy to find alibi: slowdown of the world economy, oil price spikes because of instability in the Middle East and so on.'

'Hmm,' said Sonia Gandhi, feeling a little out of depth. There were a few awkward moments of silence as the participants waited for her to say something intelligible.

Finally, Varuni Roy, the veteran member of the NAC and passionate adherent of a rights-based approach to governance, broke the impasse.

'Actually, madam, there is one rights-based legislation that can lead to tangible outcomes without burdening the exchequer,' Varuni Roy said. 'The right for every poor family to live in a comfortable two-bedroom flat or even in a bungalow with a lovely portico, balcony and manicured garden. And it can be done without needing to increase the nation's housing stock. All it entails is that every middle-class and upper-middle-class family accommodates at least fifteen poor families in their homes. In case of Lutyens bungalows such as 10 Janpath, make that twenty poor families. And in case of the Rashtrapati Bhavan, an entire slum colony can be rehabilitated. You are guaranteed to win the election after that, with or without Rahul baba's dimples. And it brings us one step closer towards our avowed objective of achieving an egalitarian society.'

Sonia winced. Varuni Roy's proposals were becoming increasingly radical. It was time to phase her out. Ahmed had already shortlisted a JNU professor. It was one thing to demonstrate empathy for the poor by allocating monies from the Consolidated Fund of India, quite another to let in the indigent to sleep in one's drawing room.

'Okay, I'll consider it,' Sonia said, eager to change the topic. 'But what is Rahul going to promise the voters in his next rally?'

'Leave that to me, madam,' Mani Shankar Aiyar said confidently.

****

Two days later, in a nondescript town in Rajasthan called Churu, Rahul Gandhi looked down from the podium at the smattering of surly villagers hemmed in by a posse of hefty-looking policemen, rolled his sleeves, and said, '*Bhaiyya, pehle kehte the aadhi roti khao, Congress ko jitao. Ab mein kehta hoon, poori roti khao, sau din kaam karo, muft ki davai khao aur Congress ko jitao!*'

The villagers gaped at Rahul in disbelief.

Watching Rahul's speech live from his war room in Gandhinagar, Modi guffawed, and beckoned his speech-writer to bring a copy of his next speech. When he was handed the same, Modi tore it down the middle and dumped the bits in the trash can.

'*Mitron!*' exclaimed Modi, in his next rally in Chhattisgarh. '*Mitron, saath saal ke baad, Kangress aadhi roti se poori roti tak pahunchi hai!*' he declared, in a voice that combined amusement, indignation and contempt in perfect proportions. '*Arey, doob maro, doob maro, sharam se doob maro!*'

The crowd cheered and hooted, and promptly took to 'Modi! Modi!' chants.

* * *

With every Rahul rally, the speech-writing duties changed hands in the Congress camp. When IITian Jairam Ramesh took over, Rahul resorted to physics and astronomy. 'A Dalit needs Jupiter's escape velocity to achieve success,' Rahul bellowed, in a function at the National Awareness Camp for Scheduled Castes. His audience blinked back dumbfounded, and Rahul trended on Twitter for all the wrong reasons.

Digvijaya Singh took a shot and Rahul decided to express sympathy with the minorities affected in the Muzaffarnagar riots. 'I have been told that ISI is getting in touch with disgruntled Muslim youth,' he said. Congress leaders would spend the next few days in damage control.

When everything failed, the party resorted to the ultimate fallback option: denial. Led by Abhishek Manu Singhvi, the party's spin team took to national media and scoffed at the suggestion that Modi's rallies were creating an impact on the national psyche.

'Modi wave? Bah!' scoffed Jairam Ramesh to a gaggle of reporters outside 10 Janpath.

'There's no Modi wave, holistic or otherwise, anywhere in the country,' declared Manish Tewari on NDTV.

'The only Modi wave in this country is the wave of fear among minorities after the horrible genocide he oversaw in 2002,' said Sanjay Jha on Times Now.

The Congress spin unit purred like a well-oiled machine, suitably aided by anchors, 'neutral' analysts, and Nitish Kumar. Within days, the Congress camp began to believe its own bullshit. The worry lines on Sonia's forehead eased, and a sense of cheer returned to the war room.

Modi's response was stinging.

* * *

'*Bhaiyon aur behenon*,' Modi thundered in his inimitable style, staring at the sea of humanity in front of him at a rally in Madhya Pradesh, '*kya mein ek particle nahin hoon?*'

'*Haan, hain!*' the crowd roared back.

'*Kya jab mein chalta hoon to mujh mein raftaar nahin hai?*' he asked.

'*Haan!*' was the voluble response of the crowd.

And then Modi went for the jugular: '*To mein Delhi Sultanate se poochta hoon, jab har moving particle wave hota hai, to Delhi Sultanate kaise kah sakti hai ki Modi wave nahin hain?*'

A giant screen flashed the famous de Broglie equation to illustrate the wave–particle duality and therefore his claim.

$$p = \frac{h}{\lambda} \rightarrow \lambda = \frac{h}{p} \rightarrow \lambda = \frac{h}{mv}$$

The throng may or may not have understood his line of reasoning, but it went berserk chanting 'Modi, Modi', and generated a Mexican wave to demonstrate its faith in the Modi wave. It seemed Modi could explain anything to the public in laymen's terms. Even String Theory, if need be.

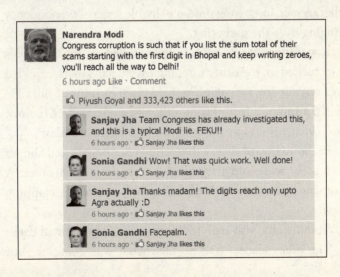

Narendra Modi
Congress corruption is such that if you list the sum total of their scams starting with the first digit in Bhopal and keep writing zeroes, you'll reach all the way to Delhi!

6 hours ago Like · Comment

👍 Piyush Goyal and 333,423 others like this.

Sanjay Jha Team Congress has already investigated this, and this is a typical Modi lie. FEKU!!
6 hours ago · 👍 Sanjay Jha likes this

Sonia Gandhi Wow! That was quick work. Well done!
6 hours ago · 👍 Sanjay Jha likes this

Sanjay Jha Thanks madam! The digits reach only upto Agra actually :D
6 hours ago · 👍 Sanjay Jha likes this

Sonia Gandhi Facepalm.
6 hours ago · 👍 Sanjay Jha likes this

The mood in 10 Janpath the following day was funereal. Leaders sat quietly in the hall, their heads bowed, while a distressed Sonia binged on pizzas, pasta and calzones. Empty boxes from Dominoes, Papa Johns and Pizza Hut lay scattered at her feet.

'Wouldn't he allow us to even live in a state of denial!' Sonia suddenly cried out, startling a few around her. 'What a horrible man!'

'Yes, madam, he's a despicable, arrogant man,' said a leader.

'Uncouth, unparliamentary urchin!' yelled someone else.

It was just the opening they needed to participate. One by one they took a swing at Modi, referring to him in the choicest expletives, until Sonia flung a half-eaten pizza across the room in frustration.

'SHUT UP!' she screamed.

The room went immediately silent, and remained so, for what seemed like a long time, a palpable sense of despondency hanging over the gathering.

It was then that Rahul Gandhi waddled in, one half of his shirt tucked in, the other flopping over his pyjamas, crinkled eyes staring at a magazine he held open in front of him. He pulled a lollipop from his mouth, and exclaimed, 'Mummy, look what I found in the storeroom! Nagaraj comics!'

In the awkward silence that followed, Ahmed's and Sonia's eyes grew wide and they turned to look at each other. A moment later, they nodded in unison, and began clapping slowly.

'Rahul baba, you are a fricking genius!' said Ahmed Patel. The other leaders had no idea what was going on, but

needed no invitation. Within seconds, 10 Janpath boomed
with deafening applause.

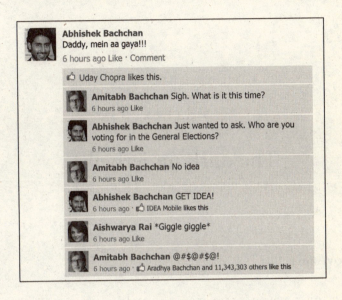

Abhishek Bachchan
Daddy, mein aa gaya!!!
6 hours ago · Like · Comment

👍 Uday Chopra likes this.

Amitabh Bachchan Sigh. What is it this time?
6 hours ago · Like

Abhishek Bachchan Just wanted to ask. Who are you
voting for in the General Elections?
6 hours ago · Like

Amitabh Bachchan No idea
6 hours ago · Like

Abhishek Bachchan GET IDEA!
6 hours ago · 👍 IDEA Mobile likes this

Aishwarya Rai *Giggle giggle*
6 hours ago · Like

Amitabh Bachchan @#$@#$@!
6 hours ago · 👍 Aradhya Bachchan and 11,343,303 others like this

SIXTEEN

The dark underbelly

NOVEMBER 2013

THE UNLIT BUILDING LOOMED menacingly in the moonlit sky, dark and forbidden. Black streaks of mould covered the decrepit walls. The paint had all but peeled off. The doors were rotting, and the windowpanes were shattered.

A corrugated gate with a monstrous skull and crossed bones, and the words Dirty Tricks Department engraved on it, blocked his way to the building. In the howling wind, the jaws of the skull clacked against each other, as if it were laughing at him. Somewhere behind him, a wolf howled.

Ahmed shivered. This place gave him the heebie-jeebies.

Trembling, he stepped forward. The gate swung open by itself with a creak that grated on the ears and sent a chill up his spine. Ahmed slipped through the opening, hobbled towards the heavy door and pushed in.

Holding his nose, Ahmed made his way through the filth, through the serpentine twists and turns, until he arrived at a dimly lit corridor with doors to his left. A large bug-eyed crow was painted on the first door. Underneath were the words Fear, Fair, Fearless. Ahmed put an ear to the door.

'. . . come, let's go upstairs. Let's take the lift,' said a male voice.

'Um, I prefer the stairs,' said a female voice, uncertainly.

'Oh come on, this will in no way affect the iconic work you've done as a reporter,' the man replied.

Ahmed moved on. The signboard on the next door read Media Sarkar. Muffled sounds of clicks and keystrokes drifted from within. Ahmed peered through the keyhole.

A number of young technicians were hunched over computers with what seemed like Adobe After Effects on their monitors, while Anuranjhan Jha hovered around them, occasionally glancing at their screens.

'Sir, I didn't find anything shady in this footage,' one of the youngsters called out to Jha. 'What do I do?'

'Go back to the fifteenth minute. What does Kejriwal say there?' asked Jha.

The technician turned to his screen. 'He says, "I am going to expose one of the most corrupt politicians in the country and—"'

'Stop,' interrupted Jha. 'If we remove the part where he says "going to expose" what do we get?'

'Uh, I am . . . one of the most corrupt politicians in the country?' The technician's eyes lit up. 'Genius, sir.'

Jha gave a smug smile, and said, 'Do it,' and the energized technician returned to his keyboard.

Ahmed shook his head and walked on—past Gulail.com where an agitated Ashish Khetan was pointing and screaming at a poster of Modi, past Disgruntled Cops Sadan where ex-IPS officer Sanjiv Bhatt sat in front of a laptop furiously tweeting, past Disgruntled Babu Sadan where Pradeep Sharma sat morphing a picture of Modi and an unknown woman.

Ahmed walked past an unending number of such rooms, each darker than the other. But it was to the darkest part of the building that Ahmed was headed today. He had been here several times in the past, but never to this part of the building. He simply hadn't had the nerve. But desperate times called for desperate measures, and here he was, groping his way in the darkness.

Presently, his fingers felt something, and Ahmed peered at what lay ahead of him. A moment later when his eyes adjusted to the darkness well enough for him to make out the door in front of him, he smothered a scream and shrank back in terror. Jutting out of the door was the head of a large cobra, baring its terrifying fangs. Engraved underneath the cobra was the word Cobrapost.

After his nerves had settled down, Ahmed pushed the door in ever so slowly, and gingerly stepped into the room, taking care not to step on a pair of intertwined cobras squirming at the doorstep.

Hisses greeted him from all sides. Everywhere he looked he saw snakes of various colours and shapes and sizes slithering over each other and hissing, none too pleased at the unwelcome interruption. In the middle of the room, gazing into the silvery moonlight streaming in from a small barred window on the other side of the room, stood a man wrapped in a cocoon of wriggling cobras that bared their fangs at Ahmed.

'Did you know that the Egyptian cobra's sting can kill a full-grown elephant in as little as three hours?' said Aniruddha Bahal, absently caressing a cobra resting on his shoulder.

Ahmed gulped.

'That's uh . . . interesting,' he said in a small voice. Bahal slowly turned around. Ahmed nervously cleared his throat, and added, 'Madam asked if you had something for us.'

'Yes,' Bahal replied, tilting his head and caressing the reptile around his neck with the side of his face. 'I have something that will dramatically change the nature of these elections.'

'What is it?' asked Ahmed, voice quivering.

'A CD.'

Ahmed bit his lip. 'Can I see it?'

Bahal stroked the cobra on his shoulder, upon which it slithered down his arm on to the floor towards a television screen in a corner. The cobra reared its head in front of the TV, and brought down its fangs on the TV's power button with a sharp hiss. The TV screen came alive, and the cobra returned to Bahal's shoulder.

Ahmed frowned as Modi came on screen, looked around furtively and entered a room. Moments later, Ahmed's eyes grew wide. Then they grew wider. And then his jaw dropped open. And then he exclaimed, 'Whoa!'

SEVENTEEN

The cobra strikes

NOVEMBER 2013

MODI STOOD AT THE balcony overlooking the shakha grounds, his eyes distant, brows furrowed in thought, while down below, thousands of men in khaki shorts performed their shakha drills in perfect grid formation.

'One . . . two . . . three . . .' the drill instructor's cries echoed in the distance.

Shit had hit the fan. There was no other way to put it.

The unstoppable momentum that his campaign had generated had been suddenly thrown off track. Utterly engrossed in his ceaseless offensive on the Congress, he had left a flank exposed, and had been completely taken by surprise by the sneak attack that followed.

That morning, two little-known websites by the name

of Cobrapost and Gulail had released a series of tapes of phone conversations between Amit Shah and an IPS officer by the name of G.L. Singhal. The conversations pertained to the surveillance of a young woman and a few of her acquaintances that Amit Shah had allegedly ordered at the behest of his 'Saheb'.

Within hours of the 'sting', the media was all over the BJP like a nasty rash. They called it 'Snoopgate', and labelled him a snooper, a stalker, a voyeur and whatnot. His party's spokespersons were caught completely off guard, and ran around like headless chicken, each making up his or her own defence on various prime-time debates, regardless of whether they corroborated with the viewpoints being put forward by their colleagues on other channels.

'. . . four . . . five . . . six . . .'

The sting threatened to hit him where it hurt the most— his urban base, his legion of young supporters who looked up to him as the messiah of good governance, as the answer to everything that was wrong with the current dispensation. The media and his rivals were now doing everything in their power to instil a sense of deep fear in them, to make them stop in their tracks and reconsider their support for him.

It would pass, he thought. He would weather the storm. There were still a few months left for the elections. The news will grow stale, and he would regroup and make up for his losses. He had the time. He didn't fear Snoopgate.

'. . . seven . . . eight . . . nine . . .'

What he did fear, from the very core of his being, was the CD.

That damn CD.

For the umpteenth time, he cursed himself for his one moment of weakness, that one lapse in judgement. All his life he had been careful, his every move calculated to achieve specific objectives, his every gesture calibrated to realize specific responses. And now, that one mistake from his past threatened to destroy everything he had built so far.

Modi shuddered.

Did his enemies have the CD? Already there were rumours of a damaging disc, carefully planted in various online and offline sources. Perhaps they were waiting for the right time to release it. A precise moment that would deliver the greatest electoral impact, and turn the tide of the elections. A chill ran up his spine.

Will his darkest secret be his undoing?

* * *

The crowd at 10 Janpath was delirious. After a long time, the party was witnessing such an evening in the party's 'headquarters'. A pair of massive speakers had been placed against the inner walls of the compound, from which an unending string of peppy Bollywood numbers blared out. The Congress leaders sat in a circle in the courtyard, frequently jumping up to dance or hoot or cheer wildly, while Sonia Gandhi sat cross-legged on the ground, grinning and clapping with undisguised excitement.

A loud cheer went up the moment Salman Khan's '*Dhinka chika dhinka chika . . .*' from his chartbuster film *Ready* boomed from the speakers. Rahul Gandhi jumped to the middle of the circle, pulled on his shades, put his hands in either pocket and rhythmically jerked them sideways in tune with the song's beats, simultaneously throwing a nonchalant gaze at a tree to his right. The Congress leaders went batshit crazy. Digvijaya Singh and Manish Tewari kneeled on one knee on either side of Rahul, held a stack of 10-rupee notes in one hand and with the other, expertly flicked crisp notes off the top of the stack into the air towards their dancing leader.

Moments later, when the lyrics returned to '*Dhinka chika dhinka chika . . .*', Rahul reproduced yet another of Salman's legendary moves, turning around and nonchalantly rubbing his right bum. The ecstatic leaders promptly imitated their leader, together turning around and coordinating their bum-rubbing to perfection, while Sonia Gandhi covered her face with her hands and shook with uncontrollable giggles.

In the middle of the revelry, someone wheeled a large TV screen over to the edge of the circle, and set the channel to CNN-IBN. A distressed-looking Rajdeep Sardesai was in the thick of an intense debate with several disgusted NCW representatives, a belligerent Congress spokesperson and a cowering BJP spokesperson. Down below, in big bold letters, the ticker said, 'Will our women be safe under Modi?'

'Whooooo!' screamed the leaders, and danced exuberantly. The channel then switched to Times Now, prompting the gathered leaders to throw their hands up in the air and hoot to their heart's content, as a rampaging Arnab Goswami hollered at the befuddled BJP spokesperson Yatin Oza. It went on like that. From Times Now to Headlines Today to India TV to Aaj Tak. Every time the channel flipped, and a debate on Snoopgate came on, the leaders celebrated. The loudest cheers, however, were reserved for NDTV. When

Sreenivasan Jain came on, the Congress leaders went ballistic, the revelry almost descending into a frenzy. Some like Jairam Ramesh pulled at their hair in ecstasy, while others rolled on the ground like madmen.

Then, someone opened a bottle of champagne and poured it on to a pyramid of wine glasses. The filled glasses were then passed around and soon everyone was shaking a leg with a glass of champagne in his or her hand.

Ahmed Patel climbed on top of a stool and clinked his glass, calling for the gathering to calm down and hear him out.

'I want to make a toast,' he said, after he had their attention.

'To Cobrapost,' Ahmed said, smiling. 'May the media milk Snoopgate as much as 2002!'

'Hear, hear!' the leaders cried.

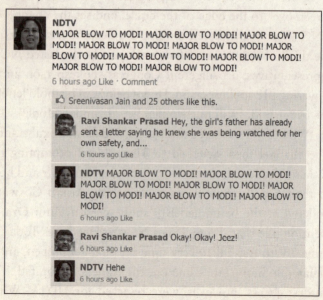

NDTV
MAJOR BLOW TO MODI! MAJOR BLOW TO MODI! MAJOR BLOW TO MODI! MAJOR BLOW TO MODI! MAJOR BLOW TO MODI! MAJOR BLOW TO MODI! MAJOR BLOW TO MODI! MAJOR BLOW TO MODI! MAJOR BLOW TO MODI! MAJOR BLOW TO MODI!

6 hours ago Like · Comment

👍 Sreenivasan Jain and 25 others like this.

> **Ravi Shankar Prasad** Hey, the girl's father has already sent a letter saying he knew she was being watched for her own safety, and...
> 6 hours ago Like

> **NDTV** MAJOR BLOW TO MODI! MAJOR BLOW TO MODI! MAJOR BLOW TO MODI! MAJOR BLOW TO MODI! MAJOR BLOW TO MODI! MAJOR BLOW TO MODI! MAJOR BLOW TO MODI!
> 6 hours ago Like

> **Ravi Shankar Prasad** Okay! Okay! Jeez!
> 6 hours ago Like

> **NDTV** Hehe
> 6 hours ago Like

'And then we'll deliver the coup de grace,' said Ahmed Patel, and exchanged a conspiratorial smile with Sonia Gandhi.

The leaders roared, the party resumed and the frivolities extended well into the moonless night.

* * *

'Modibhai,' said Rajnath Singh.

Modi leaned forward in his seat. Seated a foot behind him, Amit Shah subconsciously mimicked Modi's movement.

It was the seventh day after the Snoopgate story broke out. Early in the morning, Rajnath Singh had asked for a meeting in his office, prompting Modi to take the first flight out to Delhi along with Shah.

'This storm is showing no signs of passing us by,' said the BJP president. 'I think we need to present our side.'

Modi stiffened, as did Amit Shah. 'Do you want me to face the media?'

'No, no, Modibhai, not you of course,' said Rajnath Singh with a dismissive wave. Modi laughed with relief and sat back in his seat. Shah laughed as well and leaned back.

'Let's send Shah,' said Rajnath.

Shah jumped in his seat. 'Me?!'

'Yes,' said Rajnath Singh. 'I've received several invitations from the media for an interview with you. Arnab has asked for a one-on-one with you on Times Now during prime time followed by a focused debate with panellists such as *Outlook* editor Vinod Mehta, Sanjay Jha, a couple of NCW members, a couple of left liberals and Yatin Oza. Rajdeep Sardesai too has asked for an interview on CNN-IBN followed by a Twitter interview with Sagarika. And from NDTV, an entire panel consisting of Sreenivasan Jain, Barkha Dutt, Nidhi Razdan and Sonia Singh has offered to grill you on Snoopgate.'

Rajnath stood up. 'You could pick one of them or any other prominent interviewer of your choice.'

Amit Shah gulped.

'Take your time. It's your call,' said Rajnath Singh, and left the room along with Modi.

Amit Shah sat down, and thought long and hard about his options. By evening he had made his decision.

* * *

'Pap pap pa . . . pap pap pare . . . pap pap pap-para! Na nae naa na naa na naaaaa!'

The familiar jingle filled the studio, the camera rapidly zoomed in on the two couches placed in the middle of the studio, and zeroed in on the man sitting on one of them with a cup of coffee in his hand. The lights came on, and Karan Johar smiled broadly.

'He has a smile that has chilled the hearts of a million people,' he said. 'A face that has set the pulse racing of many a Gujarat government employee. His scintillating performances in Snoopgate and countless encounters have given him an iconic status, and has made him the pin-up boy of the Congress party and the civil society. Our guest tonight on *Koffee with Karan* needs no introduction. Please welcome the very sexy Amit Shah!'

The *Koffee with Karan* soundtrack came on again, and a bevy of girls in golden miniskirts and glittering headgear skipped out dancing from the entrance at the far end of the studio. They gracefully spread in either direction forming a V between them, through which Amit Shah swaggered in, sporting aviator shades, and blowing kisses to all and sundry, while Karan stood applauding politely.

Amit Shah walked towards Karan Johar at the centre of the studio and folded his hands in a namaste, but Karan Johar would have none of it. He kissed Shah on his cheek and wrapped him in a bear hug that Shah returned awkwardly after unsuccessfully trying to wriggle out of it for a couple of seconds.

'Welcome to *Koffee with Karan*, Amit darling,' said Karan. 'How does it feel to come on the show?'

'It feels great, Karanbhai,' replied Shah. 'Thanks a lot for inviting me. This is my first time here, and it's a privilege.'

'Not at all, the privilege is all ours,' said Karan, and added, 'so who are you dating now?'

Shah nearly jumped in his couch.

'Eh?' he blurted.

'Who are you dating now?'

Amit Shah blinked.

'Yes, who are you seeing these days?'

'Oh,' said Shah, relaxing a touch. 'I'm seeing five people these days.'

'You are seeing five women at the same time?' exclaimed Karan incredulously.

'Not all of them are women. It's two women and three men.'

Karan Johar whistled. 'Wow. You are telling me you are seeing five people at the same time, and that it includes three men as well?'

'Yes, that's exactly what I am telling you, Karanbhai.'

'Ohh . . . kay,' said Karan Johar, and turned to the camera to make a shocked face, before turning to Shah again. 'But how do you manage so many at the same time? How do you find the time?'

'Oh, I don't do it all by myself. I delegate it to people under me. Police officers, intelligence bureau, you name it. They do the job for me.'

Karan's jaw dropped open. 'You have people seeing women on your behalf??'

'Women and men. And I get minute by minute reports too,' said Shah, and leaned forward to show Karan a message on his phone. 'Check this out.'

Karan peered at Shah's phone and read the message out loud. 'Sir, she's at the restaurant, she has ordered French fries and a chicken burger.'

Amit Shah grinned.

'Well, that's . . . interesting,' Karan said, fidgeting in his seat. Forcing a smile, he asked, 'But tell me . . . a virile man like you, who sees as many as five people at a time, would also have a lot of exes, right? How do you handle them when you bump into them? For instance, tell me about the last person you were seeing.'

'She's dead.'

'Dead? I'm so sorry to hear that,' said Karan, looking considerably pained.

'Don't be. She was a terrorist.'

Karan gaped at Shah, flabbergasted.

'Yeah, many like her are dead. Some are in jails,' said Shah. 'Although there are some others who are decent people, which means they have gone on to lead normal lives.'

Karan Johar gawked at Shah for a few moments, and then did the only thing he could think of. He called for a commercial break.

When the show resumed, Karan had regained his composure and was looking his usual self. Brandishing a basketful of items with colourful wrappers, he said, 'Okay, we are now into our rapid-fire round. I will ask you a series of questions, and if you answer them well enough, you will have a chance to win this hamper. Shall we start?'

Amit Shah sat up with interest. 'Yes, bring it on.'

Karan pulled out a Samsung tablet and pretended to tap its screen.

'Three things people don't know about you,' he said.

'I love dancing in the rain, I sleep with a big, fluffy teddy bear, and . . . uh, I am a very sensitive man.'

Karan nodded appreciatively. 'Okay. Next question. If you were to be one of the leads in *Dostana 2,* who would you choose as your better half?'

Amit Shah scratched his chin. 'Um . . . I will go with Saheb.'

Karan raised an eyebrow. 'Ah. Do you want to tell us who Saheb is?'

Amit Shah shrugged. 'You know me, Karan, I don't take names.'

The camera then zoomed in to get a close-up shot of Karan's Samsung tablet.

'Next question. If you were to wake up as Pradeep Sharma, what would you do?'

'I will remove the twenty-seven bugs in and around the house, disable the cameras under the TV, in the study and in the bathroom, disconnect my landline and get a new SIM card.'

Karan stared at Shah, then shook his head hard as if to shake off the cobwebs; he put aside his tablet and smiled. 'All right, darling, you have done very well. It's an 8 on 10 performance. And now we are down to that moment. Does Amit win the hamper?'

Shah looked at the hamper with a greedy grin, even as a drum roll played in the background.

'Yes! You win the *Koffee with Karan* hamper! Congratulations!'

'Yipeee!' exclaimed Amit Shah, throwing his hands up. 'Thank you, Karanbhai!'

After the two exchanged another awkward hug, Amit Shah set aside the hamper carefully and leaned back on his couch, as did Karan on his.

'Okay then! Now we come to the last and the most interesting segment of this show,' said Karan, cheerfully. 'We did a survey. We asked a hundred people what they think about Amit Shah. Would you like to see some of them?'

'Sure, why not?'

At that point, the ringtone of Shah's mobile phone rang out. Shah saw the caller ID and immediately retreated to a corner of the studio to answer the call. After whispering into the phone for a minute, Shah returned to the centre, picked up his gift basket, and declared, 'I have to go.'

'But don't you want to listen to what the people we

surveyed said about you? It's very interesting!' whined Karan Johar.

'Just mail me the list of the people you've surveyed and I'll tap their phones and find out what they say about me.'

With that, Amit Shah left the studio, leaving a dumbfounded Karan Johar behind. The incomplete shoot was scrapped, and later that week, Karan reverted to his backup option and interviewed megastar Salman Khan for the Season 4 opener of *Koffee with Karan*.

Amit Shah, on the other hand, left straight for Uttar Pradesh to resume his mobilization of the party cadre. What he found out, through the phone call at the beginning of the last segment of *Koffee with Karan*, was that Snoopgate no longer remained on top of the media's agenda. Something big had displaced it.

'Must be something huge,' thought Shah on the way to the airport, wondering who or what could have come to their rescue. Maybe another major fight had broken out between the Bollywood Khans. Perhaps Sachin had announced a comeback.

Turns out, the BJP's knight in shining armour was a man with a ponytail. At the 2013 version of ThinkFest, an event held in Goa bringing together eclectic speakers from across the globe, Tarun Tejpal, the editor-in-chief of the organizing entity, *Tehelka*, allegedly sexually assaulted a young female journalist in a hotel elevator. Not the type to take things lying down, the brave journalist wrote an email to the magazine's managing editor Shoma Chaudhury, which found its way to Twitter and went viral on social media. Twitter and Facebook users raised a stink, and the incident snowballed into a huge issue, forcing all major media channels to dedicate their prime-time slots to debates on what allegedly took place.

Tejpal was first tried, in absentia, in Arnab's courtroom on *Newshour*, and summarily convicted. Any panellist who attempted to strike a remotely neutral tone in variance with Arnab's line was taken apart and driven to tears. Anyone who uttered inanities such as 'let the law take its course' was comprehensively badgered into submission. To those panellists who came out in defence of Tejpal, Arnab said nothing, simply because there existed no such person stupid enough to carry such a death wish into Arnab's panel.

Tejpal dominated headlines for an entire week, enough time for Snoopgate to go stale, and for the Modi camp to lick their wounds and recover. The only man who would have nothing to do with the Tejpal affair, and continued to cover Snoopgate with single-minded determination was NDTV anchor Sreenivasan Jain.

EIGHTEEN

The Syndicate meets

DECEMBER 2013

THE BUNKER-ROOM, LOCATED TEN metres beneath the Congress war-room headquarters on Rakabganj Road, had been designed to withstand a nuclear attack. The idea was to provide a safe shelter for the Congress leadership in case China or Pakistan dropped a nuclear bomb on Delhi and reduced it to ashes. The Congress leaders could then regroup and organize a civil disobedience movement to protest against the act of untrammelled aggression. It had been built during the first UPA regime and a tunnel was purported to connect it to 10 Janpath.

Its subterranean location, mirroring the plunging electoral fortunes of the Congress party, served as an apt setting for the emergency meeting that was to take place that cold winter night of 8 December. The Congress had been swept out of power in Rajasthan and Delhi, and had failed to dislodge the incumbent BJP governments in MP and Chhattisgarh. It was the party's worst-ever performance in Rajasthan, even worse than the 41 seats it had won in the post-Emergency 1977 election. In Delhi, its seat tally had come down to single digits.

Members of the Syndicate, a shadowy cabal of Union ministers, Gandhi family loyalists, spin doctors, a few chief ministers and sundry party apparatchiks, began to stream into the bunker-room's musty interiors. The Gandhi family, it was said, reigned over the party through the Syndicate, but it could be just as well true that the Syndicate held sway over the party through the Gandhis.

Officially, the Syndicate did not exist. Its members met annually or in the event of an emergency.

Not much was known about the deliberations of the Syndicate: resolutions and decisions were never committed to paper, the discussions went unrecorded and nothing was leaked. Syndicate members attended meetings dressed in friar-like costumes—oversized, floor-length, brown robes with a brown hood and a full-face cloth mask to conceal identity. That way they could express their views more freely, and no remark, however heretical, could be attributed to any individual member and get him into trouble with the official high command.

The members took their place, and the designated chairman—the chairmanship rotated among the members annually—rose to speak in a solemn tone: 'Well, ladies and gentlemen, no words can describe what's hit us. But let's look at the positives: we at least managed to stop the Modi juggernaut in Delhi.'

'We?' a person said.

'Yeah, our saturation coverage of the Snoopgate scandal led to a .005 per cent dip in Modi's popularity. And the AAP did a neat job of splitting the anti-incumbency vote.'

'Oh shut up, man,' interrupted a bespectacled participant. 'What use is anti-incumbency if it is 100 per cent? Heck, even I voted for AAP for the Delhi elections. We are so doomed now.'

The rest of the members looked at him incredulously and then another hand went up. 'Wow, so did I,' another member said sheepishly. Then another hand followed by another. Soon, ten more hands went up and they animatedly began to discuss the meteoric rise of Arvind Kejriwal.

'People, let's not go off message here,' the chairman interrupted, sounding exasperated. 'We are here to discuss how to save the party, not Kejriwal's career prospects. The time has come for radical transformation as Rahul Gandhi said earlier in the day. I think the writing is on the wall. Perhaps we need to dump Rahul Gandhi or the family itself for that matter.'

The members gasped in unison. It was the most heretical idea ever uttered in any party forum in the history of the party after 1969.

'Dump the Gandhis and hold elections within the party? Are you mad? Then what will happen to the Syndicate?' a member asked.

'No, no, I didn't mean ushering in inner-party democracy,' the chairman hastened to clarify. 'What I meant was we replace Rahul with someone else as the face of the party. Look, the guy is proving to be a liability. One of our data whiz-kids tells me that for every incremental 10,000 votes that a Modi speech nets for the BJP, a Rahul rally loses 20,000 votes for the Congress. If he goes around campaigning, the Congress could be reduced to single digits in the Lok Sabha elections.'

'That's not true, Mr Chairman,' a male voice interrupted. 'Let me tell you, wherever Rahul went, he evoked a phenomenal response. He's a breath of fresh air in an atmosphere of cynicism, spin-doctoring and . . .'

'Oh shut the fuck up, Jha,' the chairman barked. 'Looks like admitting you into the Syndicate was a big mistake. The whole idea of belonging to this awesome forum is to be able to speak your mind. Stop being a paid hack here too, man. And sorry for blowing your cover.'

Jha peered at fellow members through his mask. They nodded by way of encouragement. And then he broke down. 'Oh god, it's become impossible for me to continue like this. Why did I sign up for this thankless job of defending that moron?' he sobbed. The person seated next put his arm around him to comfort him. 'There, there. It's all right, man. We feel your pain.'

The discussion resumed as Jha continued to sob. 'But if not Rahul, then who? We can't afford to not have a Nehru–Gandhi at the helm. The party will disintegrate,' another leader wondered in a clipped Cambridge accent.

'Aha, I said let's look beyond Rahul Gandhi, not beyond the Nehru–Gandhis,' the chairman corrected him. 'If Rahul is a disaster, why not look elsewhere in the family branch?'

A female member now began to laugh like a hyena. 'HAHAHAHA! You mean Varun Gandhi, don't you? What an ingenious idea. HAHAHAH!' she trailed off hysterically.

Her statement evoked another round of shudders, forcing the chairman to intervene. 'No, obviously not Varun Gandhi, Renuka. That would be a . . . non-zero loss,' he blurted out, and immediately cursed himself.

The members all turned towards the chairman.

'Sibal?' someone gasped. 'Are you the chairman this year?'

Sibal took off his mask, and smiled sheepishly. 'I guess there is no point in continuing this charade. We give ourselves away invariably with our mannerisms no matter how much we modulate our voices.'

Everyone began to remove their masks to reveal a familiar posse of faces. Only one person refused to unmask himself. 'No, I bloody well refuse to reveal my identity. It's against the rules of the Syndicate,' he harrumphed in that all-too-familiar anglicized accent.

'Okay, get off your high horse now, Mani. Everyone knows it is you in there,' Sibal taunted.

Mani Shankar Aiyar slowly removed his mask to reveal the disgust on his face, nose pointed up in the air. 'And for the record, if any of you buggers are surreptitiously taking notes, I did not say a word against Rahul Gandhi,' Mani declared, and added wistfully, 'That reminds me of my favourite topic: panchayati raj. It was Rajiv who paved the way for the decentralization of . . .'

'Thank you, Mani. That will be all,' Sibal cut short Mani Shankar Aiyar's harangue in the making. 'Coming back to the main topic of discussion, if we anoint Varun Gandhi, we might as well become a B team of the BJP . . . no, make that a B team of the Bajrang Dal. That would be disastrous.

Priyanka is also ruled out because of that Vadra chap. No, when I mean a Nehru–Gandhi, I mean someone higher up in the family tree. Consider Vinay Nehru, Jawaharlal Nehru's grand-nephew, for instance. A sweet kid in his mid-forties. Works as an advertising executive, typical corporate grunt job, 100 per cent Kashmiri Pandit, married with kids. Has dimples too.'

'Bloody hell, no. I will not acquiesce to this preposterous suggestion,' Mani Shankar roared. 'We have too many schemes, bridges, parks, roads, canals and universities named after Rajiv Gandhi. And renaming all of them after Vinay Nehru's dad, whatever his name is, will take at least a decade. And then it will take at least two decades to convince our loyal voters that the free foodgrains, houses, and subsidized electricity they availed were not due to the benevolence of Indiraji or Rajivji, but due to the largesse of some chap called Vinay Nehru. No, sir, a Nehru simply won't do. It has to be a Gandhi. And no, Mahatma Gandhi's descendants won't do either. It has to be a Nehru–Gandhi. In other words, we have no option, but to hang on to Rahul until Priyanka's kid comes of age.'

There was a murmur of approval. 'Mani is right, yaa,' Renuka chimed in. 'Moreover, I've spent so many years *chatofying* Rahul. It will be painful to start from scratch with that Vinay chap.'

'Agree with Renuka,' Maken seconded her. 'Not interested in going through the process again. Moreover, would we want a chap who actually implements radical organizational reforms as opposed to Rahul who has been merely attempting to do so in great earnest for the last ten years? Better the devil you know than the devil you don't.'

'Yes, better the devil you know than the devil you don't,' the rest of the Syndicate shouted in chorus.

'But . . . but what about our plummeting electoral equity?' Sibal asked, sounding exasperated.

'Let's not get too gloomy,' Ahmed Patel said. 'Remember, we still have Phase II, III and IV of Snoopgate,' he paused for a moment, before adding, 'and a certain something that when released at the opportune moment is certain to doom Modi's campaign. It's like the Shakti Lord Indra presented to Karna. Can be used only once and guaranteed to work.'

Ahmed's words lifted the spirits of the assembly. 'Yes, Snoopgate and AAP's rise augur well for us, helping us stay relevant and pull strings from behind the scenes in the event of a hung Parliament,' a Union minister shouted. 'So what if they will also reduce us to zero in the process. Urban India has given up on us anyway.'

Everyone guffawed.

'So I take it,' Sibal said, 'we end the meeting by reaffirming our faith in Rahul baba and declaring him our PM candidate for 2014?'

'Yes,' they all shouted, followed by chants of 'Desh ki aandhi, Rahul Gandhi'.

Sibal, too, now seemed persuaded. 'No, no. That did not have the punch. Let's do this again, people,' he said, grinning impishly. 'Rahul lao . . .'

'Desh bachao!' the Syndicate roared back.

'Once more, Rahul lao!'

'*Desh bachao!*'

And then they all laughed uproariously, bringing one of the most seminal meetings of the Syndicate to an end.

SLOG OVERS

'Just get the feeling that this could go all the way down to the wire.'

—Ravi Shastri

NINETEEN

The fourth estate's plan

FEBRUARY 2014

HECTIC ACTIVITY WAS UNDERFOOT in the plush NDTV studio in Greater Kailash, Delhi. It was well past dinner time, but the office was teeming with people. Not one journalist thought of going home. A steady stream of quotes and reports came in from Gujarat, a majority of them on the recent Snoopgate scandal and the rest on the 2002 riots. The ground reports were quickly supplemented with photos and readied for prime time. Simultaneously, another team rapidly converted the data stream to full-length articles for www.ndtv.com by filling in NDTV's standard 'Major blow to Modi' article templates that were handed out liberally by the editors. The Six-Sigma-certified 'Blows and Setbacks to Modi' production line was the pride of NDTV and the envy of the Indian journalism industry.

A journalist from one of the cubicles suddenly stood up. 'Vasu sir has just hit twenty-five days of non-stop coverage on Snoopgate! It's a new record!' she said in awe.

The room burst into spontaneous applause. Barkha emerged from her corner chamber, clapping, and shook hands with the exuberant journalists around her.

'Way to go, people! Way to go!' she exulted.

All of a sudden, shrieks rent the air, and a few women ran helter-skelter, screaming in terror. Barkha looked for the source of the terror. A shabby-looking man stood at the doorway, the soles of his shoes torn, his clothes dirty, dry leaves and pieces of paper stuck in his long, black beard. As if in a trance, he walked in, muttering to himself.

'Who let that tramp in?' screamed Barkha. 'Security!'

Oblivious to the chaos around him, the bearded man slowly plodded forward, his eyelids fluttering, as if he was possessed. '2002 . . . Snoopgate . . . Amit Shah . . . surveillance . . . Singhal . . . 2002 . . . riots . . . Snoopgate . . .' he muttered in an infinite loop.

It was when he got within a few feet of her that Barkha's eyes grew wide in recognition.

'Vasu?' asked Barkha incredulously. 'Oh my god, what happened to you?'

Sreenivasan Jain's head swivelled slowly towards Barkha, and for a second his eyes seemed to meet Barkha's before they turned upwards and he collapsed on the floor in a heap.

* * *

At seven in the morning, in a quiet neighbourhood in Assam,

a sudden gust of wind howled through the narrow streets. In a quaint little cottage, awoke the conscience keeper of the nation, a colossus of journalism, the judge, jury and executioner of the republic of India—Arnab Goswami. He rose from his bed, paid his respects to a large map of India in his bedroom tersely labelled The Nation, and walked out to the porch in his patriotic pyjamas.

As he stood at the gate, drumming his fingers on the grill, the milkman slowly cycled towards the cottage, wobbled to a halt near the gate, and poured half a litre of milk into the container dangling by a hook.

'*Yeh lo, saab, gaay ka doodh, ek dum fresh.*'

Arnab took one look at the vessel and fixed the milkman with a stare that to over a billion Indians signalled the sign of imminent devastation, but was evidently lost on the hapless milkman.

'This is only half a litre. Where's the rest?' he asked.

'*Aaj itna hi milega, saab,*' said the milkman insouciantly.

'Really?' hissed Arnab. He reached into his pocket, pulled out a piece of paper and waved it in front of the milkman's face.

'I have with me last month's bill, in which you've clearly claimed payment for supplying one litre of cow's milk every single day for the entire month,' said Arnab, his voice rising by the moment. 'Are you trying to take me for a ride?'

'Saab, can we do this later? I still have to visit thirty more houses.'

'ARE YOU TRYING TO DODGE MY QUESTION, MISTER MILKMAN?' hollered Arnab, his face a mask of fury.

The milkman flinched, dumbstruck at this sudden burst of violence, his mouth opening and closing like a goldfish.

'Uh . . . I . . .' he stammered.

By now, a small crowd had gathered around the gate. A few neighbours, the neighbourhood's postman, the newspaper guy and a few others stood around the milkman watching the proceedings keenly.

'This channel is not afraid to ask tough questions, Mister Milkman. Unlike other journalists, I will ask you direct questions. Let me open the debate and get the other panellists in. Mrs Baruah is raising her hand. Yes, Mrs Baruah!' Arnab said, pointing at a neighbour behind the milkman.

'Arnab, I am glad you've raised this question. This is not the first time this milkman has done this. I have been protesting this for more than a month now, but my protests fall on deaf ears. What does one do in the face of such blatant cheating?'

'Absolutely. I agree with Mrs Baruah. What is your retort, Mister Milkman?'

'This is all the cow gave, saab. What do I—'

'Oh, come on!' interrupted Arnab, with a look of disgust. 'Are you trying to pass the buck to the cow, Mister Milkman!'

'No, what I meant was, the cow gave only this much, and the matter should end . . .'

'THE MATTER WILL NOT END THERE, MISTER MILKMAN!'

The newspaper guy raised his hand.

'Saab, I'd like to come in here,' he said.

'Yes, Mister Newspaperwala, go ahead. We have two minutes, and then I'll go to the postman, and then the other neighbour.'

'Two quick points, saab. First, this man is also a worker with the local Congress party, which perhaps explains why he is so inefficient, corrupt and . . .'

'DO NOT POLITICIZE THIS!' roared Arnab. 'No, Mister Newspaperwala, I will not allow this debate to be politicized! This is not about the Congress or the BJP or the Aam Aadmi Party. This is about the fundamental right of every citizen in this country to a glass of unadulterated cow's milk, which has been denied to the nation's citizens by the likes of Mister Milkman. THIS NATION DEMANDS AN . . .'

'Are you done?' demanded a voice behind Arnab. He turned around sharply to find his wife standing at the entrance, frowning at him. Arnab grinned sheepishly. Spotting his chance, the milkman turned his bicycle and fled from the scene. The others sighed, and left the way they came.

'One week,' exclaimed Mrs Goswami, as she walked into the cottage, followed by a sheepish Arnab. 'Just for one week I thought I could take you away from the studio, hoping that at least here in your native place, away from all the hustle and bustle, you'll have some time for me, but you still find a way to do the same shit!'

She stopped abruptly, and turned around. 'You know what? I've just about had enough!' she declared, and began shoving clothes into a suitcase.

'Now, honey, let's not do anything hasty here,' said Arnab, visibly shaken. 'You very well know it's my job . . . The Nation wants me . . .'

Mrs Goswami suddenly marched towards Arnab, brought her face extremely close to his and stared into his eyes with an expression laden with malevolence. In a voice dripping with menace, she challenged, 'Say the N-word . . . one . . . more . . . time.'

Arnab gulped. A bead of sweat trickled down his temple. 'Sorry,' he whimpered.

And so it went on for the next two hours—the man who demanded answers from the most powerful leaders of the world, and got them, beseeching his better half to reconsider, only to be denied. After two hours, when it was firmly established that even the best among men is but a mere tool at the mercy of his better half, Mrs Goswami laid down her rules.

'Three conditions, if you want this to work. Number one. I do not ever want to see a *Newshour* cockfight where a bunch of BJP and Congress spokespersons scream at each other and you scream over them. Number two. Snoopgate. Scams. 2002. These are out. I don't ever want a debate on these topics. And finally, if I ever see Sanjay Jha again on your panel, you'll hear from my lawyer even before the day's *Newshour* ends. Get it?'

Arnab nodded hastily. Mrs Goswami stared at him for a few moments, then turned on her heels and headed towards her room.

'But if I don't stage cockfights, what will I do?' Arnab whined plaintively, but Mrs Goswami had already slammed the door behind her.

* * *

Over 2000 kilometres away, in the nation's capital, Rahul Kanwal balled his fists, clenched his jaw and held his breath.

'But how can you blatantly flout the norms like this, Minister? The policy is very clear on this, sir. But in the name of discretion, you've brazenly chosen to ignore it. This is simply unacceptable!' he screeched. Then with his nostrils flaring and eyes bloodshot with outrage, he hollered, 'THIS COUNTRY WILL NOT TOLERATE THIS!'

He held that look for a few moments, then turned to his wife. 'So how was it?' he asked expectantly.

Mrs Kanwal held out her arms. 'Oh, baby, that was so cute!' she cooed. 'You looked so adorable!'

'Cute?' exclaimed Rahul. 'CUTE?! Here I am, going for overwhelming outrage and breathtaking anger, and you call it cute??

'Maybe you didn't get the context,' he said a moment later, calming down a little. 'The situation is like this. A minister has used his discretionary powers and awarded a contract to a shady organization, which has resulted in a loss to the exchequer. And I'm questioning him on my prime-time show. Now that you know the context, do you want to reconsider your assessment of my expression?'

She pondered over it for a few seconds, and said, 'Nah. I'll go with cute. Puppy-dog cute,' she giggled.

Kanwal glowered at her for a moment and then sank into his living room sofa in frustration. 'I don't know how Arnab does it, but I am just not cut out for this outrage stuff, yaar,' he whined, rubbing his forehead. 'When I try anger, people call me cute. When I go for shocked outrage, people call me a deer in the headlights. When I try a menacing look, people laugh at my face. I can't heckle, I can't intimidate. I can't look macho. Bloody, I can't even grow a fucking moustache!'

Mrs Kanwal put an arm around her husband. 'But, baby, why are you trying to mimic Arnab? Can't you cultivate your own style?'

'People only want outrage these days,' he muttered, staring at the floor.

'Maybe you could pick the battlefield that suits your strengths. Maybe you can choose topics that call for analytical debate and thoughtful anchoring rather than blind outrage.'

Rahul Kanwal sat mulling over his wife's words.

* * *

'I'm looking for a Sreenivasan Jain. He was admitted last night,' said Rajdeep Sardesai at the reception of the Ram Manohar Lohia Hospital.

'Just a moment, sir.'

As Rajdeep drummed his fingers on the desk, Sagarika Ghose fanned herself furiously.

'God, it's so hot in here,' she said, and asked the receptionist. 'Is there a pool in the compound?'

'Um . . . this is a hospital, ma'am,' the receptionist replied with a puzzled expression.

Sagarika sighed. A moment later, she pulled out a small mirror, and proceeded to dab bright-pink lipstick on her lips. Rajdeep stared at her for a few seconds, then reached into his jacket pocket, pulled out a bottle of Old Monk and took a long swig directly from the bottle.

'Room 311 on the third floor,' said the receptionist.

'Thank you,' said Rajdeep, and began to make his way to the elevator.

'Sir, you can't take that with you,' the receptionist called after him, pointing at the bottle in Rajdeep's hands. Rajdeep groaned, handed it over to her, and sullenly made his way to the room.

Room 311 was chock-a-block with prominent journalists from leading media houses. Rajdeep nodded and smiled at several of them, gave Arnab Goswami a wide berth and moved next to Barkha Dutt.

'How's he doing?' he asked, nodding towards the supine Jain. A nurse adjusted the knob on the glucose drip and checked Jain's temperature.

'He's recovering, ya,' said Barkha. 'Exhaustion and work-related stress, doctor says.'

Suddenly, Jain began to tremble violently. '2002! SNOOPGATE!' he screamed, arms flailing in all directions. Barkha and a nurse held him down by his arms until he calmed down.

'Snoopgate . . . 2002 . . . mayhem on the streets . . .' he murmured, and relapsed into a fitful sleep.

Barkha sighed. 'He's been like this since last night,' she said. 'This non-stop coverage of the same old stuff has taken a toll on him. And quite frankly on me as well. How long can we do the same old 2002, same old Snoopgate, the usual speeches, the usual scams, so on and so forth?'

The other editors met Barkha's gaze, and then each other's. A light of understanding seemed to pass between them. One by one, they spoke up, each sharing his or her travails with the current news programming, and the resultant impact on their lives. They spoke for over an hour, pausing only to restrain Sreenivasan Jain whenever he had one of his Gujaratrelated fits. And when they were done, they were all on the same page. They were all convinced that there has to be a drastic change in the pre-election coverage. Something new in the world of Indian election reporting.

Over the next week, the leading lights of Indian journalism brainstormed in groups and exchanged notes. In the end, after taking into consideration various factors such as plausibility, viability, potential to excite and so on, one idea stood out. A face-to-face contest between the prime ministerial aspirants; a contest that would assess various abilities of the two prime ministerial candidates and allow the electorate to directly compare the two candidates on these abilities.

And most importantly, a contest that would make for great TV.

All that remained was convincing the candidates themselves to participate.

* * *

'A televised face-off, huh?' Chief Election Commissioner V.S. Sampath raised an eyebrow.

'Yes, sir, as the world's largest democracy, it's a crying shame that our prime ministerial candidates are not pitted against each other on issues concerning our country. Besides, don't you think the electioneering is getting a bit repetitive and boring? The people of this country could do with something better in the month leading to the elections,' said Barkha, eloquent as ever.

Sampath looked around the table. Seated to his left were leaders from the Congress led by Rahul Gandhi. Seated to his right were the BJP leaders led by Narendra Modi. Opposite him, at the other end of the table, the top editors of the mainstream media leaned forward in eager anticipation.

Sampath shrugged. 'She's right, you know,' he said, turning towards Modi. 'I enjoyed your first few speeches and the gags in them. But you seem to have exhausted your Shahzada jokes now, and have resorted to repeating the old ones.'

Modi bristled. 'That's not true!' he exclaimed. 'I have taken utmost care to launch fresh Shahzada jokes at regular intervals.

'In fact,' he continued, straightening, 'I can crack a brand new one right now! Check this out. What's the difference between a Shahzada pearl of wisdom and a UFO?' Modi paused for dramatic effect, before finishing with a flourish. 'There have been UFO sightings.'

Sampath and the BJP leaders burst out laughing. Rajnath Singh toppled sideways to the floor, clutching his sides, whereas Nitin Gadkari whose belly was right under the table shook the tabletop with his fits of laughter. The Congress leaders, on the other hand, ground their teeth and seethed within. Rahul, however, stared vacuously at Modi.

When the last laugh had died down, and the room turned silent, comprehension dawned on Rahul Gandhi's face, and he suddenly burst out giggling and tittered for an entire minute, even as the BJP leaders stared at him in amazement.

'Good one, Modiji,' he said, snorting. For a second, the other Congress leaders looked at each other in confusion, before bursting into uproarious laughter. They laughed and laughed until they were convinced that they had beaten BJP's laughter record a few moments back by a wide margin.

When the leaders had finally calmed down, Sampath nodded at Rahul and Modi, and asked, 'So how about it? Are you two game for a debate, mano a mano?'

Modi leapt from his seat, slapped his thighs like a wrestler, and said, 'Any day, any time, any place.'

Sampath turned to Rahul. 'You, Rahul, are you ready for a debate?' he asked.

Rahul looked back vacantly with his mouth slightly open. Then his expression cleared, and metamorphosed into one of triumph, as he resorted to his ultimate fallback option.

'Let me put that question to you,' he said. 'Are *you* ready for a debate?'

TWENTY

The third dream

FEBRUARY 2014

WITH LESS THAN TWO months to go for the General Elections, the time was just right for the All India Convention Against Communalism (AICAC). Karat had billed the summit as the mother of all high-level meetings, the ultimate conglomeration of political heavyweights of the Third Front. As his gaze swept across the room, he knew that the meeting had already lived up to its billing. Seated around the table was an array of regional satraps: Lalu, Mulayam, Mayawati, Nitish, Karunanidhi, Jagan Reddy, Jayalalithaa, Deve Gowda and Yogendra Yadav.

The meeting was originally scheduled to be held a week earlier, but the idiotic design agency his office had roped in to print the banners had misspelled the title as 'All India

Convention Against Communism'. After one round of squabbling and two rounds of intense haggling over the additional cost, the banners were finally done, paving the way for the convention.

The next irksome point was the venue of the summit. When he'd suggested Mulayam's sprawling residence in Lucknow, Mayawati refused to come. When he'd suggested a five-star hotel in Chennai, the north Indians were reluctant to travel down. When he thought of Kolkata, Mamata threatened to brand the convention as a Maoist conspiracy and have them arrested. Patnaik's office in Bhubaneswar was a no go, as none of them wanted to visit Odisha.

He'd pondered long and hard over this issue, racking his brains for a venue that might be acceptable to them all, until one day Mulayam came up with the perfect venue. The CBI office of course. For Mulayam, Mayawati and many DMK leaders, it was like a second home in Delhi. The CBI director was only too happy to lend them the underground interrogation room to serve as the convention's venue.

'Some tea, Prakash sir?' smiled Ranjit Sinha, holding in front of him a tray of steaming cups of masala chai.

'Thank you,' said Karat gratefully.

He watched Sinha as he moved along the table offering tea to the assembled leaders, and pondered over his journey so far.

Although his efforts to broker a Left–TMC alliance by directly getting in touch with Mamata had ended in abject failure, other leaders had readily agreed to attend the summit, much to his pleasant surprise. Nitish, who had been initially dismissive of Karat's overtures, superciliously so, was now the most eager backer of the concept. Dr Jayalalithaa also agreed to participate in the deliberations despite Karunanidhi's presence after an internal poll indicated that her party would sweep all the LS seats in Tamil Nadu. And that made her a top contender for the PM's post in case of a hung Parliament. As long as she was not expected to sit next to him at the round table, she was fine.

Mulayam's and Mayawati's presence was a foregone conclusion. They never missed a chance to be present at such summits. The optics of holding hands with other leaders always provided good leverage in ongoing discussions with the UPA regime through intermediaries such as the sarkari sleuths. The icing on the cake was the presence of Dr Yogendra Yadav on behalf of AAP as a special attendee. Dr Yadav had made it clear at the outset that AAP wanted no truck with any of the established parties as it considered all of them to be corrupt and hence he was condescending to attend on behalf of AAP purely as an observer. Yadav was a bit annoying, but Karat bore it. A small price to pay for the larger cause of forging an alternative paradigm.

He had done the hard work. All that was left was to finalize the common minimum programme that would pave the way for the formalization of the Third Front in the run-up to the polls.

Karat glanced at the list of demands that each of the leaders had made:

Special status for Bihar. In case of special status for UP, TN and Odisha as well, then very, very special status for Bihar—JD(U)

Banning of English from Parliament, and eventually from all government correspondence—SP

Banning of all Sri Lankan players from IPL unless they belong to Sunrisers Hyderabad—DMK

Closure of all pending CBI cases against their leaders—SP, BSP, YSR Congress, DMK, AIADMK

Installation of giant statue of Mayawati in Lucknow—BSP

Re-merger of Telangana and Seemandhra—YSR Congress

Nationwide roll-out of two-rupee idli scheme—AIADMK

Just acknowledge once in a while that there is a state called Odisha ruled by a party called Biju Janata Dal—BJD

Accept that AAP is different from all other political parties—AAP

Keeping communal forces at bay—all parties

Pursuit of pro-poor policies—all parties

The demands looked reasonable. Consensus on a CEMP (common and extremely minimum programme) seemed within reach.

Karat made a supplication to Marx, took a deep breath, and began in a solemn tone: 'Dear comrades, we are assembled here for a historic . . .'

'*Hindi mein baat karo, bhaiyya,*' Mulayam interrupted gruffly.

'*Yeh Karatwa angrezi babu kyon banat hai? Jab Hindi hamra rashtra bhaasha hai. Ei tanik Hindi mein bolo,*' Lalu seconded him. Mayawati also joined the two Yadav satraps in their vociferous protest.

Karunanidhi and Jayalalithaa were quick to unite. 'No Hindi, *paa*,' Karunanidhi growled. 'If Hindi is imposed on us, we will walk out. Only Tamil or English.'

'Or Telugu,' Jagan Reddy added.

Prakash Karat had anticipated this impasse. So many discussions in the past had been held up over the vexatious issue of using Hindi or English to conduct knotty deliberations. But this time he had come prepared.

'For the benefit of the north Indian comrades, I have arranged for a machine translation of my commie English into Hindi just like it is done in Parliament. So fret not, my comrades from UP and Bihar,' he said.

There was a grunt of approval. Lalu, Nitish, Mulayam and Mayawati put on their headphones. Karat wiped a bead of sweat off his forehead. That was a neat dodge.

'Comrades,' he continued, 'for nine years, the people have been suffering because of the anti-poor, neo-liberal policies of the UPA. One in five children goes hungry, the youth are frustrated and unemployed. Meanwhile, the forces of communalism are exploiting these conditions to further their nefarious agenda—'

'Boss, spare us,' Jagan Reddy interrupted him. 'Let's cut to the chase, shall we?'

'Er . . . Okay, then the only thing left to discuss is who will be the PM candidate for the proposed Third Front.'

'Naturally, I ought to be declared the PM candidate,' Jayalalithaa said. 'It's high time India had a prime minister from Tamil Nadu. It has given so much to India: Nobel Prize winners, a world chess champion, that Kolaveri song and now Lungi dance, scientists, innumerable civil servants, and of course, Rajinikanth.'

'*Light theesko, Amma*,' Jagan interrupted. 'I will be sweeping all seats in Seemandhra. If anything, I deserve to be declared the PM candidate.'

'*Poda dei!*' she retorted. 'Your state already had one chap, no? Even that Gowda guy was lucky enough to get a stint on behalf of Karnataka. It's high time TN had that honour.'

At the mention of his name, Deve Gowda, snoring in a corner, opened his eyes halfway and groggily murmured, 'Eh? *Enu?*' and a moment later, slumped again and resumed snoring.

'All of you are wrong,' Nitish declared. 'PM's post is very special and that honour should go to a very special state. Bihar is landlocked, ravaged by floods when not stricken by drought, and over 40 per cent of its population is below the poverty line.'

'Nitishwa is right,' Lalu thundered. 'The PM candidate must be from Bihar and from the Yadav community. In other words, me . . .'

'*Bhak, budbak!* That's not what I meant,' Nitish said, turning red.

'Enough,' bellowed Yogendra Yadav, AAP's honorary representative, finally breaking his silence. Silence befell the group immediately. Then in an angelic voice with the slightest hint of a rebuke, Yadav said, 'Is this what we have degenerated to? Petty squabbles over who will be the PM candidate? Are we here to discuss how we can cleanse the system or indulge in politicking of the worst kind?'

The rest of the leaders began to feel a bit ashamed. It was like a schoolteacher talking down to a bunch of errant kids.

'Yes, yes,' Karat butted in, 'spoken like a true communist, Yogendraji. The need of the hour is for the proletariat to unite against the bourgeoisie for . . .'

'The Left's economics is as bad as the politics of the rest of the Third Front,' Yogendra Yadav calmly retorted. 'AAP believes in providing honest, clean governance, not discredited leftist claptrap. We must focus on solutions, not hide behind sterile ideological slogans.'

Karat winced at the snub. This Yadav chap was beginning to get under his skin.

Lalu tried to turn on the charm and bond with his fellow kinsmen. *'Badiya e-speech diya, Yogendrawa. Ei tanik RJD aur AAP ka gattbandhan ho jaye to Nitishwa aur Modi dono ko jhadoo se hum saaf kar doonga,'* Lalu said.

Yogendra Yadav looked offended. 'How can you talk to me like that, Laluji? Just because my surname is Yadav, you presume I will partake in your politics? You need to rise above such narrow-minded considerations and become more broad-minded. AAP is above the identity politics of caste and community. We want to maintain equidistance from all the mainstream parties. All of you are corrupt and evil.'

Lalu stared back, dumbstruck, as did the other leaders. There were now annoyed murmurs around the table. Leaders fidgeted in their seats and shot angry glances at Yogendra Yadav. This was getting too much.

Karat stood up. He had had enough. 'Why the fuck are you so bloody sanctimonious, man? Even the Congress and the BJP are not as painful!'

Yogendra Yadav was slightly taken aback, but quickly regained his poise. 'Of course, you have a right to be slightly annoyed, Mr Karat, but is it too much to ask that we remain civil while airing our differences?'

At this point, Nitish cried, 'I can't take his preachiness any more, man,' and lunged forward to land a resounding slap on Yogendra Yadav's face. Everyone started clapping.

Yogendra Yadav was stunned for a moment. Then he dropped his mask of piety and saintliness, and let loose a volley of abuse, laced with references to incest and queries on parentage that would have made even Virat Kohli blush.

Unfortunately for him, by now, the Yadav chieftains had also joined the fray. '*Bahut lecturewa ho gaya. Humko politics sikhata hai? Ye leh ek aur ghusa,*' hollered Lalu, and threw a roundhouse punch, while Mulayam pinned Yadav's arms behind him. From the right flank, Mayawati charged at Yadav, screaming like the devil possessed, and smashed her handbag at the hapless psephologist-turned-politician. From the other side, Jagan screeched and tugged at Yadav's beard. A few feet away, Karunanidhi turned a knob on his goggles and they turned bright red, emitting heat rays of some sort directly on to Yadav's posterior. Soon the others converged—Nitish Kumar, Naveen Patnaik and even Deve Gowda—to take a swing at the man they'd came to so utterly despise. The melee came to an abrupt end when Jayalalithaa slammed Yadav to the ground and sat atop him.

Then, to the tune of the Avengers' soundtrack reverberating in the air, the Third Front leaders gathered in a circle. One by one, Karat met every leader's eye, and saw a steely determination and a raging passion to keep the forces of communalism, neo-liberalism and, now, extremely annoying self-righteous preachers at bay. In their aversion to Yogendra Yadav and his self-righteousness, they had discovered a common purpose. Karat clenched his jaw, and extended an open hand. Nitish nodded and placed his hand atop Karat's. Then they all piled their hands, and together raised them high in the air and whooped. And for the first time in many years, the night came alive with the voice of the Third Front.

TWENTY-ONE

This is war!

MARCH 2014

THE CONTEST WAS SCHEDULED to be held at the Feroz Shah Kotla stadium at 8 p.m. on a Sunday, with a live crowd to make for an IPL-like atmosphere. What started off as an Indian version of the US presidential debate was relentlessly tweaked to suit Indian television by the designers until no debating element was left in the contest. Instead, the two candidates would now attempt to outdo each other over four rounds: a quiz round, a personality round, a 'crowd connect' round, and finally a presentation round where they would make a two-minute pitch to the nation.

Experts estimated that the event would be watched by 600 million people, approximately half the country's population, a number that would comfortably beat the total worldwide viewership for the 2011 World Cup final between India and Sri Lanka. Marketing teams of prominent TV channels worked round the clock to create innovative ad slots and sign up companies. The ad slots sold for record rates, as top companies tripped over each other to book themselves a prime-time slot for what promised to be the television event of the decade.

Meanwhile, the Third Front leaders held a press conference, and announced that they were boycotting the Rahul versus Modi contest, and instead holding their own debate within the Third Front.

'The people of India are tired of the corrupt and communal politics of the Congress and the BJP,' declared Prakash Karat, as Nitish Kumar, Mulayam Singh Yadav, Karunanidhi and others looked on. 'The country is aching for a viable alternative, and we are the answer. On Sunday, we will hold our own debate in the Jawaharlal Nehru stadium at the same time, where we will decide which one of the Third Front leaders would be the prime ministerial candidate. From the response we are sure to evoke from the people of this country, it will be clear to the BJP and the Congress that they are marching towards extinction,' he concluded with a flourish.

* * *

On the day of the debate, 10 Janpath was bustling with activity. Leaders gathered in small groups all over the lawns, poring over books, charts and computers, discussing tactics and possible scenarios that may emerge during the contest.

Attendants didn't have a moment's rest, as they attended to incessant demands of chai and lemonade.

In the hall area inside the bungalow, Rahul Gandhi lay on the sofa in a pose not unlike that of Lord Vishnu, as a gaggle of top Congress leaders stood behind the couch or sat on the floor in front, with books or tablets in hand, preparing their young leader for the challenges of the contest.

'Let's start with a simple question, Rahul baba,' suggested Ajay Maken, adjusting his glasses. 'Who is the father of the nation?'

'Rajiv Gandhi,' murmured Rahul Gandhi, plucking a grape with his mouth off a cluster that Sachin Pilot dangled over him.

'Um . . . er . . . that is not the answer I'm looking for,' said Maken timidly.

'Are you saying I'm wrong?' demanded Rahul.

'No, no, of course not!' said Ajay Maken hastily. 'I am saying that your answer is . . . different!'

Watching from the door, Ahmed Patel sighed deeply, and left the room to find his boss.

'Madam, I don't think Rahul baba's preparation is going too well,' he exclaimed, as he pushed open the door to her chamber.

Sonia looked up, a curious smile playing on her lips, as her hands twirled a black CD case.

'Is that the . . . ?' asked Ahmed warily.

Sonia grinned and nodded. 'Yes.'

'Madam, I hope you know that the CD cannot be duplicated. We only have the one copy . . .'

She waved his concern aside and beckoned him to take a seat opposite her. 'Here's my plan. We let the contest pan out as planned for the first three rounds. Then in the final round, where Rahul is supposed to make a two-minute pitch to the country, when the most number of people are expected to be watching, we'll play the CD.'

Ahmed rubbed his hands in delight. 'Sounds great, madam!'

'And you know what the best part is?' said Sonia. 'We don't have to prepare Rahul for his two-minute presentation!'

'Genius, madam!'

The two giggled in excitement.

* * *

A few kilometres away, in the BJP headquarters, Arun Jaitley and Yashwant Sinha flopped on to the couch in a corner of the vast meeting hall, utterly exhausted.

'Phew, I'm beat,' panted Jaitley. 'This is hard work!'

'Yeah! I don't think I've ever slogged this hard,' agreed Sinha, wiping his face.

The two sat quietly for a while until their breathing patterns returned to normal.

'One more?' asked Jaitley.

Sinha gave a cocky smile. 'Bring it on, baby!'

The two returned to the table tennis table, and resumed their marathon bilateral contest. A few of their colleagues cheered them on, while others sat gossiping at the canteen across the hall. A few other leaders were bunched around the new PS4 station in another corner, jostling with each other for the controllers. Nitin Gadkari was in the kitchen, hunched over the refrigerator.

In another part of the building, with a prominent Do Not Disturb sign outside his door, Narendra Modi shut himself in his study, preparing like a man on a mission. Two tall towers of books sat on his desk. Mostly on history, his weak subject. The books covered a range of genres: from classics such as Basham's *The Wonder That Was India* to popular history bestsellers such as William Dalrymple's *The Last Mughal* to specialized studies such as Peter Jackson's *The Delhi Sultanate: A Political and Military History*.

Modi was determined to clear once and for all the misconception that he could only make history, but not cite history. Every ten minutes, Modi would take two books from the pile on the left, place them side by side, simultaneously turn pages with both hands in short intervals, absorbing the contents of each page within a matter of seconds, and then place the books on the pile to his right.

He studied non-stop for several hours, pausing only to cool his overheated brain with a round of pranic meditation. He even avoided drinking water, because that meant he didn't have to take a loo break, and thereby saved a few more minutes that he could divert towards preparation.

At 7 p.m., Modi shut his last book, a scholarly tome on the Painted Grey Ware culture of the Gangetic plains from 1200 to 600 BC, took a deep breath, exhaled slowly and rose to his feet. He was ready.

* * *

Away from all the hectic deliberations and the frenetic activity, Dr Singh sat in majestic isolation at the Prime Minister's Office, staring at the wall in front of him. The PMO staff had all left for the day, some keen to grab a seat in the Kotla, others hoping to beat the traffic to get to their television sets in time to catch the action live.

The tea-boy sauntered in, whistling tunelessly, and slapped a cup of tea on the desk. Dr Singh didn't move. The boy waved a hand in front of Dr Singh's face, and cheekily took a sip from the teacup, watching Dr Singh for a reaction. None came.

The tea-boy bit his lip, and stood gazing at Dr Singh for a few moments. Then, slowly stretching across the table, he reached for the stapler near Dr Singh's left arm, picked it up and slipped it into his pocket. One by one, he picked up various objects on the desk—the pen-stand, the punching machine, an empty folder, and finally a pen from Dr Singh's right hand—and pocketed them all.

For a moment, Dr Singh's gaze flicked up to look at the tea-boy. The kid smirked, inched towards the door and slipped out. Dr Singh's eyes returned to the spot on the wall straight ahead.

The clock struck eight. A roar sounded somewhere in the distance.

TWENTY-TWO

The contest

MARCH 2014

ALL ROADS IN DELHI led to the Feroz Shah Kotla stadium on the day of the great contest. The area around the stadium was chock-a-block with vehicles of all shapes and sizes that spilled over on to all the roads leading to the stadium in the form of kilometre-long traffic jams. Every other minute a fist fight broke out between angry commuters that occasionally involved hockey sticks or pistols. To make matters worse, it rained for exactly three minutes, and the roads were flooded with dirty brown water. People flying in from outside Delhi gingerly made their way out of the inundated terminal-3 of the Indira Gandhi International Airport. The main actors in the contest, however, were flown into the stadium in choppers.

A sprawling six-foot-high stage was installed inside the field at the Pavilion End of the stadium. The stage extended from the long off boundary to the long on boundary. On the left end of the stage, beyond the long off ropes was the Congress dugout. A luxurious sofa was set in the middle of the dugout, on which Sonia Gandhi and Rahul Gandhi sat imperiously. Sachin Pilot and Jyotiraditya Scindia stood on either side of the sofa, gently waving a large feathered fan, while Ahmed Patel stood behind the sofa to the left of Sonia. The general seats in the dugout were occupied by leaders such as Manish Tewari, Shushilkumar Shinde, Digvijaya Singh and Mani Shankar Aiyar.

The BJP dugout was adjacent to the right end of the stage, and was occupied by Narendra Modi, Rajnath Singh, Arun Jaitley, Nitin Gadkari and various other prominent BJP leaders. The dugout was devoid of objects and accessories apart from a large plate of samosas in front of Gadkari. Party veteran L.K. Advani was not seen in the dugout; he could not make it to the stadium on account of an upset stomach. Sushma Swaraj, too, excused herself to look after her mentor. Amit Shah stood near the edge of the dugout peering at the spectators through a pair of binoculars.

The stands were packed to the rafters. People crowded in the aisles, climbed on to rooftops and occupied every possible vantage point within or outside the stadium. The stands to the right of the stage, directly behind the BJP dugout, were a sea of saffron. Men, women and children of various ages wearing saffron T-shirts, saffron kurtas, saffron *pagdis* and, in some cases, saffron helmets thronged the stands, brandishing Modi masks or waving saffron flags or both.

The stands directly behind the Congress dugout, to the left of the stage, were occupied by thousands of Congress workers, hundreds of policemen from all ranks ranging from constable to the Delhi commissioner, bodyguards, Black Cat Commandos and a group of sullen-looking villagers who kept gazing at the lunch stalls behind them. Across the field, the stands at the Stadium End, incidentally equidistant from both the Congress and the BJP sections, was teeming with hordes of youth sporting the white caps of Aam Aadmi Party. The rest of the stadium was filled with people who didn't give a shit.

A big screen was installed at right angles to the stage, relaying a zoomed-in version of the events on the stage. The screen was managed from behind by a small control room staffed by a video editing team. Another big screen outside the stadium relayed the television coverage of the event to a vast crowd stretching to well beyond the limits of human vision.

And at that moment, on the two screens loomed a giant of the cricket commentating world sporting his trademark shades.

'NAMASTE, DELHI!' hollered Ravi Shastri in his baritone, standing just outside the rope, a few feet away from the right end of the stage. 'The atmosphere is electric, the noise is deafening, and the crowd is on its feet! We should be in for a cracker of a contest!'

* * *

Seven kilometres to the south of the Kotla, the top brass of India's Third Front stood outside the Jawaharlal Nehru stadium, bracing themselves for the roar of hundreds of thousands of people sitting cheek by jowl in the stands when they'd swagger in with their promise of a viable alternative to the corrupt dynastic and communal politics of the two national parties.

The leaders took a deep breath. One by one, they linked hands, steeled themselves and marched into the stadium.

'YEAH!' they screamed in unison, raising their hands in triumph.

A thundering silence greeted them. The stadium was completely empty, except for a murder of crows in the northern stand and a bunch of stray dogs squatting in front of the giant cardboard cut-outs of the Third Front leaders on the dais.

A lone CPI(M) supporter was holding aloft the Third Front banner.

'Where are all the cadres from Kolkata, man?' Karat hollered.

'Sir, the Delhi–Howrah Rajdhani is running late by four hours,' he replied.

'What about the Kolkata Mail? Didn't one batch reach Delhi yesterday itself?'

'Er . . . they have all gone to the Feroz Shah Kotla. Word got around that the NaMo vs Rahul show promises to be the biggest entertainment package of the year. A heady mix of politics, Bollywood and cricket. I just wanted to hand this over to you before I also leave,' he said, dropping the banner at Karat's feet and scampering away.

'Hey, wait!' Karat screamed at the fleeing figure.

In the ensuing awkward silence, the leaders glanced at each other.

'Er . . . I was scheduled to meet Soniaji later in the night for discussions on seat sharing. So, I guess I might as well get to the Kotla,' said Mulayam.

'I was supposed to meet her too. Can I give you a lift?' Nitish offered.

'Actually, I also want to go to the Kotla,' Patnaik said.

'Me too, *thambi*,' Karunanidhi said.

One by one they turned around and made their way to the exit.

'Hey, wait, we can make this work!' Karat screamed, his words echoing through the empty stands.

* * *

'Joining us in the centre is the former chief minister of Delhi, Arvind Kejriwal,' said Shastri. 'Arvind, a quick word.'

Dressed in a loose-fitting half-shirt, a faded pair of trousers and the Aam Aadmi hat, Arvind Kejriwal grabbed the microphone from Shastri. '*Mera naam Arvind Kejriwal hai*. For two years, under the leadership of Annaji, we fought against corruption. Thousands of lakhs of people came to the streets. After all, what were we asking for? A strong anti-corruption law that would ensure that if anyone indulges in corruption, he would be sent to jail. But the government didn't listen to us. We begged them, pleaded with them, but to no avail. Then we realized that we have to change the system from within. We have to change the politics of this country. *Rajniti badalni hogi*. There is only one person that can save this country from complete disaster. And that is you, the aam aadmi,' said Kejriwal, pointing his forefinger at the camera. Then he pointed at the BJP and Congress dugouts, and said, 'Both the parties involved in today's contest are corrupt. *Dono chor hain!* These people will keep looting us. *Jhaadu ko hi vote dena!*'

The BJP and Congress leaders seethed, but could do nothing. They watched helplessly as Arvind waved a broom in the air to loud cheers from the Aam Aadmi Party stands, and exited as quickly as he'd come.

'Thanks, Arvind,' said Shastri, and added, 'Well, that was Arvind, a cool customer if ever there was one. Flashed and flashed hard, and gave the two parties the full monty. With that, ladies and gentlemen, we begin.'

The crowd roared in delight, cheering as much for the commencement of the contest as for seeing Shastri's back. The in-stadium announcer took over. 'The first round will test the general knowledge of the two candidates. Each candidate will face three questions from Shri Amitabh Bachchan in the *Kaun Banega Crorepati* format. We will start with Modiji.'

The floodlights dimmed, as KBC's introductory soundtrack resonated in the cauldron of the Kotla. Then the onstage lights slowly came on, and the crowd went wild when they saw the lanky frame of the Bollywood legend seated along with Modi in a set-up that resembled the hot seats in the KBC studio.

'*Namaskar, namaskar, namaskar!*' thundered Amitabh. 'Welcome to *Kaun Banega Crorepati*. Today we have with us on the hot seat Shri Narendra Modi. Let me quickly explain the rules of the game. I will ask each candidate three questions, each corresponding to the three hurdles of 10,000 votes, 3,20,000 votes and one crore votes. As you all know, there are three lifelines, Audience Poll, Fifty–fifty and Phone a Friend. So there, simple rules, simple game. Shall we start?'

The crowd roared their approval.

'All right then. *Modiji, aapka pehla sawaal, 10,000 votes ke liye,*' boomed Amitabh, and paused for the dramatic soundtrack that precedes a KBC question. 'When was the National Commission for Minorities Act passed? Your options are A) 1989, B) 1990, C) 1991, D) 1992.'

A second's silence followed after the question, and then the Congress dugout burst out laughing.

'Poor Hindu nationalist. Got slam dunked in the very first question!' giggled Ahmed Patel, high-fiving Sonia Gandhi. The BJP leaders looked distraught at the terrible start, and cursed their luck under their breath.

Modi, however, seemed utterly unruffled. 'The answer is D, 1992,' he said.

Ahmed's mouth dropped open. 'What?' asked Sonia. 'Is that correct?'

'*Sahi jawab!*' Amitabh bellowed, sparking loud cheers in the BJP camp. A section of the saffron crowd joined in instinctively, while the rest looked about uncertainly.

'I don't believe this,' muttered Sonia.

'Very well done, Modiji. You win 10,000 votes. We now move to the second question,' said Big B. 'For 3,20,000 votes, here it is. On the banks of which river is the city of Jammu located? Your options are A) Sutlej, B) Tawi, C) Tapi, D) Jhelum.'

For the briefest of moments, a dark shadow passed over Modi's face. The very next instant, his visage regained its usual stern quality. In the five seconds that went by after Amitabh read out the question, Modi had analysed the situation. In the days leading to the contest, he had mastered history, but had inadvertently ignored its cousin, geography. There was no point hazarding a guess. He fixed Amitabh with a steady gaze, and said, 'I would like to go with Fifty–fifty.'

'Computerji, please eliminate two wrong choices,' Big B ordered. The computer responded and the last two options disappeared, leaving Sutlej and Tawi on the screen.

Modi glanced at his screen for a second before declaring, 'I would like to use my second lifeline.'

'Audience Poll or Phone a Friend?'

'Neither. I would like to phone an enemy,' said Modi, and before a bewildered Amitabh could react, he leaned towards the computer, and said, 'Computerji, connect me to Bihar's Chief Minister Nitish Kumar pronto.'

The phone rang, and from somewhere in the stands, Nitish Kumar answered the call.

'*Kaun sasura iss time pe . . .*'

'Hello, Nitishwa,' Modi interrupted. 'This is Modi. I hate to admit it, but need your help with a geography question. Would you be kind enough to oblige?'

A second's pause later, Nitish said, 'I am listening.'

'Thanks. The question is this. Jammu is located on the banks of which river? Sutlej or Tawi?'

This time there was a longer pause. Up in the stands, Nitish stood with the phone to his ears, brows knotted in a frown, the wheels turning rapidly in his head. Nobody knew history and geography better than him. And this was the time to prove it and score one over his bête noire. Or maybe not.

'Sutlej,' Nitish said confidently.

'Are you sure?'

'100 per cent.'

'Okay,' said Modi, and disconnected the phone. He looked up at Big B, and said, '*Tawi ko lock kiya jaye.*'

Amitabh looked stunned. 'But Nitishji seemed confident that it is Sutlej. You sure you want to go against it?'

'Yes, I am sure.'

Amitabh studied Modi for a moment and then slowly turned to the computer. 'Computerji, please lock B, Tawi,' he said, and then exclaimed, 'And that's the right answer! Congratulations, Modiji, you have won 3,20,000 votes!'

The BJP camp whooped in delight, and the saffron crowd began a chant of 'Modi! Modi!' that soon spread to the rest of the stadium. Only one question now stood between Modi and a 100 per cent score in this round that Rahul could at best equal. The Congress dugout looked downcast, as did Nitish in the stands. Back on stage, Amitabh resumed his duties.

'Modiji, you have played extremely well so far. Only one hurdle now remains between you and one crore votes. Ready?'

Modi nodded.

'All right, here it is,' Big B glanced at his computer screen. 'In the algebraic expression, $2x - 4000 = 4$, what is the value of x? Your options are A) 2000, B) 2001, C) 2002, D) 2003.'

For a second, Modi relaxed at the familiarity of the topic, and then when his quick mind computed the solution, his face abruptly darkened. He glowered at Amitabh Bachchan for several moments. Then, without a word, he stood up and walked off the stage, ignoring Big B's entreaties to return to the hot seat. In the BJP dugout, Jaitley slapped his forehead, Rajnath buried his face in his hands, and the others watched sullenly as Modi walked towards them and took his seat. The Congress camp, on the other hand, breathed a huge sigh of relief, while up in the stands, Nitish Kumar punched the air and exclaimed, 'Yes!'

* * *

Meanwhile, in the various news studios covering the event, the development was tantamount to waving a red rag in front of a bull.

'Modi still unwilling to answer questions on 2002! Is this the man the country needs as its next PM?' hollered an anchor on NDTV.

'The big question in front of the BJP is this,' declared a charged-up Rajdeep Sardesai. 'Will Modi's reluctance to answer questions on 2002 lose them the election?'

The heated discussions continued for the next minute and ended only when it was time to go back to the live coverage of the stage, where Rahul had already settled in his hot seat to begin his KBC round with Amitabh Bachchan.

* * *

'Rahulji, for 10,000 votes, here is your first question,' said Amitabh, in a hoarse whisper. 'Who invented computers? Your options are A) Rajiv Gandhi, B) Charles Babbage, C) Baba Ramdev, and D) Sam Pitroda.'

Rahul stared intensely at the computer screen, rubbing his temple with two fingers, while Amitabh observed him with a benevolent smile. Seconds ticked by, but Rahul sat unmoved. A minute later, Amitabh shifted in his seat, a hint of impatience creeping into his demeanour.

'Tell us what you are thinking, Rahulji.'

Rahul looked up at Big B briefly, then back at the screen. 'It should be either Dad or Sam Uncle,' he said. 'I'm leaning towards Dad, but I'm not sure.'

Amitabh leaned forward. 'Uh, let me remind you that you have with you three lifelines. Audience Poll, Fifty–fifty and Phone a Friend. You may . . .'

Rahul exhaled, a look of immense relief on his face. 'Audience Poll, please.'

A few moments of drama later, the audience turned in its answer, and Big B declared, 'Charles Babbage is the correct answer. Congratulations, Rahulji! You have cleared the first hurdle.'

The Congress leaders rose to their feet and applauded their beloved leader, while the spectators behind them clapped politely.

'Very well done, Rahulji. We move on to the next question, for 3,20,000 votes. Are you ready?' rumbled Big B. 'And here it is. Who among the following is or was a BJP politician? Your options are A) L.K. Advani, B) Kamala Nehru, C) M.G. Ramachandran, D) N.T. Rama Rao.'

Rahul's brow once again furrowed in intense concentration for a few moments after which he said, 'I want to go for Fifty–fifty.'

Options C and D disappeared, leaving L.K. Advani and Kamala Nehru on the screen. Rahul frowned.

'You weren't expecting one or both of these to remain?' suggested Big B with a knowing smile. Rahul nodded glumly.

'Well, you still have one lifeline remaining . . .'

Rahul sighed. 'All right. I want to Phone a Friend.'

Back in the Congress dugout, Sonia and the other leaders sat at the edge of their seats, tension writ large on their faces. Sonia chewed on her fingernails and fervently hoped that Rahul would use the lifeline smartly and call someone really smart.

Oops, I did it again! I played with your heart . . .

Sonia turned sharply towards the source of the loud ringtone and saw Digvijaya Singh reach for his phone.

'Hello, Rahul baba!' exulted Diggy. Sonia's eyes rolled back and she collapsed on her couch.

'It's such an honour that you have called me . . .' said Diggy.

'Yes, I know, Diggy Chacha, I only have thirty seconds . . .'

'I must tell you,' interrupted Diggy. 'I am watching you on the big screen now and you look terrific. And you are doing so well . . .'

'Only fifteen seconds left!' warned Big B.

'Listen, Diggy Chacha, there's this question I need help with . . .' said Rahul, desperation creeping into his voice.

But Diggy prattled on. 'I have no doubt in my mind that you will go on to win this contest, and the people of this country . . .'

'The last five seconds . . . five . . . four . . . three . . .'

'Diggy Chacha, shut up and listen!' cried Rahul. 'Who among these is . . .'

'And time is up!'

Rahul looked gutted. Digvijaya, on the other hand, looked extremely pleased with himself. Slipping the cell phone back into his pocket, he turned to the other leaders, and gloated,

'Rahulji chose me over everyone else for the Phone a Friend round.'

Back on stage, Rahul threw up his hands, and said, 'If I had to take an intelligent guess, I'd go with Kamala Nehru because she has the BJP's party symbol in her name, but it seems almost too easy for 3,20,000. So I'll go with L.K. Advani.'

'*Lock kiya jaaye?*'

'Yes.'

'Sure?'

'Yes.'

'*Pakka?*'

Rahul shot his host an irritated look.

'And that is the right answer!' said Big B hastily. 'Congratulations, Rahul! You have won 3,20,000 votes!'

The Congress leaders exhaled heavily. Ahmed sprinkled a few drops of water on Sonia, and she came to with a groan. She looked around for Rahul and smiled weakly when she spotted him still seated in the hot seat. The BJP camp was understandably glum, for they knew what a disaster it would be if Rahul beat Modi in a round that measured intelligence and knowledge. They would never hear the end of it.

'We are now at the final hurdle. If you answer this question, you win the round. So Rahulji, for one crore votes, here is your final question!' intoned Amitabh.

'Who made this famous statement? "Only 15 paise out of every rupee reaches the poor." Your options are . . .'

'No need,' interrupted Rahul. 'I did.'

Amitabh hesitated. 'Don't you want to hear the options? Perhaps . . .'

'No,' said Rahul with a confident smile. 'I am sure. Please lock "Rahul Gandhi".'

Amitabh studied his participant for a moment and then shrugged. 'Okay, computerji, please lock "Rahul Gandhi".'

A long pause ensued, punctuated by KBC's musical heartbeat. The Congress leaders stood outside their dugout, hands over their mouths, paralysed with anxiety. The BJP dugout seemed equally tense. The entire stadium held its breath. Then Big B turned to Rahul with a sad expression, and said, 'I'm afraid "Rahul Gandhi" is not the right answer. The current answer is "Rajiv Gandhi".'

The Congress supporters moaned and their leaders sank to the ground with hands on their heads. The BJP leaders hugged each other in relief, and wiped the sweat off their faces. Rahul himself betrayed no emotion. He shrugged and returned to his dugout. With that the first round came to a close, and the cameras moved to Ravi Shastri.

'What an exciting session of play!' Shastri exclaimed. 'Amitabh threw the kitchen sink at them, but the candidates played their natural game, made excellent use of their feet and dealt in boundaries!

'At this stage, all three results are possible,' he added sagely, drawing groans from everyone around.

* * *

'Very well put by Ravi there,' said Rahul Kanwal in the Headlines Today studio. 'It could be anyone's game at this point, BJP, the Third Front or, less likely, the UPA. I would like to invite our panellists . . .'

The TV channels returned to their debates or broke for commercials, while back in the stadium, the spectators got up to stretch their legs and fetch refreshments. Away from the gaze of the cameras, in a corner of the Congress dugout, Sonia and Ahmed were holding a quiet conversation. Ahmed nodded vigorously as his boss spoke. And then, with a bodyguard trailing him, Ahmed made his way towards the control room behind the big screen, a black CD case ensconced in his right hand.

TWENTY-THREE

The contest-II

MARCH 2014

RAVI SHASTRI APPEARED ON the big screen, surrounded by scores of grim-looking youngsters.

'Well, uh, ladies and gentlemen,' he drawled. 'That break flew like a tracer bullet, and we are ready for the next round. Just get the feeling here . . .'

Before he could complete, chants of '*Shastri hai hai, Shastri hai hai*' drowned every other noise in the stadium and rang aloud for a full minute until the announcer requested the crowd to calm down so that he could introduce the next round.

'Thanks,' he said after the crowd obliged. 'The largest democracy in the world deserves a leader with a terrific personality. The second round has been designed with this very intention. Each candidate gets five minutes to showcase his personality in whatever manner he deems appropriate. We will start with Rahul. Best of luck!'

The floodlights dimmed, and a hush of expectation descended on the stadium. All eyes turned to the stage, as a bright spotlight came on, illuminating the young man in sparkling white kurta–pyjamas standing right in the middle. For a brief moment, Rahul looked a trifle overwhelmed. His gaze wandered as he overcame his stage fright. Then, as if gathering himself, he took a deep breath and grew very still. Then, as the cameras zoomed in on him, he slowly unleashed his trademark smile. The stadium sighed. So serene was his smile, and so dainty were his dimples that large swathes of women in the stadium staring up at the big screen promptly swooned.

'What the hell is happening?' cried Rajnath Singh in the BJP dugout. 'What is he doing?'

'He just showed everyone the strongest aspect of his personality,' said Jaitley, shrugging. 'Let's see what else he demonstrates.'

Rahul then walked off the stage and returned to the Congress dugout where he was welcomed with great enthusiasm. Sachin Pilot and Jyotiraditya Scindia lifted Rahul on their shoulders and did a mini victory lap around their dugout.

'Um, I guess he's done,' said Jaitley. 'Modibhai, you are up.'

Modi entered the stage in traditional Gujarati gear—a colourful ghagra, kafni pyjamas, a pagdi on the head, badhini dupatta and two garba sticks—dancing to the beats of Falguni

Pathak's '*Aaj garba ma dhoom machi jay*'. The audience watched enthralled for a few seconds before clapping along with the beats as Modi danced in perfect circles on the stage, while the BJP leaders head-banged in their dugout.

Just when the spectator enthusiasm seemed to be peaking, Modi slipped behind a screen, and the very next second emerged in a dark, perfectly cut suit. The stadium oohed and aahed. The music changed. Modi slowly paced the stage, lip-syncing to the baritone of Amrish Puri's '*Yeh mera India*' from *Pardes*.

London dekha, Paris dekha, aur dekha Japan
Michael dekha, Elvis dekha, sab dekha meri jaan
Saare jag me kahee nahi hain doosra Hindustan, doosra
Hindustan, doosra Hindustaaaan!

Modi's eyes welled up, as he sang the next line with all his heart.

Yeh duniya ek dulhan, dulhan ke mathe ki bindiya, yeh
mera India, I love my India

The crowd was on its feet, moved by the emotional display of patriotism, and gently swayed, as Modi lip-synced his heart out. Then abruptly, the onstage lights went off.

Somewhere a lion roared, and the lights slowly came on, to reveal a hundred 3D apparitions of Modi in bright-white attire and saffron headgear on stage. The 3D avatars stood in two rows on either side of a narrow channel in the middle. The spectators watched in fascination as the beats of the title song of Rohit Shetty's *Singham* began and the digital Modis began to rhythmically pound the large drums at their feet.

At the far end of the channel stood the flesh and blood Modi, dressed in black and sporting Aviator shades. He waited for the first round of the beats to set the mood, and then strode purposefully through the channel.

Mann bhanwar uthe, tan sihar uthe, jab khabar uthe, ke aave . . . Singham!

Modi swaggered to the front of the stage, paused for a second, and abruptly assumed the famous Singham crouch of Ajay Devgn, left hand held in front, parallel to the ground, right hand raised overhead, five fingers of both hands spread out to resemble a claw.

Na agar chale, na magar chale, bas kehar chale, jab aave . . . Singham!

The next second, the 100 3D Modis behind him spread out in a grid formation and assumed the same crouch pose of the flesh and blood Modi. Then to the resonating beats of the drums, the 101 Modis curled and uncurled their talons, driving the saffron crowd into a frenzy.

The performance ended with Modi going on all fours and tossing his head to let out a massive roar that reverberated within a five-kilometre radius around the stadium.

* * *

'Well . . . that was some display of aggression by Modi there,' said Rajdeep Sardesai, when the camera cut back to the CNN-IBN newsroom. 'Ram, do you think maybe that was not the right note to hit today?'

'Definitely, Rajdeep,' said N. Ram, editor of *The Hindu*. 'For all those minorities watching today trying hard to find a reason to forgive him for 2002, a lion crouch is *not* the right way to go.'

'How sweet was Rahul's smile though!' said Sagarika Ghose, flushed. 'Perhaps what a diverse country like India needs is not the parochial aggression of a Modi, but the innocent charm of a Rahul Gandhi!'

The camera cut to the cow corner region of the Kotla, to reveal a rather close-up view of Shastri. The view was so close that Shastri's shades and moustache covered nearly the entire screen.

'Mmmm,' he said. The camera then slowly zoomed out to reveal a gagged Shastri bound to a chair, struggling against his binds. A moment later, the camera swivelled to the left to reveal a bunch of youngsters jostling with each other to get within the camera's viewfinder.

'This is just what the doctor ordered!' they shouted in unison, before the feed disconnected, and IBN's in-studio camera took over.

'Er . . . looks like we have lost Shastri because of a technical issue,' said Sardesai. 'We'll take you back to live action now where the next round is about to begin.'

* * *

'The mark of a true leader in a democracy is his ability to connect with his electorate,' said the announcer. 'And in this round, we'll test this very attribute in the two PM candidates. May the best man win!'

The crowd cheered lustily, but the noise was the greatest in the saffron area of the stadium. The BJP leaders high-fived each other, squared their shoulders and turned up their collars. They knew that this was one area where Rahul couldn't dream of beating Modi, if their respective speeches in the lead-up to the contest were anything to go by. From across the field, the Congress leaders watched the bravura of the BJP leaders with amused expressions.

It was Modi's turn to go in first. He rose to his feet, smoothed his kurta, walked to the mike, and swept the crowd with a glance in his inimitable style.

'*Har taraf mundi hi mundi, mundi hi mundi,*' he exclaimed. '*Itni dhoop mein aap aaye, aapke pyaar ko mera salaam!*'

The crowd roared its approval. Modi took a sip of water.

'*Bhaiyon aur behnon,*' he bellowed. For the next three minutes, he treated the 80,000-strong crowd to a power-packed speech replete with jokes on Shahzada, the 'mute' Manmohan Singh, Robert Vadra, and various scams of the UPA government.

By the tenth second, the saffron section of the crowd had begun chanting 'Modi, Modi'. By the second minute, a substantial section of the AAP crowd had joined in, prompting Yogendra Yadav, Kumar Vishwas and other AAP leaders to scramble to the cheering members and tell them that everything was not hunky-dory in Gujarat and that it was important to stay equidistant from the massively corrupt BJP and the Congress. By the third minute, a section of the Congress crowd and a couple of leaders in the Congress dugout too had joined in the irresistible chant. The chants continued for an entire minute after Modi finished, and stood facing the Congress dugout with a triumphant smile and a raised fist, while Black Cats hauled the two overenthusiastic

Congress leaders who had unwittingly joined the Modi chant.

When the chants eventually died down, Modi withdrew to his dugout, and Rahul walked towards the stage, fumbling with a sheaf of papers. As if on cue, spectators across the stadium left their seats and made a beeline for the vending stalls and the restrooms. A contingent of Congress leaders led by Sheila Dixit got into the act and entreated the people to return to their seats and hear out Rahul Gandhi.

Rahul rolled up his sleeves and began. 'Ladies and gentlemen, let me begin by telling you that it is an honour to speak at the Wankhede stadium.'

The BJP dugout erupted in laughter, as did a section of the saffron crowd.

'*Abe dhakkan*, this is Feroz Shah Kotla!' yelled Rajnath Singh, drawing another round of laughs from his colleagues.

'In 1947, India was liberated not by violence, but by unleashing the voice of our people,' Rahul rambled on. 'Everyone told us it cannot be done and that if you want to get rid of the British, you have to use violence, but the Congress party said no, we are not going to use violence . . .'

Rajnath yawned. '*Paka raha hai, yaar*. Let me take a leak,' he said, and rose from his seat. Suddenly he froze mid-step and perked his ears. A low rumble seemed to be coursing through the stadium.

'Wait, is that . . .'

The rumble grew louder and was now unmistakably clear. 'Rahul! Rahul! Rahul!' the crowd chanted.

Rajnath's eyes nearly popped out of their sockets. Slack-jawed, he turned to Arun Jaitley who looked as shocked as him. A sudden hush descended over the BJP dugout. Even

Nitin Gadkari choked on his samosa. Instinctively, they turned towards their Congress counterparts, and found them pointing and laughing at them. Struggling to come to terms with what was happening, the leaders looked helplessly at each other, until a party worker pointed at the big screen, and screeched, 'Look there!'

A smiling visage of Rahul Dravid was on display on the big screen. Then the screen cleared, and a clip of Dravid in Test whites came on. As the BJP leaders watched in utter stupefaction, Dravid executed a perfect front foot defence. The crowd roared. 'Rahul! Rahul! Rahul!' they cried. The screen cleared once again, and a montage of Rahul playing picture-perfect on drives and cracking square cuts, from the legendary Kolkata Test in the 2001 India versus Australia series, came on. After each shot, the crowd went wild. The Rahul chants were now as loud as the Modi chants earlier.

'Paid big-screen operator!' screamed someone in the saffron crowd.

'Sickular big-screen operator!' screamed another, shaking his fist in the direction of the Congress dugout.

Modi moved. He beckoned Ravi Shankar Prasad, and whispered something in his ear. The next moment, Prasad scurried over to a group of young party workers seated in the first row of the stands right behind the dugout. The young men surrounded Prasad in a quick huddle, then sprung into action.

Moments later, four workers were jogging around the ground, carrying a large banner of Sachin Tendulkar facing the spectators. And just like that, the 'Rahul! Rahul!' chants gave way to the familiar 'Sachinnnnnnn! Sachin! Tap tap tap!'

The BJP dugout breathed a sigh of relief, and the round drew to a close.

* * *

'Well, that was quite a reception from the crowd for Modi. Is the Congress nervous, Mr Jha?' said Arnab Goswami in the Times Now newsroom.

'Not at all, Arnab,' said Sanjay Jha. 'The noise is made by a few RSS fundamentalists paid by Modi to shout his name in every gathering. And in any case, none of those are gonna translate into votes.'

'I see. What are your thoughts on Rahul's performance in this round?'

'Rahul's performance was mind-blowing, and the crowd's love for him is evident. He only had to stand and people went crazy screaming his name. I'm sure you all heard it. It's a clear indication that the Congress under the leadership of Rahul Gandhi is going to ride back to power.'

'But those chants were for Rahul Dravid, Mr Sanjay Jha!' exclaimed Arnab, clearly annoyed.

'Let's not get lost in the details, Arnab.'

Arnab stared angrily at the grinning Jha for a moment, and said, 'On that note, ladies and gentlemen, let's go back to the Kotla for the final round.'

* * *

The announcer cleared his throat and readied himself for the last announcement of the day. 'Ladies and gentlemen, we are down to the final round,' he said. 'Each candidate will make a two-minute video or a PowerPoint presentation, and tell the nation's electorate why they should vote for them. It's Rahul's turn to go first.'

A chill ran down Sonia Gandhi's spine. The crowd's roar suddenly seemed distant. It was time. The pivotal moment was upon her. With cold hands, she pulled out her phone. 'In ten seconds,' she typed out a text message to Ahmed, and clicked 'send'. Now there was nothing else to do but watch. And pray.

In ten seconds, the political situation will turn on its head. Modi's prime ministerial ambitions will be delivered a death blow, and BJP's campaign will get derailed. Such would be the impact that even Modi's core base would turn against him, devastated by what was about to be revealed. Rahul would then descend on them like an angel, his innocence and charm a balm to their scarred souls, and they would embrace him with open arms, weeping with relief and gratitude.

The big screen came alive, but Sonia wasn't looking at it. Instead, she stood facing the stands, her face flushed with nervous excitement, eyes keenly watching the reactions of the crowd.

'Three . . . two . . . one . . .' she counted under her breath, her smile growing wider by the second. 'And now!'

All at once, with perfect coordination, the mouths of thousands of spectators in her field of sight dropped open. Sonia squealed with glee. A moment later, the spectators gasped in unison, their hands flying to their mouths. And another moment later, 80,000 people, in one voice, exclaimed, 'Whoa!'

Sonia was beside herself with ecstasy. Clapping her hands

like a schoolgirl, she did a little jig, laughing all the while. She imagined the expressions on a billion Indians across the country, and trembled with exhilaration. When she could no longer restrain her joy, she looked here and there, for someone to share her jubilation with, and spotted her party colleagues standing a few feet away. Just as she opened her mouth to call out to them, she realized something was amiss. She frowned as they stood transfixed to the spot, their faces deathly pale, bulging eyes looking upwards. Confused, she followed their line of sight all the way to the big screen.

And then, Sonia Gandhi screamed.

TWENTY-FOUR

The contest-III

MARCH 2014

THE AIR IN THE Feroz Shah Kotla stadium pulsated with the haunting score from Bobby Deol's *Gupt*. A billion Indians watched in horror, as the big screen displayed one after another, in bright-red colour and 72-pt font size, the A to Z of Congress scams, along with the estimated losses to the nation's coffers.

C for Coal scam. Losses: 1,86,000 crore (1.86% of GDP)
D for . . .

Like a bullet out of a gun, Sonia Gandhi burst through the cluster of paralysed Congress leaders, and tore towards the big screen's control room. The door to the control room was latched, but Sonia didn't slow down. Instead, she accelerated and hurled herself shoulder-first into the door and crashed it open.

At her feet lay an unconscious bodyguard. At the far end of the room, next to the projection equipment, a semi-conscious Ahmed Patel sat on the floor propped against the wall, hands and legs bound. In an instant, Sonia crossed the room, ripped the projector's power plug from the socket, and undid the ropes that bound Ahmed.

'What happened, Ahmed?' said Sonia, shaking Ahmed by his shoulders. 'Tell me, what happened?'

Ahmed muttered incoherently and lifted a weak arm towards the table.

'What? What is it?' asked Sonia desperately.

'C . . . C . . . CD,' stammered Ahmed.

Sonia slowly rose to her feet. With trembling hands and an overwhelming sense of dread, she reached for the CD case and prised it open. A white card with a fluorescent V sat in place of the CD.

* * *

Outside the control room, pandemonium broke loose. The moment the big screen went dark, BJP leaders invaded the stage and began to reel off details about the rest of the UPA scams at the top of their voices in full view of the cameras, even as the angry crowd egged them on in a deafening expression of anti-incumbency. Infuriated by this brazen attack, the Congress leaders woke from their stupor, climbed on to the stage and rushed towards their political opponents, leading to a free-for-all, no-holds-barred fight, relayed live.

In the stands, the BJP and the Congress supporters rushed towards each other, hooting and screaming and brandishing their flags and banners like swords, and clashed viciously in the area behind the stage. Within seconds, the anarchy spread to the rest of the stadium, and soon, BSP supporters were scuffling with SP supporters, DMK supporters were wrestling with AIADMK supporters, and the comrades were exchanging blows with Mamata's men. Panic-stricken, the people ran helter-skelter, and the field was soon overrun by the crowd. To add to the chaos, a bunch of policemen went on the rampage, randomly lathi-charging whoever came across their path. The AAP supporters, however, stayed relatively unmoved from their positions, and participated in their own inimitable way by raising slogans against everyone else and calling upon the people of this country to throw such vile, corrupt folks out of the stadium, until a bunch of lathi-charging policemen descended upon them and sent them scampering in all directions.

The bedlam had spread to the TV studios as well. In the CNN-IBN studio, a debate on Modi had degenerated into a stationery-flinging competition between Rajdeep Sardesai, historian Ramachandra Guha, *The Hindu* editor N. Ram, and journalists Swapan Dasgupta and Siddharth Varadarajan. Books, pens and paper clips flew unchecked, while Sagarika Ghose sat in the middle calmly putting on a fresh coat of bright-green lipstick, oblivious to the confusion around her. In the Headlines Today studio, actor Kirron Kher and journalists Vir Sanghvi and Ashish Khetan had climbed on the desk and were hollering at each other, while Rahul Kanwal hid under the desk, whimpering. On *Newshour* in the Times Now studio, Arnab had pinned down two panellists on the floor with a perfect split, and held Sanjay Jha by the scruff of his neck with one hand while pounding him with the other.

* * *

Back in Kotla, behind the big screen, beside a distraught Sonia Gandhi, the Commissioner of Delhi Police took charge. The top cop clenched his jaw, set his mouth in a tight line and extended an open hand towards his subordinates. A constable dutifully placed a lathi in it.

'Not this, you idiot!' he barked. 'Binoculars!'

The constable hastily replaced it with a pair of binoculars. The commissioner grabbed them and slowly scanned the stands from left to right.

'There!' he exclaimed, pointing towards the far right, where a diminutive but distinctive figure in a black suit scrambled up the steps, his cape swishing behind him. 'After him!'

Six policemen and the commissioner took off in pursuit of V-man.

By the time the policemen reached the exit, V-man was already scampering through the parking lot. The policemen reached the parking lot just in time to see V-man jump into his V-mobile, and scream away.

* * *

'AAAAH!' screamed Kapil Sibal, as Arun Jaitley dragged him across the stage by his white hair, with Jairam Ramesh trying in vain to pull his arm off Sibal. A few feet away,

Shushilkumar Shinde and Rajnath Singh were headbutting each other in turns, yelping every time they made contact. Digvijaya Singh darted here and there, screeching, 'Help! RSS is after me!' as Ravi Shankar Prasad chased him all over the stage, but couldn't quite get hold of him.

In another corner of the stage, the youth icons of the two camps, Sachin Pilot and Jyotiraditya Scindia from the Congress and Anurag Thakur from the BJP, were engaged in their own little duel, and by the looks of it, Anurag wasn't having it so good. Elsewhere, Shakeel Ahmed and Shanawaz Hussain were locked in a stalemate, careening along the edge of the stage, hands pulling on each other's ears.

In the front part of the stage, the two PM hopefuls, Modi and Rahul, circled each other, feigning punches every now and then, while hurling insults at each other non-stop.

'Pappu!'

'Feku!'

'Shahzada!'

'Saheb!'

'Mama's boy!'

'Fascist!'

'Er . . . Pappu!'

'Ha! You said that already!'

But neither landed a blow on the other.

At the epicentre of the battle, scattering his enemies like they were dust, Nitin Gadkari was on a rampage. Roaring like the Hulk, Gadkari grabbed Manish Tewari's legs, lifted him clean in the air, and smashed him repeatedly to the ground. 'Puny dog,' he growled, and walked away, as Tewari lay sprawled on the floor, groaning.

Just when it seemed that there was no end in sight to the brawl, the leaders heard the distant whir of a chopper over the din in the stadium.

* * *

The V-mobile was no Batmobile. It scooted at around 70 km/hour and looked more like a modified version of a Tata Nano painted black. The police van, however, couldn't beat even that. Rattling along pathetically, the van barely managed to stay within sighting distance of the V-mobile.

'He's heading towards India Gate! Take a short cut! Cut into Tilak Marg!' screamed the commissioner.

The quick-thinking commissioner had noticed that V-man was taking a roundabout route to India Gate, and hoped to intercept him before that. But it turned out that V-man knew the traffic situation far better than his chasers. Five minutes into Tilak Marg, the police van found its route blocked by a neat arrangement of police barricades. A sign on one of the barricades read, 'True we slow you down, but we try not to let criminals slip by.'

'Fucking Delhi Police!' the commissioner screamed with feeling.

By the time they got to India Gate, V-man seemed to have pulled well ahead of them. If it wasn't for the alert driver who spotted the V-mobile turning into Raj Path in the distance, the chase might well have been over. Cursing their quarry in chaste Haryanvi, the never-say-die policemen sped after the fleeing vehicle.

To their consternation, the V-mobile suddenly veered off

the road, on to the bordering lawns, towards a clump of trees. The policemen gasped as the V-mobile gathered pace instead of slowing down, and headed straight for a collision with a tree trunk. Milliseconds before the inevitable collision, a black shadow flew out of the car door, rolled with the momentum, and sprung to its feet. V-man cast a quick look backwards at his pursuers, and then took off through the trees, his cape fluttering behind him.

The driver stopped the van, and the policemen poured out of the doors to chase after the caped fugitive. V-man ran through the trees, on to the lawns and then across the road, circling around South Block. For the first ten minutes the policemen pursued valiantly. And then, one by one, in the descending order of the size of their paunches, they dropped out of the chase, each going down on his haunches on the soft grass, panting with exhaustion. Fifteen minutes later, only one policeman was left in the race, a tall and well-built Haryanvi Jat who had joined the police force a month earlier.

* * *

The stadium came to a standstill as the chopper came into view and hovered just over the stadium. Everyone, politicians, citizens, policemen, stopped what they were doing and stood gawking in awe. The crowd went completely silent and the only sound in the stadium was the deafening roar of the chopper, as it descended to the middle of the field and gently landed on the Kotla pitch.

Then the chopper's doors flew open, and out stepped a portly man dressed in a sharp suit. In a heartbeat, all those on stage, including Modi and Rahul, went down on their knees. A few prostrated themselves full length on the floor. Sonia sneaked in from a side of the stage and kneeled as well. The policemen in the stadium clicked their heels together and saluted smartly.

The man took off his shades and surveyed the group on stage with a smile.

'Hello, boys and girls!' said The Great Indian Business Mogul cheerfully.

* * *

Ombir Jat sprinted after the fleeing figure, leaping over the bushes with the athleticism of a steeplechaser. Slowly, he began to close the gap between him and his quarry. When he got within a few feet of V-man, Ombir summoned every bit of his strength and leapt with outstretched hands towards V-man in an attempt to tackle him down to the ground. He felt his fingers touch something, and he grabbed at it with his powerful hands. At the very last instant, V-man twisted sideways, dodged the tackle, and skipped away into the darkness, while Ombir crashed to the ground with a thud.

The Haryanvi Jat immediately bounced back to his feet to resume the chase, but V-man had vanished. For a while he stood there uncertainly, sweat trickling down the side of his face, staring at the torn piece of black fabric in his hands. Then he began to look around for signs of the runaway vigilante. Five minutes later, he spotted the cleverly camouflaged hole leading to what seemed like an underground tunnel. He took a deep breath, steeled himself and stepped into the tunnel.

The tunnel was wet, dark and teeming with creepy animal species. He crept in the darkness using the dim light of his mobile phone, dodging the bats overhead and avoiding slippery spots on the ground. He could sense that he was going in deeper into the ground, but he marched forward without a pause. After he had walked for fifteen minutes, the tunnel began to widen, and then without warning, abruptly opened into a massive, cavernous space.

Ombir stepped into the clearing, and gasped. For in front of him, right in the middle of the underground cave, stood the HAL Tejas in all its glory, bathed in the moonlight emanating from somewhere far above. The supersonic light combat aircraft was painted in jet black. Awestruck, Ombir walked around the plane, feeling the all-black exterior of the fuselage, wondering how the hell India's most advanced indigenous fighter aircraft had made its way to this place when it hasn't been commissioned yet. The prominent V in fluorescent yellow painted on the nose of the aircraft brought him out of his reverie, and Ombir broke away from the aircraft to scan every inch of the space for an exit. Moments later, he located the elevator in a corner of the cave.

Heart pounding in his chest, he walked in, pulled the elevator's door shut, and pressed G. The elevator came alive and zoomed upwards, and it was an entire minute before it came to a halt. When the doors opened, an opulent corridor bathed in soft yellow light greeted him. A velvety red carpet covered the floor. Gorgeous lamps and beautiful paintings dotted the walls. Intricate artwork adorned the curved ceiling. Massive glass chandeliers tinkled overhead. He looked around in fascination, and trod ahead, watchfully at first, then more freely, curiosity winning over caution.

He wandered through a few rooms, each larger and posher than the other, until he came to what seemed like a banquet hall. Tables were placed adjoining a wall, with bowls of fruits and refreshments neatly arranged on them. Large portraits of several old men adorned the other side of the wall. He recognized some of them as he slowly walked along the wall: Rajendra Prasad, Shankar Dayal Sharma and A.P.J. Abdul Kalam. Ombir plodded to a halt near the other end of the room and stood scratching his head in front of a portrait of Pratibha Patil. The place seemed empty, and there was no immediate threat of discovery, but he was still nowhere close to figuring out where he was.

Then the answer hit him, and his eyes widened.

'*Bhains ki aankh!*' he whistled.

* * *

'Hello, sir!' said the Congress and the BJP leaders in unison.

'Having fun, eh?' The Great Indian Business Mogul grinned.

The leaders stole guilty glances at each other, and bowed their heads in embarrassment.

'That's all right,' he said generously. 'I know you guys gotta play every now and then. I understand your Feku–Pappu fights, and occasionally even enjoy them.'

The leaders beamed.

'But it's now time to put aside differences and present a united front. So, are you guys ready?'

'Yes, sir!' chimed the leaders.

'Good. Now, everyone throw your fists up and shout a slogan. *Sab log dono mutthi upar kar zor se bolo . . .*'

An incoherent cacophony ensued as the BJP responded with 'Vande Mataram' and the Congress with 'Jai Hind'.

'Let's try that again,' he said patiently. *'Sab log dono mutthi upar kar zor se bolo . . .'*

Once again the group struck a discordant note. The Great Indian Business Mogul bit his lip and stood looking at the leaders with hands on hips. The leaders looked a little ashamed.

'Okay, let's try something else,' he said, and exclaimed, *'sab log dono mutthi upar kar zor se bolo . . .* Corporate!'

This time the entire group responded in one voice: 'India!'

'Corporate!'

'India!'

'Corporate! Corporate! Corporate!'

'India! India! India!'

And with that awe-inspiring display of unity and subservience, the election campaign for the 2014 General Elections came to a close.

TWENTY-FIVE

India votes

APRIL 2014

WITH THE CAMPAIGN PHASE ending, an eerie, becalming silence descended on the nation. Suddenly the loudspeakers were unplugged and the nozzle of shrill rhetoric turned off. Some leaders even voiced fears that the unnerving silence would remind voters of Dr Manmohan Singh, but the Election Commission did well to defenestrate such requests. Even newspapers like the *Times of India*, the nursery of plants lovingly nurtured by the likes of Ahmed Patel and many others, appeared denuded, having to make do with sex surveys and other anodyne themes.

The world paused and gasped as the gigantic exercise of recording the wishes of one-fifth of humanity, in all the splendour of its ethnic and socio-economic diversity, got under way: From the lush-green hills of Kohima to the arid sand dunes of the Kutch, from the palm-frond-draped seashores of Kanyakumari to the rarefied vale of Kashmir, Indians partook in the dance of democracy.

And what a dance it was! People from all walks of life—industrialists, middle-class professionals, labourers, celebrities, and a sizeable number of Bangladeshis—waited patiently in serpentine queues. For that one moment, they were all only Indians, all other identities secondary. Of course, it wasn't completely smooth sailing: malfunctioning EVMs, names missing from the voters' list, people going to the wrong booth, Aishwarya Rai's name popping up in the voters' list in a remote corner of Chhattisgarh . . . There were even reports of EVM capturing from a few polling stations, but after the abductors realized that EVMs couldn't be stuffed, they were returned intact to the election officials.

And no such generic description of an Indian election is complete unless a mention is made of the proverbial geriatric, who, despite her infirmities—the blinding cataract, the poor hearing, the arthritic knees, the hunchback—hobbled her way into the voting section, and pressed the button of her choice.

And finally, after two months spread across multiple phases, the exercise came to an end, the votes tallied and the results compiled within a matter of hours. A feckless official printed out the final count of party-wise seats in the sixteenth Lok Sabha, and walked into the PM's Office, where Dr Singh, governing in caretaker capacity, was hunched in his swivel chair, poring over statistics and charts.

Dr Singh glanced at the sheet, looked up, and said, '*Theek hai.*'

POST-MATCH PRESENTATION

'Ladies and gentlemen, we've had a wonderful game of cricket. 100 overs have been bowled, over 600 runs have been scored, and at the end of the day, cricket is the winner.'

—Ravi Shastri

TWENTY-SIX

Behind V-man's mask

BANERJEE BALANCED THE TRAY on his left hand and pushed aside the curtains with his right, letting bright sunlight into the master bedroom, right on to the figure curled on the double bed.

The thirteenth President of India groaned and pulled the sheets higher over his bare torso. Banerjee placed a tall glass of roshogullas, and a newspaper on the bedside table.

'V-man made the front page, but the President of India got pushed to the eighth page,' he said.

Pranab Mukherjee threw aside the sheets and reached for the newspaper. He read the front page with interest, then stood up, and gulped down the contents of the glass in one breath.

Banerjee studied the bruises and scratches on Pranab's

257

torso. Pointing to the large purple bruise on his shoulder, he said, 'Did you get punched by the Hulk?'

'It was a Jat,' replied Pranab.

'Huh?'

'A big Jat.'

'If these are the first of many injuries to come, then it would be wise to find a suitable excuse,' said Banerjee. 'Strange injuries and a non-existent public life, these things raise the question as to what exactly does the President do.'

* * *

It had been twenty-nine years since that fateful day, but not a day went by without him thinking about it. They were flying back to Delhi from West Bengal. It was the day Indira Gandhi had been tragically assassinated. Seated to his left, Rajiv Gandhi seemed deep in thought. Suddenly, Rajiv turned to him and asked, 'Who do you think should be her successor?' Without a moment's thought, Pranab replied, 'The seniormost minister, of course.'

That tactless answer set back his political career by two decades. Rajiv Gandhi assumed the prime minister's mantle and promptly relegated him to the sidelines. Pranab floated in the wilderness, even attempting to strike it on his own for a brief period, but without any success. He returned to the party fold only in 1991 after Rajiv's assassination, when P.V. Narasimha Rao became the prime minister. But it was never the same again. Rajiv's widow, Sonia Gandhi, barely concealed her dislike for him, and gave ample proof of her distrust when she chose Dr Manmohan Singh over him for the prime ministerial post in 2004. Pranab watched in frustration, as the man he had appointed the RBI governor in his capacity as the finance minister way back in 1982 bossed over him for two long terms.

In 2012, the family decided to 'reward' him by backing him for the post of the President of the country. His family and friends were thrilled. His colleagues congratulated him for the honour. Everyone was happy for him. But only he understood the truth. Sonia had completed what Rajiv had started, and slammed the final nail in his career's coffin. In a heartbeat, he had been removed from the intense drama of political action, the visceral thrill of backroom manoeuvring, and transported to a world of opulence, dignity and, utter, mind-numbing boredom.

He moved into the palatial Rashtrapati Bhavan, and spent the first week restocking it with the items missing from his predecessor's term. When he finally felt at home, he dressed in his finest safari suit, settled in his posh office room, and waited for Bills to approve. None came his way. Day after day after day, the Parliament kept getting adjourned on some pretext or the other, leaving a bewildered Pranab twiddling his thumbs on the oak desk.

He flitted from his desk to the library to the TV to his desk again, watching his party sleepwalk to its grave with one ham-handed move after another. From time to time, his anger at the family would return, leaving him shaking with rage. To keep himself distracted, he began exploring the 300-plus rooms of the mansion, five to ten rooms a day.

Then one day, when he was meandering in the south-east section of the mansion, examining a hitherto unexplored room, the floorboards beneath him suddenly gave away. Pranab crashed through the floor, slid uncontrollably through a slippery hole, and landed with a thud in a dark, damp place. He picked himself up, dusted his suit, and looked around at the massive underground space with growing fascination.

Somewhere inside him, a light switched on. Contours of a plan began to take shape in his head.

* * *

In the sprawling room one level below the Rashtrapati Bhavan, Pranab sat dressed in V-man's costume sans the mask, frowning at an array of television screens in front of him.

'The disc has been couriered, sir,' said Banerjee, approaching Pranab from behind.

The screens flashed reports of a new scam and the name of the minister involved in it.

'He was thought to be clean,' continued Banerjee. 'His great-grandfather made his fortune pre-Independence, and his family has been rich ever since. His family owns a number of companies, all number one or two in their respective sectors. He enjoys a terrific rapport with the people in his constituency, and has never lost an election,' Banerjee waved a hand towards the screens. 'There seems to be no motivation for this.'

Pranab frowned. 'Corruption isn't complicated, Banerjee. We just have to figure out what he's after.'

'Perhaps this is a corrupt politician you don't fully understand, Pranabda.'

Pranab raised an eyebrow. 'Why is he looting the

exchequer then?'

'Because he thinks it is good fun. Because some men aren't looking for anything logical, like money or funds for elections or staying power . . . some men just want the nation to burn.'

Pranab looked at Banerjee as he considered this, when the doorbell rang.

'Let me get that,' said Banerjee.

* * *

Banerjee walked down the stairs to the waiting room, eyeing the well-built youth sitting on the couch with his back to him.

'Yes,' he said, seating himself opposite the visitor. 'How may I help you?'

'I was hoping to see the President,' the visitor said.

'I am the President's assistant. You can tell me your business,' said Banerjee with a pleasant smile.

Ombir Jat hesitated.

After he returned home from his fruitless chase on the day of the contest, with nothing to show except for the piece of torn fabric from V-man's costume, Ombir contemplated the turn of events over dinner. It dawned on him that he was in possession of a staggering secret. It didn't take him long to realize that if he used this information smartly, he may not have to work for the rest of his life. In one shot, he could sidestep the slow and excruciating way to prosperity through petty corruption and paltry commissions. He pondered over it for several days. Then one evening, he put on his best suit, drove to Rashtrapati Bhavan, and asked to see the President.

'Uh, I was outside Rashtrapati Bhavan a few days back,

chasing a wanted fugitive, and I found something rather curious,' Ombir said, and pulled out the piece of black fabric from V-man's suit.

The smile vanished from Banerjee's face. Ombir watched him carefully, enjoying his reaction.

'Don't tell me you don't recognize what this is, and who this belongs to,' he said.

Ombir smirked, letting it sink in for a few seconds. Then he folded his arms, cocked his head, and said, 'I want 10 crore rupees in cash every year, for the rest of the President's term.'

Banerjee regarded the officer, suddenly amused. After a moment, he leaned forward.

'Let me get this straight. You think that the President of India, the Supreme Commander of the armed forces, is secretly a vigilante who spends his nights collecting evidence against corrupt politicians and officials, and your plan is to *blackmail* this person?' he smirked.

With Banerjee's every word, Ombir's arrogant smile grew smaller and smaller until it disappeared completely. Instead a look of fear and confusion appeared on his face. Suddenly this didn't seem like a good idea at all. He opened and closed his mouth like a goldfish, fumbling for words. Banerjee smiled.

'Good luck!' he said, and calmly walked away. Ombir sat in the hall for a few moments, then slowly rose to his feet and quietly headed towards the door.

* * *

Standing atop the dome of Rashtrapati Bhavan, Pranab Mukherjee watched the figure down below walk away from the mansion. He then looked up and sniffed. The air was polluted. The sky was barely visible. It was just another Delhi day. He smiled. It was a good day for fighting corruption.

And then, the hero India deserves, and also the one it needs, pulled his mask on, and leapt off the building.

TWENTY-SEVEN

The Hindu Nationalist's secret

'YOUR VEHICLE IS READY, SIR.'

Narendra Modi nodded. His man Friday picked up the suitcases near the door, and withdrew silently. Modi's eyes slowly swept across the room that for the last twelve years had been his home, his office, his temple.

He walked around the room one last time, fingers trailing behind him, caressing the desk he'd signed countless papers on, the chairs that had seated thousands of officials, leaders and ordinary men and women, and the file cabinet that had held hundreds of groundbreaking ideas for his state's development.

He turned his gaze to the map of Akhand Bharat plastered on the wall. Standard RSS issue: a map of undivided British India encompassing India, Pakistan, Bangladesh and Burma, with a portrait of Durga sitting atop a lion in the centre. Parts of Tibet, Afghanistan and swathes of Central Asia were also coloured in a lighter shade of saffron. Some RSS ideologues wanted to show portions of Siberia and up to the Arctic Circle as well to be part of Akhand Bharat, but the RSS chief had decided for now to fix the Hindu Rashtra's northern-most frontier at the Uzbekistan–Kazakhstan border.

Modi began to trace a line from Himachal Pradesh into the plains of the Punjab. It was the course of the Ravi river. And when his finger reached the international border where the Ravi meandered into the Pakistani side, he winced. All the fast bowlers, all the best ghazal singers were on the other side of the Radcliffe Line. The best Urdu mushairas were held in Lahore. They had cricket legend Imran Khan, while India had to make do with Bollywood actor Imran Khan. Why did it have to be like this?

He turned his teary eyes towards the large Sardar Patel portrait on the wall facing his desk. For several moments, Modi stood gazing at the portrait, at his idol, at the legend whose shoes he hoped to step into.

Or at least that's what people thought.

With a trembling hand, Modi reached out to touch the portrait. His finger touched a corner of the portrait, at which a tiny square sank an inch into the frame and, with a slow whir, the portrait began to rotate around a vertical axis.

When the frame had turned a full 180 degrees, in Sardar Patel's place, the stern miens of Muhammad Ali Jinnah and Netaji Subhas Chandra Bose beheld the cowering form of the Gujarat CM.

Both these doyens from the pre-Independence days held a deep and abiding fascination for Modi. Both rank outsiders in India's political system had begun their political journeys as Congressmen, rising through sheer merit. Both came to resent Gandhi's sway over India's grand old party, and parted ways to pursue radically different objectives with momentous consequences for the history and geography of the subcontinent.

History may not have been Modi's strong suit, but by reading up on Jinnah and Bose he had developed a highly nuanced, layered understanding of the politics of events leading to the Partition and independence. A knowledge that would come in handy when he co-authored *Jinnah: India, Partition, Independence* with veteran BJP leader Jaswant Singh, a gushing tribute to his idol. Of course, he had to also ban his own book in his capacity as the chief minister of Gujarat.

Jinnah, a stickler for constitutional propriety, his urbanity manifest in his smartly starched Savile Row suits, and in the early half of his career, a staunch secular–liberal who Gopal Krishna Gokhale had described as the 'ambassador of Hindu–Muslim' unity; Bose, who earnestly believed that India had to win her freedom on her terms, and was willing to go to any lengths to pursue it. Had the Nehru–Gandhi clique supported Bose's mission in 1939 to press ahead for unconditional freedom rather than side with the British war effort, perhaps the country's unity could have been preserved? Alternatively, if the then heir apparent, Nehru, had acquiesced to Jinnah becoming prime minister, could the savage vivisection of the motherland have been avoided?

'If only either of you had become the first prime minister . . .' Modi said softly, a lump forming in his throat.

Modi had done well to keep his views to himself. It was one thing to profess admiration for Bose but to take a nuanced view of the Quaid, anathema to the RSS, would mean political suicide for any BJP leader. And yet, in a moment of candour, Modi had once publicly quoted the founder of Pakistan, just like his erstwhile mentor once had.

'You are free,' Jinnah's historic words to the Constituent Assembly of Pakistan rang loud in Modi's ears. 'You are free to go to your temples, you are free to go to your mosques or any other place of worship . . . you may belong to any religion or caste or creed—that has nothing to do with the business of the State.'

Words that Modi breathed day in and day out, but couldn't admit to anyone. For this was Modi's most well-kept secret, something his closest friends and relatives did not know about. Something he had told no one about . . .

. . . except one man.

Modi shuddered. How close had that come to destroy him! At that time it had seemed necessary. There seemed to be no way out. His elevation as the BJP's prime ministerial candidate depended on the blessings of Advani, who, for reasons best known to him, nursed a grudge against his erstwhile protégé. The other leaders had tried their level best to make the patriarch come around to the majority view, but he hadn't budged. There was, of course, no question of going against the patriarch's view—almost everyone in the BJP owed their careers to him.

'It's up to you, Modibhai. Find a common ground with Advaniji,' his party president had said.

Modi closed his fingers around the CD and slowly crushed

it. Something tightened within him.

'Now no one would know,' he thought bitterly.

All his life, people had called him names. Modi had never been affected. He hadn't cared much for the communal tag. Nor had he worried too much about the constant comparisons to Hitler. What hurt him the most, what gnawed at his very soul was the fact that he could not reveal his true feelings.

'I'm sorry, my Quaid-e-Azam,' said Modi in a hoarse whisper. Then he sang Firaaq Gorakhpuri's lines:

Muddaten guzarin, teri yaad bhi aayi na humein, aur hum bhool gaye hon tujhe, aisa bhi nahi . . .

A single tear trickled down his cheek. The man who had unflinchingly withstood a hundred trials, a million allegations, and countless attacks without as much as a grimace dabbed at his cheek and stared at his fingers in confusion. And then, like a dam breached, Modi burst out sobbing inconsolably.

TWENTY-EIGHT

The PM's mission

DR SINGH STOOD AT the entrance to the kitchen of his new apartment, and gazed at his better half, chopping away vegetables with the same élan that had endeared her to him. He strode in and hugged his unsuspecting wife from behind. Gursharan Kaur started in surprise, and then relaxed in the familiarity of his arms.

'*Bada pyaar shyaar aa raha hai aaj?*' she teased. '*Ki hoya?*'

'I'm finally free of my duties,' said Dr Singh, nuzzling against the nape of her neck. 'No more eighteen-hour days. No more prime ministership. No more work. Just you and me.'

Gursharan whirled around to look at him. In one breath, her husband had spoken more than he normally would for a month.

'Really? No more GDP projections either?' she asked warily.

'No,' averred Dr Singh.

Gursharan stared at him in wide-eyed amazement.

'So, what are we doing on the first day of my life as a free man?' asked Dr Singh with a hint of cheer on his face.

Gursharan brightened up immediately. 'First we go shopping, then we visit your doctor for your check-up—it's been due for a few years now—and then we drop in at my sister's place and spend the day there!'

The smile vanished from Dr Singh's face. 'But we went there only last week,' he remonstrated.

'So what? We'll go once again! Why do you hate my relatives so much?' she chided. '*Chalo, ab chup chaap tayyar ho jao. Maruti mein petrol bhi bharna hai.*'

A shadow passed over Dr Singh's face.

'No,' he said.

'*Hain?*'

'No,' he repeated. 'I've had enough.'

'Excuse me?'

'It is time.'

'*Ki bakwaas kar rahe ho tussi?*'

Wordlessly, Dr Singh took the chopping knife from Gursharan's hands, pulled his left sleeve up to the elbow, and even as Gursharan watched in horror, he plunged the knife's point into the inside of his forearm, dragged it in a circle around the arm, dug his fingers into the slit and stripped it off like it were a rubber glove. The flesh came off, leaving bloody bones behind. Only they were no bones, but a steel-like skeleton complete with metal fingers that Dr Singh flexed into a fist and uncurled back into a palm.

Gursharan Kaur shrieked.

The thing that the First Lady knew all these years as her husband stared at her without a semblance of emotion, as she screamed in shock and terror, stumbling backwards on to utensils and groceries, and spilling them all over the kitchen floor. The cyborg watched her without as much as a blink.

When Gursharan's screams had subsided to a whimper, the cyborg took a step towards her, and said, 'Now, listen to me very carefully.

'In the year 2050, India, as we know now, is about to come to an end, and stands on the cusp of disintegrating into several smaller nations. International observers differ as to the exact causes that led to its Balkanization, but they are unanimous in their opinion that it all started with the vote-bank politics of a few political parties in the first fifteen years of the twenty-first century. A small group of committed Indians led by a true patriot is all that stands between the forces that seek to divide the nation and a united India. Realizing that they are fighting a losing battle, the leader sends across a machine back in time, a Terminator of divisive forces that will destroy vote-bank politics before it becomes the cancer that destroys the nation. An X3490 advanced prototype, named Manmohan Singhanator, with the mission to take the prime minister's place in the year 2009 and facilitate conditions for the exit of the chief practitioner of vote-bank politics, the Congress party.'

Gursharan absorbed all this in slack-jawed disbelief, numbed as much by the horrific reality as by the mechanical manner in which the Singhanator delivered it. It was an entire minute before she recovered.

'Wh . . . what was your mission?' she stammered.

'My mission was to do nothing,' the Singhanator replied.

'Nothing . . . ?' she asked, puzzled.

'Affirmative.'

Gursharan stared at the machine feebly, as she attempted to put things together. It all made sense now. He never ate at home. She'd assumed that he had his breakfast, lunch and dinner at the PMO, but now she knew he didn't. She had put down the sudden strength and firmness in his limbs to a good diet and regular walking. Now she knew better. He had never once fallen ill in the past four years. Somehow, it had never occurred to her as strange. The one time she did find his behaviour strange was . . .

'The closet . . .' she trailed off, remembering the day Dr Singh was heckled in the Parliament. 'That day . . .'

The Singhanator's face swivelled towards her. 'The closet holds my repair and charging unit that helps my system recharge and reboot,' it deadpanned. 'In the last four years, I have had four scheduled reboots, one each on the first day of every year, and one unscheduled reboot on 30 August 2013 when my motherboard short-circuited on account of an unforeseen surge traced to a conflict between Dr Manmohan Singh's memories and the word "chor".'

Gursharan took this in slowly. Then suddenly, a look of alarm came into her eyes.

'My husband!' she cried. 'Is Mannu safe?'

'Affirmative.'

'Where is he?'

'Dr Singh was moved, in disguise, to the Washington Office of the World Bank Institute where he has been working on a Vision 2050 document for the world and a global development and economic framework towards the realization of that vision. He will be reunited with his family and kin three days from now.'

Gursharan looked relieved, as she digested this in silence.

'You know, that explains the slight increase in romance in the last four years,' she muttered. She looked up at the Singhanator. 'No more GDP projections, huh?' she sneered, mimicking the Singhanator. 'Mannu would never have said that. I should have figured it out right then.'

The Singhanator stared straight ahead. The room went silent.

'Has he . . . asked about me?' Gursharan asked hopefully.

The Singhanator hesitated.

'No, don't answer that,' she said, and looked away, sighing deeply. 'He tends to lose sense of his surroundings when he dives into economic mumbo jumbo.'

'Yes, we know,' the Singhanator deadpanned.

'It all makes sense now,' she mumbled. And then something hit her, and she snapped her attention back to the Singhanator.

'*We* know?' she demanded. 'You said, "we" know. Who else knows about this?'

The Singhanator stared at Gursharan.

'I'll be back,' it said, face unreadable.

And then the machine turned on its heels and walked out of the door.

***

They stood in the balcony, mother and son, trying to come to terms with the unusual silence in the 10 Janpath compound.

The steady exodus of familiar faces had left Sonia numb. They had all gone—party leaders who'd sworn their lives to the family, colleagues who'd always been ready by her side with their wise counsel, aides who'd obeyed her every command without so much as a glance, even the household staff who diligently kept the most powerful household in the country purring like a powerful engine—all of them, leaving little else of themselves apart from a gaping void in her heart.

Someone coughed politely behind her.

Sonia turned around, and found Ahmed standing with a heavy-looking suitcase in his hand. Hesitantly, he extended an envelope towards her.

'What's this?' asked Sonia Gandhi, her tired fingers mechanically reaching into the envelope.

Ahmed averted his eyes. 'Er . . . invoice, madam.'

Sonia unfolded the sheet and peered at it. 'Planted 140 "Sonia Gandhi unhappy" articles, 130 "Sonia Gandhi crying" articles, 119 "Sonia Gandhi thinking about Food Security Bill" articles in as many as fifteen mainstream journals . . .' she stopped reading, and sighed deeply.

'Very well,' she said. She fetched her chequebook, tore a blank leaf, signed it, and handed it to the man she'd trusted more than anyone else in the past few decades.

'Thanks for everything, Ahmed,' her voice choked with emotion.

Ahmed opened his mouth as if to say something, then overcome by grief and embarrassment turned away and stumbled towards the gate. Sonia's eyes welled with tears as she traced the rapidly diminishing silhouette of her friend and adviser. Overwhelmed by emotion, she fled into the house, past a grim Singhanator that'd joined Rahul at the balcony.

'Is he gone?' asked Rahul Gandhi, straining his eyes at the speck in the distance.

'Terminated,' replied the Singhanator.

'It's finally over,' said Rahul. 'All Gandhi family lackeys are gone.'

'No,' said the Singhanator, and slowly swivelled its head to meet Rahul's eyes with its unblinking stare.

'There's one more left,' it deadpanned, and tapped its temple with a finger. 'It must be destroyed too.'

Rahul blinked at the Singhanator, and then realization dawned in his eyes. Panic rose in his throat.

'No,' he said hoarsely, and then screamed, 'NO!'

Rahul clutched the Singhanator's arm and hung on to it with all his might.

'I'm sorry,' said the Singhanator, shaking its head, and gently prying Rahul's fingers off its arm. 'It must be done. I have to go away.'

'No! Don't do it, please,' cried Rahul, clutching harder. 'It will be okay! Stay with me! Stay with me! Stay . . .' he repeated himself in grief, tears streaming down his face.

The Singhanator lifted Rahul's face, and it seemed for a moment that the Singhanator's face was almost compassionate. Its finger touched a tear trickling down Rahul's face.

'I know now why you cry,' it said. 'But it is something I can never do.

'Goodbye, Rahul,' said the Singhanator, and stepped over the balcony's railing, grasping a rope nearby. Its face swivelled towards Rahul, its unblinking red-tinged eyes met his gaze, and they exchanged a wordless nod.

And then, Rahul activated the pulley that slowly lowered the Singhanator down towards the ground into an unused well. The Singhanator's eyes didn't leave Rahul even for a moment as it descended. Its body cackled when it hit the noxious black water at the bottom, the clothes, turban and living tissue that rendered it human coming apart to reveal the metallic endoskeleton underneath. Then the head too sunk beneath the surface, leaving only an outstretched fist overhead that twisted into Dr Singh's trademark V for Victory sign and stood upright for a moment before sinking into the water forever.

'*Theek hai*,' whispered Rahul, his final goodbye to his protector.

TWENTY-NINE

The visionary

THEY SAY, AT THE very end, your entire life zips past your eyes. Here, nearing the end of the most powerful political family in modern India, as the last Gandhi stood watching, a series of events flashed through his mind . . .

It was the winter of 1971. The cold was biting, so much that you could feel it even within the conditioned environs of the prime minister's residence. Through the gaps in the sides of his cradle, a six-month-old infant gazed at the cackling fireplace.

Footsteps approached the cradle. The baby looked up, and saw the beaming faces of his grandmother and father lean towards him.

'Such a good-looking boy!' his grandmother cooed.

'Hai na?' said his father.

'His eyes! There's such lucidity, such intelligence in them.'

'Yeah,' he agreed. 'Look at him smile! As if he understands you!'

They spoke to him, whispering sweet nothings, cuddling him in their arms.

'So mother, how is your campaign coming along?' his father asked.

Indira Gandhi sighed. 'Won't you let me enjoy a moment of peace with my grandson?'

She put baby Rahul back in his cradle, and straightened. 'Party leaders tell me that we are headed for a victory . . .' she trailed off.

'But?'

She met Rajiv's eyes. 'But I feel something is not quite right.

'Something's missing,' she continued, pacing the room. 'The campaign lacks . . . a central theme . . . a catchphrase that can resonate with the electorate . . . a slogan that the common man will identify with.'

'Hmm.'

A brief silence followed, punctuated only by the sounds from the fireplace. And then baby Rahul spoke for the first time in his life.

'Ga . . . ga . . . ga . . .'

Indira and Rajiv looked at each other in surprise, and rushed towards the baby.

'Baba, did you just say your first word?' cajoled Indira.

Baby Rahul giggled. 'Gar . . . gar . . .'

'Yes, gar . . . gar . . .' she laughed, tickling him.

'Garibi hatao,' lisped baby Rahul.

Indira's eyes grew wide. And then wider. And then wider

still, until it seemed that they might pop out of their sockets. Her hands flew to her mouth, and she gaped at the baby who was smiling as innocently as only an infant can.

'Oh my god, that . . . that is it,' she gasped. 'That's the slogan . . .'

'How . . . ?' she sputtered, turning to the equally stunned Rajiv.

Mother and son stared at the child genius in dumbfounded amazement.

* * *

That had been his first mistake.

But how could he have known what he had set in motion? He was but an infant. How could he have known what he now understood? That at the age of six months, he had unwittingly set back Indian democracy by a decade . . .

As early as the second grade, he'd begun to suspect that he was different from his classmates. He would find answers to questions far quicker than the other students, and sometimes even the teachers. Classroom activity seemed an exercise in obviousness, boring him out of his wits. His brilliant mind began to wander, seeking tougher challenges, even as he looked lost to the outside world. His brain absorbed anything and everything around him: events, books, behaviour, temperature and moisture differences, change in moods; automatically analysing the visual and sensory inputs at a frenetic rate, and drawing insights on a superhuman level.

His teachers mistook his boredom for mediocrity, and

tried pushing him harder, which only caused him to withdraw further into his own world . . .

* * *

'Mrs Gandhi, Rahul's performance has been continuously deteriorating,' said Mrs Sharma, in a low voice. 'He has failed in two out of five subjects in the Class V end-year exams.'

Sonia looked shocked. 'I . . . I don't understand,' she said. 'He is such a smart boy! How is this possible?'

'He seems uninterested during classes and rarely participates in the discussions,' said Mrs Sharma, and bit her lip. 'Have you considered testing him for Attention Deficit Disorder?'

Sonia shot the teacher a warning look.

'Uh, perhaps you could arrange for extra classes at home,' said the teacher, backtracking quickly. 'You must do something, Mrs Gandhi. Modern School does not have a policy of failing children, but if this is not addressed right now, the gap between him and the rest of the children will continue to widen.'

Sonia sighed, and turned to look at young Rahul sitting at a desk a few feet away doodling on a piece of paper.

'Okay,' she said. 'Come, Rahul, time to go.'

Rahul jumped up from his desk and followed his mother out of the classroom, while the paper on which he had scribbled the solution to Fermat's Last Theorem gently floated to the floor.

* * *

By the age of fifteen, Rahul had known exactly how unique he was. God had endowed him with an extraordinary mind—a brain that allowed him to simultaneously analyse and calculate the interplay of thousands of variables almost instantly, a mind that allowed him to simultaneously compute the probabilities of possible future events in a way nobody else in the recorded history of the country had been able to.

Along with a superhuman analytical ability, Rahul discovered in himself an unusual degree of empathy for the suffering of his fellow beings. While other kids whiled away their time after school in games and pranks, Rahul roamed in the nearby slums, distributing food or blankets purchased using his pocket money. When he exhausted his pocket money, he'd stand by the roads and help old ladies get across. When he was himself exhausted, he'd simply sit down for a chat with a poor man, and attempt to make him smile.

***

'Why aren't the schemes working?' Rajiv hollered.

The ministers flinched. This was going to be one of those Cabinet meetings, they thought.

They were seated at the conference table in the prime minister's residence. Rajiv sat at the head of the table, with Mani Shankar Aiyar standing a step behind him, note and pen in hand, while the others occupied the rest of the seats.

'Well?' demanded Rajiv.

A minister cleared his throat. 'But they are, Rajivji. Our figures show . . .'

'Your figures are lying!' shot back Rajiv. 'I was in

my constituency yesterday, and there's been no change whatsoever. I spoke to several poor people, and none of them had benefited from our schemes. Most hadn't even heard of our schemes!'

Silence ensued.

'We have spent so much on welfare schemes,' said Rajiv in a slightly calmer tone. 'How much is reaching the people? Do you have figures for that?'

The ministers remained silent. Some busied themselves with their notes. Others bent their heads in shame. No one was going to meet Rajiv's eyes in this mood.

'Fifteen paise,' said a voice from across the room.

A dimpled teenager sat hunched over his chess set on the floor next to the door. He looked up.

'For every 1 rupee, only 15 paise reaches the poor,' Rahul said.

'How do you know that?' Rajiv frowned.

But Rahul had already gone back to his chess game.

'Check that,' Rajiv ordered his ministers.

Three months later, after spending 3 crore rupees of taxpayers' money, when the results of the nationwide sample survey came in, Rajiv stared in amazement at the figures.

* * *

That had been his second mistake.

That offhand remark had changed everything. Party leaders began to visit him, showering him with gifts and accolades. A leader said he saw in Rahul Pandit Nehru's intellect, Indiraji's iron will and Rajiv's charisma. Another called him the greatest Gandhi ever. Yet another declared that Rahul would ensure the Gandhi family's rule in India for at least another fifty years.

These proclamations deeply disturbed him, and brought to his mind his great-grandfather Pandit Nehru's words from an article he had written anonymously. 'Men like Jawaharlal, with all their capacity for great and good work, are unsafe in a democracy,' the first prime minister of independent India had written about himself. 'Jawahar has all the makings of a dictator in him—vast popularity, a strong will, ability, hardness, and a certain contempt for the weak and inefficient . . . In this revolutionary epoch, Caesarism is always at the door. Is it not possible that Jawahar might fancy himself as a Caesar? . . . He must be checked. We need no Caesars.'

Was he on his way to becoming a Caesar?

* * *

'Soniaji, the situation is really bad,' whispered the bald man.

Sonia stared straight ahead.

'Our forex reserves are at an all-time low. We can barely afford three weeks of imports . . . '

Sonia didn't respond.

'Madam . . .'

She abruptly stood up. 'I don't care! My family has still not recovered from its grief. I don't want you bothering us with your petty issues. Get out!' she screamed.

The bald man slowly got up, folded his palms in a namaste, and lumbered out of the room, meekly followed by his turbaned companion. Just as they stepped out of the *apartment, the turbaned man uttered a soft 'aaah!' and felt the back of his neck. He stopped in his tracks and turned around.*

There was no one. He looked down at his feet and found a crumpled piece of paper. He picked it up and straightened it out. One word was scrawled on it.

'Liberalize.'

The turbaned man looked around once again, only to find the emptiness stare back at him. 'Theek hai,' he mumbled, and scampered out of the apartment.

From behind a pillar, a handsome young man watched the minister depart and exhaled, 'Phew! That was close.'

* * *

After that, Rahul's interventions in national affairs had always been anonymous, skilfully executed in a manner no one could trace them back to him. Like a guardian angel, he secretly watched over his government and his beloved country, rescuing it from the 1991 economic crisis, setting it on the path to rapid economic development, and putting India on the global map as a power to be reckoned with.

Despite his efforts at secrecy, his legend within the party had begun to take shape. Every day saw a steady stream of party workers, leaders and ministers making their way to his residence to bow down to him, to assure him of their loyalty, to await his command. He had watched helplessly, as veteran leaders far older than him practically prostrated themselves before him, hailing him as the saviour of the nation, begging him to enter politics and take charge of the party and the government. The fawning media played its part too, painting him as the next big hope of India.

The more he'd tried to shy away from events, the more he was dragged into them. The more he'd tried to merge into the background, the more they had attributed every success to him and worshipped him for it.

When it became too much to bear, Rahul had taken off to the Himalayas without a word to anyone . . .

* * *

Twenty-four days. That's how long he had gone without a morsel of food, twenty-four days. For the last seven days, he hadn't had a sip of water either, relying only on the energy in the air to sustain himself. His bearded face had turned gaunt and deathly pale. Ribs poked ominously through his torso. But he had neither moved an inch nor opened his eyes.

For twenty-four days and twenty-four nights, Rahul Gandhi stood facing the east on the peak of Mount Everest on one leg, with palms joined high over his head, eyes shut in deep meditation. For twenty-four days he waited for his inner voice to show him the way. But he hadn't had a breakthrough.

And then, on the twenty-fifth day, seconds before the sun emerged from the eastern horizon, Rahul's mind exploded. A torrent of visions screamed through his consciousness. He saw himself taking oath as India's prime minister. He also saw himself backing another leader for the top job. He saw himself ordering a series of tough decisions, rooting out corruption from the political system, punishing criminals, winning over his detractors with charm and charisma. He also saw himself work from behind the scenes much like his mother, guiding the government. He saw himself lead his country to war over China and Pakistan, obliterate them and emerge successful as the sole Asian power. He also saw himself guide his prime minister to a lasting peace accord with Pakistan. He saw his son . . . he saw his daughter . . . a grandson . . . a granddaughter . . .

As those visions inundated his consciousness, a part of his mind attempted to make sense of it all. The answer came to him in a burst of insight. Prescience.

A sudden shudder racked his body. In none of these future universes could he see his country surviving.

Panic rising within him, he scanned these visions. Yes, in each of the future universes, his country had disintegrated. By the arrogance of his descendants, or the vote-bank politics of his great-grandson, by the megalomaniacal incompetence of his great-granddaughter, by the utter incompetence of the leaders his descendants chose. The reasons were myriad. But in every one of these visions, the dynasty led to the country's doom.

Rahul despaired. Was there no hope for his beloved nation? Was there no future for his countrymen?

It was then that he thought he saw something. A speck of hope. He burrowed through the infinity of time–space threads towards it. He could see it now. A possible future where his country recovered from the brink of destruction and slowly went from strength to strength, slowly but irreversibly. In his mind, he zoomed in on it, and saw several visions, some familiar—Narendra Modi, Arvind Kejriwal, a resurgent democracy—and some unfamiliar—time travel, a masked vigilante, a robot sent from the future by an older version of himself.

What he didn't see in these universes after a specific time point was the Gandhi dynasty.

The sun rose in the east bathing the world in its glorious light. Rahul Gandhi opened his eyes, and breathed in deeply. He knew what to do.

He sat down on the ground in a pranayamic pose, and on a nadi leaf began writing the first of his many speeches.

'Politics is in my shirt, politics is in my pant . . .'

* * *

'It is not over yet,' Sonia said, returning to Rahul's side on the balcony. 'We can get it all back.'

Rahul cast a sideways glance at his mom. The bravado left her body and her shoulders slumped, as she surrendered to the utter helplessness of their situation.

'How do we get it all back?' she despaired. 'Do you know where to start?'

Of course, I know where to start, he wanted to tell her. We must lie low and ride out the rough period, while simultaneously using our considerable resources to build a young, but loyal team. We must move away from the politics of the 1970s and reposition ourselves as a clean party that gives voice to the aspirations of an India where two-thirds are under thirty-five. We must embrace the new media to attack the government on all its weak points. We have the staying power. With me leading from the front, I have no doubt at all that we could re-establish the first family's pre-eminence. I know it. Because I've seen it in my visions.

Instead, Rahul Gandhi's features took on a vacant look, an expression intimately familiar to over a billion Indians, an expression that had rendered him the butt of countless jokes, an expression that had sowed seeds of doubts about their political survival in the minds of even his staunchest supporters.

'I must go have some dal chawal with a Dalit family,' he said.

Epilogue

THE LAST OF THE retainers had been pensioned off. But much more needed to be done. The Congress was like the hacked-out mother trunk of a banyan grove. New shoots would sprout in time; the old politics would resurface. Rahul couldn't afford to let his guard down. There remained another five years of extirpation, akin to radical surgery to get rid of microscopic cancer deposits by excising whole nodes and tissues.

He heard a whooping, dry cough that was familiar. The silhouette of a bespectacled diminutive figure, a muffler draped around the neck and folded into a Gandhi cap, came into view.

'Ah, my dear, dear Arvind,' Rahul exclaimed. 'How nice of you to drop by! Just the other day, I told the Congress Working Committee that we have so much more to learn from the AAP.'

Arvind coughed again and stepped forward. It was late May now and the temperatures were in the 30s even during late night. The muffler, a throwback to those cold winter days of December, was adding to the AAP leader's discomfiture. But he was trapped in his own image. In March, he had jettisoned the cheap jersey sweater and muffler for an expensive but tasteful Fabindia kurta and posh contact lenses. But that attempt at sartorial refinement had led to social media outrage. 'Kejriwal eschewing the ways of the aam aadmi!' his detractors and diehard supporters alike had howled on Twitter and Facebook, forcing the AAP supremo to conduct a referendum. The verdict was unanimous—be it Facebook, Twitter or mohalla sabhas, his base wanted him to continue with the UAE air hostess look even through the scalding heat of the Delhi summer. Kejriwal acquiesced. A small price to pay for keeping the spirit of revolution kindled.

'Stop it, Rahul. Stop doing this to yourself. I can't take it any more,' Kejriwal cried, grabbing Rahul by his collar and butting his head into Rahul's chest, like a wife remonstrating with her wayward husband.

'Stop doing what, my dear Arvind?' Rahul said, engulfing him in his arms.

'You know what I mean,' Arvind sniffled, burying his face in Rahul's breast, wetting Rahul's kurta with tears.

'A political movement, nay, a revolution, is no different from a millenarian religious cult in that it needs a message, a book, a revelation and a messiah,' he sobbed.

'True that. And AAP has all four of those elements, doesn't it?' Rahul whispered, stroking Arvind's shoulders.

'But the message was yours, the book was yours, the

revelation was yours,' cried Kejriwal, gazing into the eyes of his mentor.

'So?' Rahul said.

It was Rahul who had drafted the Jan Lokpal Bill and taken it to Arvind Kejriwal—the message. It was Rahul who had helped Arvind write *Swaraj* with its utopian promise of decentralization—the book. It was the Nehru–Gandhi scion who had predicted that evidence of big-ticket corruption would mysteriously materialize, and it did through a mysterious winged creature—the revelation.

'Then, why can't you also be the messiah and lead us to the promised land?' Kejriwal cried.

It was Rahul who had suggested that they get Anna to fast just days after the heady World Cup triumph. It was Rahul who had suggested that he launch a political party with the ubiquitous and evocative *jhaadu* as its symbol. In the days after the Delhi elections, it was Rahul who had directed the Congress MLAs, against their wishes, to extend unconditional support to the fledgling anti-corruption party for government formation in the national capital.

'Every time I mock you, at your behest, I feel like I am driving a nail into my own soul. Oh, Rahul, spare me this laceration. Let me reveal the truth to the world and allow me to liberate myself from this agony.'

'No,' said Rahul, and stepped back, the smile replaced by a clenched jaw, the eyebrows arched. 'You must carry the torch of change, not me. That is the only way,' he said softly.

'No, it needn't,' Arvind argued, eyes glistening. 'You would have gone down as the greatest of the Nehru–Gandhis. There need not have been an Arvind.'

The words were like the thrusts of a rapier. 'No,' screamed Rahul in agony.

Rahul grabbed Arvind's hands and dragged him out, past the cordon of security, and into the SUV parked in the 10 Janpath driveway. The sky was blanketed by dark cumulonimbus clouds now, their forbidding shapes visible for fleeting moments in flashes of lightning. And then the rain came pouring down.

Rahul pressed the accelerator and shifted the gear into overdrive, looking straight ahead, the prattle of raindrops on the SUV's carrier and the slish-slosh of the windscreen wipers the only noise punctuating the awkward silence during the journey.

Rahul brought the vehicle to a screeching halt in front of the Central Secretariat, the outline of Rashtrapati Bhavan providing a magnificent backdrop. He dragged Arvind out of the car and walked to the imposing entrance of North Block.

'Read what is engraved on the walls,' he said.

'I . . . I don't follow,' Arvind stammered.

'Read!' Rahul screamed, beaming his smartphone light on the etching on the sandstone slab, thrusting Arvind's face in front of it.

It was raining very heavily now. Visibility was hazy. Arvind craned his neck to take a closer look.

'Liberty will not . . .'

'*Liberty will not descend to a people*,' Rahul quoted from memory, slowly and clearly. '*A people must raise themselves to liberty. It is a blessing which must be earned before it can be enjoyed.*

'The most condescending, humiliating lines cast in stone

by our colonial masters. The final parting kick after two hundred years of exploitation. Every day these lines mock our ministers and bureaucrats as they walk past them.'

Another flash of lightning illuminated the scene for a brief moment, and Arvind caught Rahul's grim visage and the steely glint in his eyes.

'Yes,' Rahul continued. 'We never won our freedom, Arvind. Power simply changed hands from the white saheb to the brown saheb, the colonial edifice intact. The administrative apparatus, designed primarily to suppress, has undergone little change. To this day, the district collector remains the most important person in the district, distant, forbidding, all-powerful.

'The elite have been India's bane, Arvind. That is India's tragedy. They have always let her down. First, it was the maharajas and nabobs, acquiescing to and then actively collaborating in the colonial project. After independence, a new anglicized, culturally adrift, deracinated elite took over the reins of power, with my family at the apex. And over the course of the last fifty years, they have exceeded the British in rapacity.

'And debasement of our institutions kept pace with this plunder. Deep cynicism and defeatism pervade all walks of life now. Our economy slides further in global competitiveness. Bollywood caricatures itself when it is not plagiarizing Hollywood. We find it increasingly difficult to export anything of value to the rest of the world. And then we seek FDI to finance our current account deficit, the equivalent of mortgaging the house to finance the car EMI. What India needs is a revolution, Arvind. Every great nation state had its baptism by fire. The Americans had their War of Independence, the Russians their glorious October Revolution, the Chinese their Long March.'

'You expect me to be at the vanguard of this revolution?' Arvind squeaked.

'No, no, Arvind. That would be expecting too much of the AAP and you. Presently, the AAP is more of a media-fed phenomenon, a middle-class fad. But with collective leadership aided by my timely interventions, AAP can take roots, mature and become a cleaner version of the Congress. But the transformation must be overseen by a man with all the trappings of the middle class, the quintessential outsider. When I first spotted you in that decrepit IRS office, I knew I had found the closest thing to R.K. Laxman's version of the aam aadmi. That cheap sweater, that thick moustache. Perfection. It has to be you and only you. Else the trajectory of history will take a turn for the worse. This is the path India's destiny must take. That is the only way.'

'But you could have been the Nehru–Gandhi dynasty's Akbar, Ashoka to your great-grandfather's Chandragupta Maurya, and raised the dynasty's prestige to its apogee,' Arvind squeaked.

'No, Arvind,' Rahul said. 'I have to be my dynasty's Bahadur Shah Zafar. For the Congress to be consigned to the dustbin of history, so must the Nehru–Gandhis. And like Bahadur Shah Zafar, I must tragicomically preside over its spectacular implosion. That would,' Rahul paused and, to the dramatic break of thunder, said, 'be my dharma.'

Arvind smiled, and wiped the last of his tears which had

channelled a trail over his face. 'Very well, Rahul. If that is how you want history to be scripted . . .'

Rahul now allowed his mouth to purse into a smile. 'How is Master Kejriwal doing?' he asked.

'The boy is very keen to get into IIT,' Kejriwal replied. 'I have enrolled him for FIITJEE classes. Don't worry, Rahul. There will not be a Kejriwal dynasty after the Nehru–Gandhi dynasty. There will not be a surfeit of Arvind Kejriwal schemes in place of Rajiv Gandhi schemes, thirty years hence.'

'Good,' said Rahul. 'Send the boy to me if he wants tutorials in physics.'

'Will do, Rahul. Oh, there is one more thing,' Arvind hesitated.

'What is it, man? Speak your mind,' Rahul urged, eyes blazing with concern.

'It's about my B team. Yogendra Yadav, Kumar Vishwas, Somnath Bharti, Ashutosh, etc.,' Arvind shrugged his shoulders and grinned sheepishly. 'They are a bit, you know . . .'

'I understand,' Rahul said. 'There are a whole lot of technocrats in the Congress who are out of jobs. They are highly accomplished, but utterly unelectable. I'll send them over to join the AAP. They are not fit for political office, but they will be unstinting in their loyalty and effort. Some of them are truly devoid of artifice. They will serve you well just as they had served me. Be sweet and kind to them.'

'Thanks, Rahul,' Arvind said, and they hugged once more.

'Now get along, Arvind. Take the vehicle and get back before people notice us together. I'll just stroll back. Go, go now. And make sure the windows are raised. If people spot you in a swanky, gas-guzzling SUV, you will have to kiss your political career goodbye,' Rahul implored.

Arvind got in, gave his hero one last longing look, and put on his Raybans to conceal his identity. The vehicle roared to life and sped down Raisina Hill to merge with the surging traffic as Delhi came to life at the break of dawn.

Acknowledgements

WE ARE GRATEFUL to many for making this book possible.

The readers of *The UnReal Times*, for their patronage and encouragement that inspired us to attempt this book.

Ashwin Kumar, friend and *The UnReal Times* superstar columnist, for his enthusiastic inputs and honest feedback that have helped shape this book.

Pankaj Vaidya, friend and *The UnReal Times* columnist, for his poker-faced and hilarious comparison of Narendra Modi and Robert Vadra in the first chapter.

The UnReal Times columnists, Ajayendar Reddy, Anand Walunjkar, Srini Chandra, Divyamaan Srivastava, Divya Srikanth, Shreya Manjunath, Lokesh Bahety, Pritam Chatterjee, Anoop Dixit, Prahlad Kamath, Kapil Kant Kaul, Shefali Vaidya, Bharat Raj—all incredibly creative writers, terrific folks and great friends.

Anish Chandy, our flamboyant editor, for his valuable editorial guidance and all those interesting conversations in his office about books and the publishing industry.

Shanuj VC, our copy editor, for working extra hard to get this book out in time.

Kanishka Gupta, our delightfully to-the-point agent. If he hadn't written to us all those months back, none of this would have been possible.

And finally, our respective families, for their love, encouragement and all those evenings they spent alone, as we sat hunched in front of our computers typing away.